THE IMAGE

THE IMAGE

BOOKS BY DANIEL J. BOORSTIN

The Creators

*

Hidden History

*

The Discoverers

*

The Americans: The Colonial Experience
The Americans: The National Experience
The Americans: The Democratic Experience

*

The Mysterious Science of the Law
The Lost World of Thomas Jefferson
The Genius of American Politics
America and the Image of Europe
The Image: A Guide to Pseudo-Events in America
The Decline of Radicalism
The Sociology of the Absurd
Democracy and Its Discontents
The Republic of Technology
The Exploring Spirit

*

For young readers:
The Landmark History of the American People
A History of the United States (with Brooks M. Kelley)

THE IMAGE

A Guide to Pseudo-Events in America

DANIEL J. BOORSTIN

25TH ANNIVERSARY EDITION
WITH A NEW FOREWORD BY THE AUTHOR
AND AN AFTERWORD BY
GEORGE F. WILL

*Technology ... the knack of so arranging the world
that we don't have to experience it.* MAX FRISCH

❁

Vintage Books
A Division of Random House, Inc.
New York

First Vintage Books Edition, September 1992

The author thanks the following for permission to use various quotations:

Michael Flanders and Donald Swann for four lines from "Song of
Reproduction"; Grove Press, Inc. for a passage from *The Stars,* by Edgar
Morin, translated by Richard Howard; Harcourt, Brace & World for a
quotation from *Senator Joe McCarthy,* by Richard Rovere; Houghton
Mifflin Company for a selection from *The Fourth Branch of Government,*
by Douglass Cater; Alfred A. Knopf, Inc. for passages from *Struggles and
Triumphs,* by P. T. Barnum, copyright 1927 by Alfred A. Knopf, Inc.;
Paul S. Nathan for passages from his feature "Rights and Permissions"
in *Publishers' Weekly; Saturday Review* for quotations from "Why Write
It When You Can't Sell It to the Pictures," by Budd Schulberg, and
"Music to Hear, but Not to Listen To," by Stanley Green.

Library of Congress Cataloging-in-Publication Data
Boorstin, Daniel J. (Daniel Joseph), 1914–
The image: a guide to pseudo-events in America / Daniel J.
Boorstin. — 1st Vintage Books ed.
p. cm.
Originally published: 25th anniversary ed. New York: Atheneum, 1987.
Includes bibliographical references and index.
ISBN 0-679-74180-1 (pbk.)
1. National characteristics, American. 2. United States —
Civilization — 1945– 3. United States — Popular Culture —
History — 20th century. I. Title.
E169.12.B66 1992
973.9 — dc20 92-50080
CIP

Designed by Harry Ford

Manufactured in the United States of America

20 19 18 17 16 15 14

"My money affairs are in a bad way. You remember before the wedding, Anisim brought me some new rubles and half rubles? I hid one packet, the rest I mixed with my own. . . . But now I can't make out which is real money and which is counterfeit, it seems to me they are all false coins. . . . When I take a ticket at the station, I hand three rubles, then I think to myself: Are they false? And I'm frightened. I can't be well."

ANTON CHEKHOV, *The Hollow*

Foreword to the 25th Anniversary Edition

WHEN THIS BOOK first appeared a quarter-century ago, television still had the charm of novelty and public relations was only in process of becoming one of the most powerful forces in American life. "The Image" was not yet a cliché. This book was my own exploration of the momentous changes in the American view of reality. For the present edition I have left in the examples I used then, so that the reader, in sharing my own sense of discovery at that time, may also sense that present fashions have their roots in history. The reader can have the added pleasure of finding new examples every day.

This book has had a surprising vogue. It was not a best seller when it appeared, but it continues to live, to be quoted and to be assigned in colleges. It has been translated into the principal Western European languages and is in its thirtieth printing in Japanese.

Perhaps it is not surprising that it has had an even wider and more enthusiastic audience outside the United States than here at home. For we Americans are sensitive to any suggestion that progress may have its price. When the book appeared in 1962, I happened to be out of the country on a lecture engagement. *Time*, in reviewing *The Image*, said it was no wonder that the author left the country just before his slander on the United States was published.

Others have not been so hypersensitive about the facts of our life. Many have welcomed the vocabulary offered in this book for the new rhetoric of democracy. "Pseudo-event," the expression I introduced here, has entered our dictionaries (and the Oxford English Dictionary), along with "well-known-ness," and these have entered the Western European vernacular. The definition of a celebrity as "a person who is known for

vii

his well-knownness" has almost become a familiar quotation.

Meanwhile our technology has reinforced the tendencies described in this book. Is there any advance—from VHS and Cable TV to their unimaginable successors—that has not multiplied and vivified pseudo-events? Is there any advance in transportation—from the Walkman and the cellular telephone to supersonic planes and their successors—that has not erased the differences between transportation and communication? Every day seeing there and hearing there takes the place of being there.

Still, the author never really knows what his book means. Especially today the author's view of what he has done, like everybody else's, is clouded by the blurring together of images and realities, the disorder that eyedoctors call diplopia. It is a fair testimony to this book that it has continued to puzzle, pique, and amuse quite a few. But my Foreword to this 25th anniversary edition, insisting on the book's well-knownness, is only another evidence of how hard it is for any of us to escape the passion for pseudo-events that has accelerated, and still accelerates into the foreseeable future.

DANIEL J. BOORSTIN
June, 1987

Foreword to the First Edition

THIS IS a "how-not-to-do-it" book. It is about our arts of self-deception, how we hide reality from ourselves. One need not be a doctor to know he is sick, nor a shoemaker to feel the shoe pinch. I do not know what "reality" really is. But somehow I do know an illusion when I see one.

This is a large subject for a small book. Yet it is too large for a big book. If I pretended in this volume to survey or comprehend all the bewitching unrealities of American life in the twentieth century, I would misrepresent the vastness of the subject. The task of disenchantment is finally not the writer's but the reader's. The complete survey must be made intimately by each American and for himself.

This book arises out of some very personal convictions. First, an affection for America and an amazement at America: acquired over the half century of my life, increased by periods of living abroad, and deepened by having spent my adult life studying the American past. Having read a good deal about the villains who are said to be responsible for our perplexity—the hidden persuaders, the organization men, Madison Avenue, Washington bureaucracy, the eggheads, the anti-intellectuals, the power élite, etc., etc., etc.—I am unimpressed by their villainy. But I remain impressed by the perplexity of life in twentieth-century America. I have long suspected that our problems arise less from our weaknesses than from our strengths. From our literacy and wealth and optimism and progress.

Yet it is a mistake to believe that a wholesale problem can find a wholesale solution. From the beginning, the great promise of America was to open doors, so that men could try to work out their problems for themselves—not necessarily alone, but in communities of their choosing, and toward often-uncertain ends which appealed to them.

I am suspicious of all mass medicines for national malaise and national purposelessness. The bigger the committee, the more "representative" its membership, the more collaborative its work, the less the chance that it will do more than ease or disguise our symptoms. The problem of "national purpose" is largely an illusion—although one of the most popular illusions of our time. Our real problem is personal.

I try in this book to give the reader a representative sample of his illusions. These come out of my own experience, an experience I share with nearly all Americans. I notice here only a few of the many new varieties of unreality which clutter our experience and obscure our vision. Because I cannot describe "reality" I know I risk making myself a sitting duck for my more profound philosopher-colleagues. But I remain confident that what dominates American experience today is not reality. If I can only dispel some of the mists, the reader may then better discover his own real perplexity. He may better see the landscape to find whatever road he chooses.

Contents

Extravagant Expectations

IN THIS BOOK I describe the world of our making; how we have used our wealth, our literacy, our technology, and our progress, to create the thicket of unreality which stands between us and the facts of life. I recount historical forces which have given us this unprecedented opportunity to deceive ourselves and to befog our experience.

Of course, America has provided the landscape and has given us the resources and the opportunity for this feat of national self-hypnosis. But each of us individually provides the market and the demand for the illusions which flood our experience.

We want and we believe these illusions because we suffer from extravagant expectations. We expect too much of the world. Our expectations are extravagant in the precise dictionary sense of the word—"going beyond the limits of reason or moderation." They are excessive.

When we pick up our newspaper at breakfast, we expect —we even demand—that it bring us momentous events since the night before. We turn on the car radio as we drive to work and expect "news" to have occurred since the morning newspaper went to press. Returning in the evening, we expect our house not only to shelter us, to keep us warm in winter and cool in summer, but to relax us, to dignify us, to encompass us with soft music and interesting hobbies, to be a playground, a theater, and a bar. We expect our

3

two-week vacation to be romantic, exotic, cheap, and effortless. We expect a faraway atmosphere if we go to a nearby place; and we expect everything to be relaxing, sanitary, and Americanized if we go to a faraway place. We expect new heroes every season, a literary masterpiece every month, a dramatic spectacular every week, a rare sensation every night. We expect everybody to feel free to disagree, yet we expect everybody to be loyal, not to rock the boat or take the Fifth Amendment. We expect everybody to believe deeply in his religion, yet not to think less of others for not believing. We expect our nation to be strong and great and vast and varied and prepared for every challenge; yet we expect our "national purpose" to be clear and simple, something that gives direction to the lives of nearly two hundred million people and yet can be bought in a paperback at the corner drugstore for a dollar.

We expect anything and everything. We expect the contradictory and the impossible. We expect compact cars which are spacious; luxurious cars which are economical. We expect to be rich and charitable, powerful and merciful, active and reflective, kind and competitive. We expect to be inspired by mediocre appeals for "excellence," to be made literate by illiterate appeals for literacy. We expect to eat and stay thin, to be constantly on the move and ever more neighborly, to go to a "church of our choice" and yet feel its guiding power over us, to revere God and to be God.

Never have people been more the masters of their environment. Yet never has a people felt more deceived and disappointed. For never has a people expected so much more than the world could offer.

We are ruled by extravagant expectations:

(1) *Of what the world holds.* Of how much news there is, how many heroes there are, how often masterpieces are made, how exotic the nearby can be, how familiar the exotic can become. Of the closeness of places and the farness of places.

(2) *Of our power to shape the world.* Of our ability
to create events when there are none, to make
heroes when they don't exist, to be somewhere else
when we haven't left home. Of our ability to make
art forms suit our convenience, to transform a
novel into a movie and vice versa, to turn a
symphony into mood-conditioning. To fabricate
national purposes when we lack them, to pursue
these purposes after we have fabricated them. To
invent our standards and then to respect them as
if they had been revealed or discovered.

By harboring, nourishing, and ever enlarging our extravagant expectations we create the demand for the illusions
with which we deceive ourselves. And which we pay others
to make to deceive us.

The making of the illusions which flood our experience
has become the business of America, some of its most honest
and most necessary and most respectable business. I am
thinking not only of advertising and public relations and
political rhetoric, but of all the activities which purport to
inform and comfort and improve and educate and elevate
us: the work of our best journalists, our most enterprising
book publishers, our most energetic manufacturers and
merchandisers, our most successful entertainers, our best
guides to world travel, and our most influential leaders in
foreign relations. Our every effort to satisfy our extravagant
expectations simply makes them more extravagant and makes
our illusions more attractive. The story of the making of our
illusions—"the news behind the news"—has become the
most appealing news of the world.

We tyrannize and frustrate ourselves by expecting more
than the world can give us or than we can make of the world.
We demand that everyone who talks to us, or writes for us,
or takes pictures for us, or makes merchandise for us, should
live in our world of extravagant expectations. We expect this
even of the peoples of foreign countries. We have become so

accustomed to our illusions that we mistake them for reality. We demand them. And we demand that there be always more of them, bigger and better and more vivid. They are the world of our making: the world of the image.

Nowadays everybody tells us that what we need is more belief, a stronger and deeper and more encompassing faith. A faith in America and in what we are doing. That may be true in the long run. What we need first and now is to disillusion ourselves. What ails us most is not what we have done with America, but what we have substituted for America. We suffer primarily not from our vices or our weaknesses, but from our illusions. We are haunted, not by reality, but by those images we have put in place of reality.

To discover our illusions will not solve the problems of our world. But if we do not discover them, we will never discover our real problems. To dispel the ghosts which populate the world of our making will not give us the power to conquer the real enemies of the real world or to remake the real world. But it may help us discover that we cannot make the world in our image. It will liberate us and sharpen our vision. It will clear away the fog so we can face the world we share with all mankind.

I

From News Gathering

to News Making:

A Flood of Pseudo-Events

ADMIRING FRIEND:
"My, that's a beautiful baby you have there!"
MOTHER:
"Oh, that's nothing—you should see his photograph!"

THE SIMPLEST of our extravagant expectations concerns
the amount of novelty in the world. There was a time when
the reader of an unexciting newspaper would remark, "How
dull is the world today!" Nowadays he says, "What a dull
newspaper!" When the first American newspaper, Benjamin
Harris' *Publick Occurrences Both Forreign and Domestick*,
appeared in Boston on September 25, 1690, it promised to
furnish news regularly once a month. But, the editor explained, it might appear oftener "if any Glut of Occurrences
happen." The responsibility for making news was entirely
God's—or the Devil's. The newsman's task was only to give
"an Account of such considerable things as have arrived
unto our Notice."

Although the theology behind this way of looking at events
soon dissolved, this view of the news lasted longer. "The
skilled and faithful journalist," James Parton observed in
1866, "recording with exactness and power the thing that

has come to pass, is Providence addressing men." The story is told of a Southern Baptist clergyman before the Civil War who used to say, when a newspaper was brought in the room, "Be kind enough to let me have it a few minutes, till I see how the Supreme Being is governing the world." Charles A. Dana, one of the great American editors of the nineteenth century, once defended his extensive reporting of crime in the New York *Sun* by saying, "I have always felt that whatever the Divine Providence permitted to occur I was not too proud to report."

Of course, this is now a very old-fashioned way of thinking. Our current point of view is better expressed in the definition by Arthur MacEwen, whom William Randolph Hearst made his first editor of the San Francisco *Examiner:* "News is anything that makes a reader say, 'Gee whiz!'" Or, put more soberly, "News is whatever a good editor chooses to print."

We need not be theologians to see that we have shifted responsibility for making the world interesting from God to the newspaperman. We used to believe there were only so many "events" in the world. If there were not many intriguing or startling occurrences, it was no fault of the reporter. He could not be expected to report what did not exist.

Within the last hundred years, however, and especially in the twentieth century, all this has changed. We expect the papers to be full of news. If there is no news visible to the naked eye, or to the average citizen, we still expect it to be there for the enterprising newsman. The successful reporter is one who can find a story, even if there is no earthquake or assassination or civil war. If he cannot find a story, then he must make one—by the questions he asks of public figures, by the surprising human interest he unfolds from some commonplace event, or by "the news behind the news." If all this fails, then he must give us a "think piece"—an embroidering of well-known facts, or a speculation about startling things to come.

This change in our attitude toward "news" is not merely a basic fact about the history of American newspapers. It is a symptom of a revolutionary change in our attitude toward what happens in the world, how much of it is new, and surprising, and important. Toward how life can be enlivened, toward our power and the power of those who inform and educate and guide us, to provide synthetic happenings to make up for the lack of spontaneous events. Demanding more than the world can give us, we require that something be fabricated to make up for the world's deficiency. This is only one example of our demand for illusions.

Many historical forces help explain how we have come to our present immoderate hopes. But there can be no doubt about what we now expect, nor that it is immoderate. Every American knows the anticipation with which he picks up his morning newspaper at breakfast or opens his evening paper before dinner, or listens to the newscasts every hour on the hour as he drives across country, or watches his favorite commentator on television interpret the events of the day. Many enterprising Americans are now at work to help us satisfy these expectations. Many might be put out of work if we should suddenly moderate our expectations. But it is we who keep them in business and demand that they fill our consciousness with novelties, that they play God for us.

I

THE NEW kind of synthetic novelty which has flooded our experience I will call "pseudo-events." The common prefix "pseudo" comes from the Greek word meaning false, or intended to deceive. Before I recall the historical forces which have made these pseudo-events possible, have increased the supply of them and the demand for them, I will give a commonplace example.

The owners of a hotel, in an illustration offered by Edward L. Bernays in his pioneer *Crystallizing Public Opinion*

(1923), consult a public relations counsel. They ask how to increase their hotel's prestige and so improve their business. In less sophisticated times, the answer might have been to hire a new chef, to improve the plumbing, to paint the rooms, or to install a crystal chandelier in the lobby. The public relations counsel's technique is more indirect. He proposes that the management stage a celebration of the hotel's thirtieth anniversary. A committee is formed, including a prominent banker, a leading society matron, a well-known lawyer, an influential preacher, and an "event" is planned (say a banquet) to call attention to the distinguished service the hotel has been rendering the community. The celebration is held, photographs are taken, the occasion is widely reported, and the object is accomplished. Now this occasion is a pseudo-event, and will illustrate all the essential features of pseudo-events.

This celebration, we can see at the outset, is somewhat—but not entirely—misleading. Presumably the public relations counsel would not have been able to form his committee of prominent citizens if the hotel had not actually been rendering service to the community. On the other hand, if the hotel's services had been all that important, instigation by public relations counsel might not have been necessary. Once the celebration has been held, the celebration itself becomes evidence that the hotel really is a distinguished institution. The occasion actually gives the hotel the prestige to which it is pretending.

It is obvious, too, that the value of such a celebration to the owners depends on its being photographed and reported in newspapers, magazines, newsreels, on radio, and over television. It is the report that gives the event its force in the minds of potential customers. The power to make a reportable event is thus the power to make experience. One is reminded of Napoleon's apocryphal reply to his general, who objected that circumstances were unfavorable to a proposed campaign: "Bah, I make circumstances!" The modern public relations counsel—and he is, of course, only one of many twentieth-century creators of pseudo-events—has come close to fulfilling Napoleon's idle boast. "The counsel on public relations," Mr. Bernays explains, "not only knows what news value is, but knowing it, he is in a position to *make news happen*. He is a creator of events."

The intriguing feature of the modern situation, however, comes precisely from the fact that the modern news makers are not God. The news they make happen, the events they create, are somehow not quite real. There remains a tantalizing difference between man-made and God-made events.

A pseudo-event, then, is a happening that possesses the following characteristics:

(1) It is not spontaneous, but comes about because someone has planned, planted, or incited it. Typically, it is not a train wreck or an earthquake, but an interview.

(2) It is planted primarily (not always exclusively) for the immediate purpose of being reported or reproduced. Therefore, its occurrence is arranged for the convenience of the reporting or reproducing media. Its success is measured by how widely it is reported. Time relations in it are commonly fictitious or factitious; the announcement is given out in advance "for future release" and written as if the event had occurred in the past. The question, "Is it real?" is less important than, "Is it newsworthy?"

(3) Its relation to the underlying reality of the situation is ambiguous. Its interest arises largely from this very ambiguity. Concerning a pseudo-event the question, "What does it mean?" has a new dimension. While the news interest in a train wreck is in *what* happened and in the real consequences, the interest in an interview is always, in a sense, in *whether* it really happened and in what might have been the motives. Did the statement really mean what it said? Without some of this ambiguity a pseudo-event cannot be very interesting.

(4) Usually it is intended to be a self-fulfilling prophecy. The hotel's thirtieth-anniversary celebration, by saying that the hotel is a distinguished institution, actually makes it one.

I I

IN THE last half century a larger and larger proportion of our experience, of what we read and see and hear, has come to consist of pseudo-events. We expect more of them and we are given more of them. They flood our consciousness. Their multiplication has gone on in the United States at a faster rate than elsewhere. Even the rate of increase is increasing every day. This is true of the world of education, of consumption, and of personal relations. It is especially true of the world of public affairs which I describe in this chapter.

A full explanation of the origin and rise of pseudo-events would be nothing less than a history of modern America. For our present purposes it is enough to recall a few of the more revolutionary recent developments.

The great modern increase in the supply and the demand for news began in the early nineteenth century. Until then newspapers tended to fill out their columns with lackadaisical secondhand accounts or stale reprints of items first published elsewhere at home and abroad. The laws of plagiarism and of copyright were undeveloped. Most newspapers were little more than excuses for espousing a political position, for listing the arrival and departure of ships, for familiar essays and useful advice, or for commercial or legal announcements.

Less than a century and a half ago did newspapers begin to disseminate up-to-date reports of matters of public interest written by eyewitnesses or professional reporters near the scene. The telegraph was perfected and applied to news reporting in the 1830's and '40's. Two newspapermen, William M. Swain of the Philadelphia *Public Ledger* and Amos Kendall of Frankfort, Kentucky, were founders of the national telegraphic network. Polk's presidential message in 1846 was the first to be transmitted by wire. When the Associated Press was founded in 1848, news began to be a salable commodity. Then appeared the rotary press, which could print on a continuous sheet and on both sides of the paper at the same time. The New York *Tribune*'s high-speed press, installed in the 1870's, could turn out 18,000 papers per hour. The Civil War, and later the Spanish-American War, offered raw materials and incentive for vivid up-to-the-minute, on-the-spot reporting. The competitive daring of giants like James Gordon Bennett, Joseph Pulitzer, and William Randolph Hearst intensified the race for news and widened newspaper circulation.

These events were part of a great, but little-noticed, revolution—what I would call the Graphic Revolution. Man's ability to make, preserve, transmit, and disseminate precise images—images of print, of men and landscapes and events, of the voices of men and mobs—now grew at a fantastic pace. The increased speed of printing was itself revolutionary. Still more revolutionary were the new techniques for making direct images of nature. Photography was destined soon to give printed matter itself a secondary role. By a giant leap Americans crossed the gulf from the daguerreotype to color television in less than a century. Dry-plate photography came in 1873; Bell patented the telephone in 1876; the phonograph was invented in 1877; the roll film appeared in 1884; Eastman's Kodak No. 1 was produced in 1888; Edison's patent on the radio came in 1891; motion pictures came in and voice was first transmitted by radio around 1900; the first national political convention widely broadcast by radio was that of 1928; television became commercially important in 1941, and color television even more recently.

Verisimilitude took on a new meaning. Not only was it now possible to give the actual voice and gestures of Franklin Delano Roosevelt unprecedented reality and intimacy for a whole nation. Vivid image came to overshadow pale reality. Sound motion pictures in color led a whole generation of

pioneering American movie-goers to think of Benjamin Disraeli as an earlier imitation of George Arliss, just as television
has led a later generation of television watchers to see the
Western cowboy as an inferior replica of John Wayne. The
Grand Canyon itself became a disappointing reproduction of
the Kodachrome original.

The new power to report and portray what had happened
was a new temptation leading newsmen to make probable
images or to prepare reports in advance of what was expected
to happen. As so often, men came to mistake their power
for their necessities. Readers and viewers would soon prefer
the vividness of the account, the "candidness" of the photograph, to the spontaneity of what was recounted.

Then came round-the-clock media. The news gap soon
became so narrow that in order to have additional "news"
for each new edition or each new broadcast it was necessary to plan in advance the stages by which any available
news would be unveiled. After the weekly and the daily
came the "extras" and the numerous regular editions. The
Philadelphia *Evening Bulletin* soon had seven editions a day.
No rest for the newsman. With more space to fill, he had to
fill it ever more quickly. In order to justify the numerous
editions, it was increasingly necessary that the news constantly change or at least seem to change. With radio on the
air continuously during waking hours, the reporters' problems
became still more acute. News every hour on the hour, and
sometimes on the half hour. Programs interrupted any time
for special bulletins. How to avoid deadly repetition, the
appearance that nothing was happening, that news gatherers
were asleep, or that competitors were more alert? As the costs
of printing and then of broadcasting increased, it became
financially necessary to keep the presses always at work and
the TV screen always busy. Pressures toward the making
of pseudo-events became ever stronger. News gathering
turned into news making.

The "interview" was a novel way of making news which
had come in with the Graphic Revolution. Later it became

elaborated into lengthy radio and television panels and quizzes of public figures, and the three-hour-long, rambling conversation programs. Although the interview technique might seem an obvious one—and in a primitive form was as old as Socrates—the use of the word in its modern journalistic sense is a relatively recent Americanism. The Boston *News-Letter*'s account (March 2, 1719) of the death of Blackbeard the Pirate had apparently been based on a kind of interview with a ship captain. One of the earliest interviews of the modern type—some writers call it the first—was by James Gordon Bennett, the flamboyant editor of the New York *Herald* (April 16, 1836), in connection with the Robinson-Jewett murder case. Ellen Jewett, inmate of a house of prostitution, had been found murdered by an ax. Richard P. Robinson, a young man about town, was accused of the crime. Bennett seized the occasion to pyramid sensational stories and so to build circulation for his *Herald;* before long he was having difficulty turning out enough copies daily to satisfy the demand. He exploited the story in every possible way, one of which was to plan and report an actual interview with Rosina Townsend, the madam who kept the house and whom he visited on her own premises.

Historians of journalism date the first full-fledged modern interview with a well-known public figure from July 13, 1859, when Horace Greeley interviewed Brigham Young in Salt Lake City, asking him questions on many matters of public interest, and then publishing the answers verbatim in his New York *Tribune* (August 20, 1859). The common use of the word "interview" in this modern American sense first came in about this time. Very early the institution acquired a reputation for being contrived. "The 'interview,' " *The Nation* complained (January 28, 1869), "as at present managed, is generally the joint product of some humbug of a hack politician and another humbug of a reporter." A few years later another magazine editor called the interview "the most perfect contrivance yet devised to make journalism an offence, a thing of ill savor in all decent nostrils." Many objected to the practice as an invasion of privacy. After the American example it was used in England and France, but in both those countries it made much slower headway.

Even before the invention of the interview, the news-making profession in America had attained a new dignity as well as a menacing power. It was in 1828 that Macaulay called the gallery where reporters sat in Parliament a "fourth estate of the realm." But Macaulay could not have imagined the prestige of journalists in the twentieth-century United States. They have long since made themselves the tribunes of the people. Their supposed detachment and lack of partisanship, their closeness to the sources of information, their articulateness, and their constant and direct access to the whole citizenry have made them also the counselors of the people. Foreign observers are now astonished by the almost constitutional—perhaps we should say supra-constitutional —powers of our Washington press corps.

Since the rise of the modern Presidential press conference, about 1933, capital correspondents have had the power regularly to question the President face-to-face, to embarrass him, to needle him, to force him into positions or into public refusal to take a position. A President may find it inconvenient to meet a group of dissident Senators or Congressmen; he seldom dares refuse the press. That refusal itself becomes news. It is only very recently, and as a result of increasing pressures by newsmen, that the phrase "No comment" has become a way of saying something important. The reputation of newsmen—who now of course include those working for radio, TV, and magazines—depends on their ability to ask hard questions, to put politicians on the spot; their very livelihood depends on the willing collaboration of public figures. Even before 1950 Washington had about 1,500 correspondents and about 3,000 government information officials prepared to serve them.

Not only the regular formal press conferences, but a score of other national programs—such as "Meet the Press" and "Face the Nation"—show the power of newsmen. In 1960

David Susskind's late-night conversation show, "Open End," commanded the presence of the Russian Premier for three hours. During the so-called "Great Debates" that year between the candidates in the Presidential campaign, it was newsmen who called the tune.

The live television broadcasting of the President's regular news conferences, which President Kennedy began in 1961, immediately after taking office, has somewhat changed their character. Newsmen are no longer so important as intermediaries who relay the President's statements. But the new occasion acquires a new interest as a dramatic performance. Citizens who from homes or offices have seen the President at his news conference are then even more interested to hear competing interpretations by skilled commentators. News commentators can add a new appeal as dramatic critics to their traditional role as interpreters of current history. Even in the new format it is still the newsmen who put the questions. They are still tribunes of the people.

III

THE BRITISH CONSTITUTION, shaped as it is from materials accumulated since the middle ages, functions, we have often been told, only because the British people are willing to live with a great number of legal fictions. The monarchy is only the most prominent. We Americans have accommodated our eighteenth-century constitution to twentieth-century technology by multiplying pseudo-events and by developing professions which both help make pseudo-events and help us interpret them. The disproportion between what an informed citizen needs to know and what he can know is ever greater. The disproportion grows with the increase of the officials' powers of concealment and contrivance. The news gatherers' need to select, invent, and plan correspondingly increases. Thus inevitably our whole system of public information produces always more "packaged" news, more pseudo-events.

A trivial but prophetic example of the American penchant for pseudo-events has long been found in our *Congressional Record*. The British and French counterparts, surprisingly enough, give a faithful report of what is said on the floor of their deliberative bodies. But ever since the establishment of the *Congressional Record* under its present title in 1873, our only ostensibly complete report of what goes on in Congress has had no more than the faintest resemblance to what is actually said there. Despite occasional feeble protests, our *Record* has remained a gargantuan miscellany in which actual proceedings are buried beneath undelivered speeches, and mountains of the unread and the unreadable. Only a national humorlessness—or sense of humor—can account for our willingness to tolerate this. Perhaps it also explains why, as a frustrated reformer of the *Record* argued on the floor of the Senate in 1884, "the American public have generally come to regard the proceedings of Congress as a sort of variety performance, where nothing is supposed to be real except the pay."

The common "news releases" which every day issue by the ream from Congressmen's offices, from the President's press secretary, from the press relations offices of businesses, charitable organizations, and universities are a kind of *Congressional Record* covering all American life. And they are only a slightly less inaccurate record of spontaneous happenings. To secure "news coverage" for an event (especially if it has little news interest) one must issue, in proper form, a "release." The very expression "news release" (apparently an American invention; it was first recorded in 1907) did not come into common use until recently. There is an appropriate perversity in calling it a "release." It might more accurately be described as a "news holdback," since its purpose is to offer something that is to be held back from publication until a specified future date. The newspaperman's slightly derogatory slang term for the news release is "handout," from the phrase originally used for a bundle of stale food handed out from a house to a beggar. Though this meaning of the word is now in common use in the news-gathering professions, it is so recent that it has not yet made its way into our dictionaries.

The release is news pre-cooked, and supposed to keep till needed. In the well-recognized format (usually mimeographed) it bears a date, say February 1, and also indicates, "For release to PM's February 15." The account is written in the past tense but usually describes an event that has not yet happened when the release is given out. The use and interpretation of handouts have become an essential part of the newsman's job. The National Press Club in its Washington clubrooms has a large rack which is filled daily with the latest releases, so the reporter does not even have to visit the offices which give them out. In 1947 there were about twice as many government press agents engaged in preparing news releases as there were newsmen gathering them in.

The general public has become so accustomed to these procedures that a public official can sometimes "make news" merely by departing from the advance text given out in his release. When President Kennedy spoke in Chicago on the night of April 28, 1961, early editions of the next morning's newspapers (printed the night before for early-morning home delivery) merely reported his speech as it was given to newsmen in the advance text. When the President abandoned the advance text, later editions of the Chicago *Sun-Times* headlined: "Kennedy Speaks Off Cuff . . ." The article beneath emphasized that he had departed from his advance text and gave about equal space to his off-the-cuff speech and to the speech he never gave. Apparently the most newsworthy fact was that the President had not stuck to his prepared text.

We begin to be puzzled about what is really the "original" of an event. The authentic news record of what "happens" or is said comes increasingly to seem to be what is given out in advance. More and more news events become dramatic performances in which "men in the news" simply act out more or less well their prepared script. The story prepared "for future release" acquires an authenticity that competes with that of the actual occurrences on the scheduled date.

In recent years our successful politicians have been those most adept at using the press and other means to create pseudo-events. President Franklin Delano Roosevelt, whom Heywood Broun called "the best newspaperman who has ever been President of the United States," was the first modern master. While newspaper owners opposed him in editorials which few read, F.D.R. himself, with the collaboration of a friendly corps of Washington correspondents, was using front-page headlines to make news read by everybody. He was making "facts"—pseudo-events—while editorial writers were simply expressing opinions. It is a familiar story how he employed the trial balloon, how he exploited the ethic of off-the-record remarks, how he transformed the Presidential press conference from a boring ritual into a major national institution which no later President dared disrespect, and how he developed the fireside chat. Knowing that newspapermen lived on news, he helped them manufacture it. And he knew enough about news-making techniques to help shape their stories to his own purposes.

Take, for example, these comments which President Roosevelt made at a press conference during his visit to a Civilian Conservation Corps camp in Florida on February 18, 1939, when war tensions were mounting:

> I want to get something across, only don't put it that way. In other words, it is a thing that I cannot put as direct stuff, but it is background. And the way—as you know I very often do it—if I were writing the story, the way I'd write it is this—you know the formula: When asked when he was returning [to Washington], the President intimated that it was impossible to give any date; because, while he hoped to be away until the third or fourth of March, information that continues to be received with respect to the international situation continues to be disturbing, therefore, it may be necessary for the President to return [to the capital] before the third or fourth of March. It is understood that this

information relates to the possible renewal of demands
by certain countries, these demands being pushed, not
through normal diplomatic channels but, rather, through
the more recent type of relations; in other words, the
use of fear of aggression.

F.D.R. was a man of great warmth, natural spontaneity,
and simple eloquence, and his public utterances reached the
citizen with a new intimacy. Yet, paradoxically, it was under his administrations that statements by the President attained a new subtlety and a new calculatedness. On his
production team, in addition to newspapermen, there were
poets, playwrights, and a regular corps of speech writers.
Far from detracting from his effectiveness, this collaborative
system for producing the impression of personal frankness
and spontaneity provided an additional subject of newsworthy interest. Was it Robert Sherwood or Judge Samuel
Rosenman who contributed this or that phrase? How much
had the President revised the draft given him by his speech-
writing team? Citizens became nearly as much interested in
how a particular speech was put together as in what it said.
And when the President spoke, almost everyone knew it
was a long-planned group production in which F.D.R. was
only the star performer.

Of course President Roosevelt made many great decisions and lived in times which he only helped make stirring.
But it is possible to build a political career almost entirely
on pseudo-events. Such was that of the late Joseph R. Mc-
Carthy, Senator from Wisconsin from 1947 to 1957. His
career might have been impossible without the elaborate,
perpetually grinding machinery of "information" which I
have already described. And he was a natural genius at
creating reportable happenings that had an interestingly ambiguous relation to underlying reality. Richard Rovere, a reporter in Washington during McCarthy's heyday, recalls:

> He knew how to get into the news even on those rare
> occasions when invention failed him and he had no un-

facts to give out. For example, he invented the morning press conference called for the purpose of announcing an afternoon press conference. The reporters would come in—they were beginning, in this period, to respond to his summonses like Pavlov's dogs at the clang of a bell—and McCarthy would say that he just wanted to give them the word that he expected to be ready with a shattering announcement later in the day, for use in the papers the following morning. This would gain him a headline in the afternoon papers: "New McCarthy Revelations Awaited in Capital." Afternoon would come, and if McCarthy had something, he would give it out, but often enough he had nothing, and this was a matter of slight concern. He would simply say that he wasn't quite ready, that he was having difficulty in getting some of the "documents" he needed or that a "witness" was proving elusive. Morning headlines: "Delay Seen in McCarthy Case—Mystery Witness Being Sought."

He had a diabolical fascination and an almost hypnotic power over news-hungry reporters. They were somehow reluctantly grateful to him for turning out their product. They stood astonished that he could make so much news from such meager raw material. Many hated him; all helped him. They were victims of what one of them called their "indiscriminate objectivity." In other words, McCarthy and the newsmen both thrived on the same synthetic commodity.

Senator McCarthy's political fortunes were promoted almost as much by newsmen who considered themselves his enemies as by those few who were his friends. Without the active help of all of them he could never have created the pseudo-events which brought him notoriety and power. Newspaper editors, who self-righteously attacked the Senator's "collaborators," themselves proved worse than powerless to cut him down to size. Even while they attacked him on the editorial page inside, they were building him up in front-page headlines. Newspapermen were his most potent allies, for they were his co-manufacturers of pseudo-events. They were caught in their own web. Honest newsmen and the unscrupulous Senator McCarthy were in separate branches of the same business.

In the traditional vocabulary of newspapermen, there is a well-recognized distinction between "hard" and "soft" news. Hard news is supposed to be the solid report of significant matters: politics, economics, international relations, social welfare, science. Soft news reports popular interests, curiosities, and diversions: it includes sensational local reporting, scandalmongering, gossip columns, comic strips, the sexual lives of movie stars, and the latest murder. Journalist-critics attack American newspapers today for not being "serious" enough, for giving a larger and larger proportion of their space to soft rather than to hard news.

But the rising tide of pseudo-events washes away the distinction. Here is one example. On June 21, 1960, President Eisenhower was in Honolulu, en route to the Far East for a trip to meet the heads of government in Korea, the Philippines, and elsewhere. A seven-column headline in the Chicago *Daily News* brought readers the following information: "What Are Ike's Feelings About Trip? Aides Mum" "Doesn't Show Any Worry" "Members of Official Party Resent Queries by Newsmen." And the two-column story led off:

HONOLULU—President Eisenhower's reaction to his Far Eastern trip remains as closely guarded a secret as his golf score. While the President rests at Kaneohe Marine air station on the windward side of the Pali hills, hard by the blue Pacific and an 18-hole golf course, he might be toting up the pluses and minuses of his Asian sojourn. But there is no evidence of it. Members of his official party resent any inquiry into how the White House feels about the whole experience, especially the blowup of the Japanese visit which produced a critical storm.

The story concludes: "But sooner or later the realities will intrude. The likelihood is that it will be sooner than later."

Nowadays a successful reporter must be the midwife—or more often the conceiver—of his news. By the interview technique he incites a public figure to make statements which will sound like news. During the twentieth century this technique has grown into a devious apparatus which, in skillful hands, can shape national policy.

The pressure of time, and the need to produce a uniform news stream to fill the issuing media, induce Washington correspondents and others to use the interview and other techniques for making pseudo-events in novel, ever more ingenious and aggressive ways. One of the main facts of life for the wire service reporter in Washington is that there are many more afternoon than morning papers in the United States. The early afternoon paper on the East Coast goes to press about 10 A.M., before the spontaneous news of the day has had an opportunity to develop. "It means," one conscientious capital correspondent confides, in Douglass Cater's admirable *Fourth Branch of Government* (1959), "the wire service reporter must engage in the basically phony operation of writing the 'overnight'—a story composed the previous evening but giving the impression when it appears the next afternoon that it covers that day's events."

What this can mean in a particular case is illustrated by the tribulations of a certain hard-working reporter who was trying to do his job and earn his keep at the time when the Austrian Treaty of 1955 came up for debate in the Senate. Although it was a matter of some national and international importance, the adoption of the Treaty was a foregone conclusion; there would be little news in it. So, in order to make a story, this reporter went to Senator Walter George, Chairman of the Senate Foreign Relations Committee, and extracted a statement to the effect that under the Treaty Austria would receive no money or military aid, only long-term credits. "That became my lead," the reporter recalled. "I had fulfilled the necessary function of having a story that seemed to be part of the next day's news."

The next day, the Treaty came up for debate. The debate was dull, and it was hard to squeeze out a story. Luckily, however, Senator Jenner made a nasty crack about President Eisenhower, which the reporter (after considering what other wire service reporters covering the story might be doing) sent off as an "insert." The Treaty was adopted by the Senate a little after 3:30 P.M. That automatically made a bulletin and required a new lead for the story on the debate. But by that time the hard-pressed reporter was faced with writing a completely new story for the next day's morning papers.

But my job had not finished. The Treaty adoption bulletin had gone out too late to get into most of the East Coast afternoon papers except the big city ones like the Philadelphia *Evening Bulletin,* which has seven editions. I had to find a new angle for an overnight to be carried next day by those P.M.'s which failed to carry the Treaty story.

They don't want to carry simply a day-old account of the debate. They want a "top" to the news. So, to put it quite bluntly, I went and got Senator Thye to say that Jenner by his actions was weakening the President's authority. Actually, the Thye charge was more lively news than the passage of the Austrian Treaty itself. It revealed conflict among the Senate Republicans. But the story had developed out of my need for a new peg for the news. It was not spontaneous on Thye's part. I had called seven other Senators before I could get someone to make a statement on Jenner. There is a fair criticism, I recognize, to be made of this practice. These Senators didn't call me. I called them. I, in a sense, generated the news. The reporter's imagination brought the Senator's thinking to bear on alternatives that he might not have thought of by himself.

This can be a very pervasive practice. One wire service reporter hounded Senator George daily on the foreign trade question until he finally got George to make the suggestion that Japan should trade with Red China as an alternative to dumping textiles on the American market. Then the reporter went straightway to Senator Knowland to get him to knock down the suggestion. It made a good story, and it also stimulated a minor policy debate that might not have got started otherwise. The "overnight" is the greatest single field for exploratory reporting for the wire services. It is what might be called "milking the news."

The reporter shrewdly adds that the task of his profession today is seldom to compose accounts of the latest events at lightning speed. Rather, it is shaped by "the problem of packaging." He says: "Our job is to report the news but it is also to keep a steady flow of news coming forward. Every Saturday morning, for example, we visit the Congressional leaders. We could write all the stories that we get out of these conferences for the Sunday A.M.'s but we don't. We learn to schedule them in order to space them out over Sunday's and Monday's papers."

An innocent observer might have expected that the rise of television and on-the-spot telecasting of the news would produce a pressure to report authentic spontaneous events exactly as they occur. But, ironically, these, like earlier improvements in the techniques of precise representation, have simply created more and better pseudo-events.

When General Douglas MacArthur returned to the United States (after President Truman relieved him of command in the Far East, on April 11, 1951, during the Korean War) he made a "triumphal" journey around the country. He was invited to help Chicago celebrate "MacArthur Day" (April 26, 1951) which had been proclaimed by resolution of the City Council. Elaborate ceremonies were arranged, including a parade. The proceedings were being televised.

A team of thirty-one University of Chicago sociologists, under the imaginative direction of Kurt Lang, took their posts at strategic points along the route of the MacArthur parade. The purpose was to note the reactions of the crowd and to compare what the spectators were seeing (or said they were seeing) with what they might have witnessed on television. This ingenious study confirmed my observation that we tend increasingly to fill our experience with contrived content. The newspapers had, of course, already prepared people for what the Chicago *Tribune* that morning predicted to be "a triumphant hero's welcome—biggest and warmest in the history of the middle west." Many of the actual spectators jammed in the crowd at the scene complained it was hard to see what was going on; in some places they waited for hours and then were lucky to have a fleeting glimpse of the General.

But the television perspective was quite different. The video viewer had the advantage of numerous cameras which were widely dispersed. Television thus ordered the events in its own way, quite different from that of the on-the-spot confusion. The cameras were carefully focused on "significant" happenings—that is, those which emphasized the drama of the occasion. For the television watcher, the General was the continuous center of attraction from his appearance during the parade at 2:21 P.M. until the sudden blackout at 3:00 P.M. Announcers continually reiterated (the scripts showed over fifteen explicit references) the unprecedented drama of the event, or that this was "the greatest ovation this city has ever turned out." On the television screen one received the impression of wildly cheering and enthusiastic crowds before, during, and after the parade. Of course the cameras were specially selecting "action" shots, which showed a noisy, waving audience; yet in many cases the cheering, waving, and shouting were really a response not so much to the General as to the aiming of the camera. Actual spectators, with sore feet, suffered long periods of boredom. Many groups were apathetic. The video viewer, his eyes fixed alternately on the General and on an enthusiastic crowd, his ears filled with a breathless narrative emphasizing the interplay of crowd and celebrity, could not fail to receive an impression of continuous dramatic pageantry.

The most important single conclusion of these sociologists was that the television presentation (as contrasted with the actual witnessing) of the events "remained true to form until the very end, interpreting the entire proceedings according to expectations. . . . The telecast was made to conform to what was interpreted as the pattern of viewers' expectations." Actual spectators at the scene were doubly disappointed, not only because they usually saw very little (and that only briefly) from where they happened to be standing, but also because they knew they were missing a much better performance (with far more of the drama they expected) on the television screen. "I bet my wife saw it much better over television!" and "We should have stayed home and watched it on TV" were the almost universal forms of dissatisfaction. While those at the scene were envying the viewers of the pseudo-event back home, the television viewers were, of course, being told again and again by the network commentators how great was the excitement of being "actually present."

Yet, as the Chicago sociologists noted, for many of those actually present one of the greatest thrills of the day was the opportunity to be on television. Just as everybody likes to see his name in the newspapers, so nearly everybody likes to think that he can be seen (or still better, with the aid of videotape, actually can see himself) on television. Similarly, reporters following candidates Kennedy and Nixon during their tours in the 1960 Presidential campaign noted how many of the "supporters" in the large crowds that were being televised had come out because they wanted to be seen on the television cameras.

Television reporting allows us all to be the actors we really are. Recently I wandered onto the campus of the University of Chicago and happened to witness a tug of war between teams of students. It was amusing to see the women's team drench the men's team by pulling them into Botany Pond.

Television cameras of the leading networks were there. The victory of the women's team seemed suspiciously easy to me. I was puzzled until told that this was not the original contest at all; the real tug of war had occurred a day or two before when telecasting conditions were not so good. This was a re-enactment for television.

On December 2, 1960, during the school integration disorders in New Orleans, Mayor de Lesseps S. Morrison wrote a letter to newsmen proposing a three-day moratorium on news and television coverage of the controversy. He argued that the printed and televised reports were exaggerated and were damaging the city's reputation and its tourist trade. People were given an impression of prevailing violence, when, he said, only one-tenth of 1 per cent of the population had been involved in the demonstration. But he also pointed out that the mere presence of telecasting facilities was breeding disorder. "In many cases," he observed, "these people go to the area to get themselves on television and hurry home for the afternoon and evening telecasts to see the show." At least two television reporters had gone about the crowd interviewing demonstrators with inflammatory questions like "Why are you opposed to intermarriage?" Mayor Morrison said he himself had witnessed a television cameraman "setting up a scene," and then, having persuaded a group of students to respond like a "cheering section," had them yell and demonstrate on cue. The conscientious reporters indignantly rejected the Mayor's proposed moratorium on news. They said that "Freedom of the Press" was at stake. That was once an institution preserved in the interest of the community. Now it is often a euphemism for the prerogative of reporters to produce their synthetic commodity.

I V

IN MANY subtle ways, the rise of pseudo-events has mixed up our roles as actors and as audience—or, the philosophers would say, as "object" and as "subject." Now we can oscillate between the two roles. "The movies are the only business," Will Rogers once remarked, "where you can go out front and applaud yourself." Nowadays one need not be a professional actor to have this satisfaction. We can appear in the mob scene and then go home and see ourselves on the television screen. No wonder we become confused about what is spontaneous, about what is really going on out there!

New forms of pseudo-events, especially in the world of politics, thus offer a new kind of bewilderment to both politician and newsman. The politician (like F.D.R. in our example, or any holder of a press conference) himself in a sense composes the story; the journalist (like the wire service reporter we have quoted, or any newsman who incites an inflammatory statement) himself generates the event. The citizen can hardly be expected to assess the reality when the participants themselves are so often unsure who is doing the deed and who is making the report of it. Who is the history, and who is the historian?

An admirable example of this new intertwinement of subject and object, of the history and the historian, of the actor and the reporter, is the so-called news "leak." By now the leak has become an important and well-established institution in American politics. It is, in fact, one of the main vehicles for communicating important information from officials to the public.

A clue to the new unreality of the citizen's world is the perverse new meaning now given to the word "leak." To leak, according to the dictionary, is to "let a fluid substance out or in accidentally: as, the ship leaks." But nowadays a news leak is one of the most elaborately planned ways of emitting information. It is, of course, a way in which a government official, with some clearly defined purpose (a leak, even more than a direct announcement, is apt to have some definite devious purpose behind it) makes an announcement, asks a question, or puts a suggestion. It might more accurately be called a *"sub rosa* announcement," an "indirect statement," or "cloaked news."

The news leak is a pseudo-event par excellence. In its origin and growth, the leak illustrates another axiom of the world of pseudo-events: pseudo-events produce more pseudo-events. I will say more on this later.

With the elaboration of news-gathering facilities in Washington—of regular, planned press conferences, of prepared statements for future release, and of countless other practices—the news protocol has hardened. Both government officials and reporters have felt the need for more flexible and more ambiguous modes of communication between them. The Presidential press conference itself actually began as a kind of leak. President Theodore Roosevelt for some time allowed Lincoln Steffens to interview him as he was being shaved. Other Presidents gave favored correspondents an interview from time to time or dropped hints to friendly journalists. Similarly, the present institution of the news leak began in the irregular practice of a government official's helping a particular correspondent by confidentially giving him information not yet generally released. But today the leak is almost as well organized and as rigidly ruled by protocol as a formal press conference. Being fuller of ambiguity, with a welcome atmosphere of confidence and intrigue, it is more appealing to all concerned. The institutionalized leak puts a greater burden of contrivance and pretense on both government officials and reporters.

In Washington these days, and elsewhere on a smaller scale, the custom has grown up among important members of the government of arranging to dine with select representatives of the news corps. Such dinners are usually preceded by drinks, and beforehand there is a certain amount of restrained conviviality. Everyone knows the rules: the occasion is private, and any information given out afterwards must be communicated according to rule and in the technically proper vocabulary. After dinner the undersecretary, the general, or the admiral allows himself to be questioned. He may recount "facts" behind past news, state plans, or declare policy. The reporters have confidence, if not in the ingenuousness of the official, at least in their colleagues' respect of the protocol. Everybody understands the degree of attribution permissible for every statement made: what, if anything, can be directly quoted, what is "background," what is "deep background," what must be ascribed to "a spokesman," to "an informed source," to speculation, to rumor, or to remote possibility.

Such occasions and the reports flowing from them are loaded with ambiguity. The reporter himself often is not clear whether he is being told a simple fact, a newly settled policy, an administrative hope, or whether perhaps untruths are being deliberately diffused to allay public fears that the true facts are really true. The government official himself (who is sometimes no more than a spokesman) may not be clear. The reporter's task is to find a way of weaving these threads of unreality into a fabric that the reader will not recognize as entirely unreal. Some people have criticized the institutionalized leak as a form of domestic counter-intelligence inappropriate in a republic. It has become more and more important and is the source today of many of the most influential reports of current politics.

One example will be enough. On March 26, 1955, *The New York Times* carried a three-column headline on the front page: "U.S. Expects Chinese Reds to Attack Isles in April; Weighs All-Out Defense." Three days later a contradictory headline in the same place read: "Eisenhower Sees No War Now Over Chinese Isles." Under each of these headlines appeared a lengthy story. Neither story named any person as a source of the ostensible facts. The then-undisclosed story (months later recorded by Douglass Cater) was this. In the first instance, Admiral Robert B. Carney, Chief of Naval Operations, had an off-the-record "background" dinner for a few reporters. There the Admiral gave reporters what they (and their readers) took to be facts. Since the story was "not for attribution," reporters were not free to mention some very relevant facts—such as that this was the opinion only of Admiral Carney, that this was the same Admiral Carney who had long been saying that war in Asia was inevitable, and that many in Washington (even in the Joint Chiefs of Staff) did not agree with him. Under the ground rules the first story could appear in the papers only by being given an impersonal authority, an atmosphere of official unanimity which it did not merit. The second, and contradictory, statement was in fact made not by the President himself, but by the President's press secretary, James Hagerty, who, having been alarmed by what he saw in the papers, quickly called a second "background" meeting to deny the stories that had sprouted from the first. What, if anything, did it all mean? Was there any real news here at all—except that there was disagreement between Admiral Carney and James Hagerty? Yet this was the fact newsmen were not free to print.

Pseudo-events spawn other pseudo-events in geometric progression. This is partly because every kind of pseudo-event (being planned) tends to become ritualized, with a protocol and a rigidity all its own. As each type of pseudo-event acquires this rigidity, pressures arise to produce other, derivative, forms of pseudo-event which are more fluid, more tantalizing, and more interestingly ambiguous. Thus, as the press conference (itself a pseudo-event) became formalized, there grew up the institutionalized leak. As the leak becomes formalized still other devices will appear. Of course the shrewd politician or the enterprising newsman knows this and knows how to take advantage of it. Seldom for outright deception; more often simply to make more "news," to provide more "information," or to "improve communication."

For example, a background off-the-record press conference, if it is actually a mere trial balloon or a diplomatic device (as it sometimes was for Secretary of State John Foster Dulles), becomes the basis of official "denials" and "disavowals," of speculation and interpretation by columnists and commentators, and of special interviews on and off television with Senators, Representatives, and other public officials.

Any statement or non-statement by anyone in the public eye can become the basis of counter-statements or refusals to comment by others. All these compound the ambiguity of the occasion which first brought them into being.

Nowadays the test of a Washington reporter is seldom his skill at precise dramatic reporting, but more often his adeptness at dark intimation. If he wishes to keep his news channels open he must accumulate a vocabulary and develop a style to conceal his sources and obscure the relation of a supposed event or statement to the underlying facts of life, at the same time seeming to offer hard facts. Much of his stock in trade is his own and other people's speculation about the reality of what he reports. He lives in a penumbra between fact and fantasy. He helps create that very obscurity without which the supposed illumination of his reports would be unnecessary. A deft administrator these days must have similar skills. He must master "the technique of denying the truth without actually lying."

These pseudo-events which flood our consciousness must be distinguished from propaganda. The two do have some characteristics in common. But our peculiar problems come from the fact that pseudo-events are in some respects the opposite of the propaganda which rules totalitarian countries. Propaganda—as prescribed, say, by Hitler in *Mein Kampf* —is information intentionally biased. Its effect depends primarily on its emotional appeal. While a pseudo-event is an ambiguous truth, propaganda is an appealing falsehood. Pseudo-events thrive on our honest desire to be informed, to have "all the facts," and even to have more facts than there really are. But propaganda feeds on our willingness to be inflamed. Pseudo-events appeal to our duty to be educated, propaganda appeals to our desire to be aroused. While propaganda substitutes opinion for facts, pseudo-events are synthetic facts which move people indirectly, by providing the "factual" basis on which they are supposed to make up their minds. Propaganda moves them directly by explicitly making judgments for them.

In a totalitarian society, where people are flooded by purposeful lies, the real facts are of course misrepresented, but the representation itself is not ambiguous. The propaganda lie is asserted as if it were true. Its object is to lead people to believe that the truth is simpler, more intelligible, than it really is. "Now the purpose of propaganda," Hitler explained, "is not continually to produce interesting changes for a few blasé little masters, but to convince; that means, to convince the masses. The masses, however, with their inertia, always need a certain time before they are ready even to notice a thing, and they will lend their memories only to the thousandfold repetition of the most simple ideas." But in our society, pseudo-events make simple facts seem more subtle, more ambiguous, and more speculative than they really are. Propaganda oversimplifies experience, pseudo-events overcomplicate it.

At first it may seem strange that the rise of pseudo-events has coincided with the growth of the professional ethic which obliges newsmen to omit editorializing and personal judgments from their news accounts. But now it is in the making of pseudo-events that newsmen find ample scope for their individuality and creative imagination.

In a democratic society like ours—and more especially in a highly literate, wealthy, competitive, and technologically advanced society—the people can be flooded by pseudo-events. For us, freedom of speech and of the press and of broadcasting includes freedom to create pseudo-events. Competing politicians, competing newsmen, and competing news media contest in this creation. They vie with one another in offering attractive, "informative" accounts and images of the world. They are free to speculate on the facts, to bring new facts into being, to demand answers to their own contrived questions. Our "free market place of ideas" is a place where people are confronted by competing pseudo-events and are allowed to judge among them. When we speak of "informing" the people this is what we really mean.

V

UNTIL RECENTLY we have been justified in believing Abraham Lincoln's familiar maxim: "You may fool all the people some of the time; you can even fool some of the people all the time; but you can't fool all of the people all the time." This has been the foundation-belief of American democracy. Lincoln's appealing slogan rests on two elementary assumptions. First, that there is a clear and visible distinction between sham and reality, between the lies a demagogue would have us believe and the truths which are there all the time. Second, that the people tend to prefer reality to sham, that if offered a choice between a simple truth and a contrived image, they will prefer the truth.

Neither of these any longer fits the facts. Not because people are less intelligent or more dishonest. Rather because great unforeseen changes—the great forward strides of American civilization—have blurred the edges of reality. The pseudo-events which flood our consciousness are neither true nor false in the old familiar senses. The very same advances which have made them possible have also made the images—however planned, contrived, or distorted—more vivid, more attractive, more impressive, and more persuasive than reality itself.

We cannot say that we are being fooled. It is not entirely inaccurate to say that we are being "informed." This world of ambiguity is created by those who believe they are instructing us, by our best public servants, and with our own collaboration. Our problem is the harder to solve because it is created by people working honestly and industriously at respectable jobs. It is not created by demagogues or crooks, by conspiracy or evil purpose. The efficient mass production of pseudo-events—in all kinds of packages, in black-and-white, in technicolor, in words, and in a thousand other forms —is the work of the whole machinery of our society. It is the daily product of men of good will. The media must be fed! The people must be informed! Most pleas for "more information" are therefore misguided. So long as we define information as a knowledge of pseudo-events, "more information" will simply multiply the symptoms without curing the disease.

The American citizen thus lives in a world where fantasy is more real than reality, where the image has more dignity than its original. We hardly dare face our bewilderment, because our ambiguous experience is so pleasantly iridescent, and the solace of belief in contrived reality is so thoroughly real. We have become eager accessories to the great hoaxes of the age. These are the hoaxes we play on ourselves.

Pseudo-events from their very nature tend to be more interesting and more attractive than spontaneous events. Therefore in American public life today pseudo-events tend to drive all other kinds of events out of our consciousness, or at least to overshadow them. Earnest, well-informed citizens seldom notice that their experience of spontaneous events is buried by pseudo-events. Yet nowadays, the more industriously they work at "informing" themselves the more this tends to be true.

In his now-classic work, *Public Opinion,* Walter Lippmann in 1922 began by distinguishing between "the world outside and the pictures in our heads." He defined a "stereotype" as an oversimplified pattern that helps us find meaning in the world. As examples he gave the crude "stereotypes we carry about in our heads," of large and varied classes of people like "Germans," "South Europeans," "Negroes," "Harvard men," "agitators," etc. The stereotype, Lippmann explained, satisfies our needs and helps us defend our prejudices by seeming to give definiteness and consistency to our turbulent and disorderly daily experience. In one sense, of course, stereotypes—the excessively simple, but easily grasped images of racial, national, or religious groups—are only another example of pseudo-events. But, generally speaking, they are closer to propaganda. For they simplify rather than complicate. Stereotypes narrow and limit experience in an emotionally satisfying way; but pseudo-events embroider and dramatize experience in an interesting way. This itself makes pseudo-events far more seductive; intellectually they are more defensible, more intricate, and more intriguing. To discover how the stereotype is made— to unmask the sources of propaganda—is to make the stereotype less believable. Information about the staging of a pseudo-event simply adds to its fascination.

Lippmann's description of stereotypes was helpful in its day. But he wrote before pseudo-events had come in full flood. Photographic journalism was then still in its infancy. Wide World Photos had just been organized by *The New York Times* in 1919. The first wirephoto to attract wide attention was in 1924, when the American Telephone and Telegraph Company sent to *The New York Times* pictures of the Republican Convention in Cleveland which nominated Calvin Coolidge. Associated Press Picture Service was established in 1928. *Life,* the first wide-circulating weekly picture news magazine, appeared in 1936; within a year it had a circulation of 1,000,000, and within two years, 2,000,000. *Look* followed, in 1937. The newsreel, originated in France by Pathé, had been introduced to the United States only in 1910. When Lippmann wrote his book in 1922, radio was not yet reporting news to the consumer; television was of course unknown.

Recent improvements in vividness and speed, the enlargement and multiplying of news-reporting media, and the public's increasing news hunger now make Lippmann's brilliant analysis of the stereotype the legacy of a simpler age. For stereotypes made experience handy to grasp. But pseudo-events would make experience newly and satisfyingly elusive. In 1911 Will Irwin, writing in *Collier's,* described the new era's growing public demand for news as "a crying primal want of the mind, like hunger of the body." The mania for news was a symptom of expectations enlarged far beyond the capacity of the natural world to satisfy. It required a synthetic product. It stirred an irrational and undiscriminating hunger for fancier, more varied items. Stereotypes there had been and always would be; but they only dulled the palate for information. They were an opiate. Pseudo-events whetted the appetite; they aroused news hunger in the very act of satisfying it.

In the age of pseudo-events it is less the artificial simplification than the artificial complication of experience that confuses us. Whenever in the public mind a pseudo-event competes for attention with a spontaneous event in the same field, the pseudo-event will tend to dominate. What happens on television will overshadow what happens off television. Of course I am concerned here not with our private worlds but with our world of public affairs.

Here are some characteristics of pseudo-events which make them overshadow spontaneous events:

(1) Pseudo-events are more dramatic. A television debate between candidates can be planned to be more suspenseful (for example, by reserving questions which are then popped suddenly) than a casual encounter or consecutive formal speeches planned by each separately.

(2) Pseudo-events, being planned for dissemination, are easier to disseminate and to make vivid. Participants are selected for their newsworthy and dramatic interest.

(3) Pseudo-events can be repeated at will, and thus their impression can be re-enforced.

(4) Pseudo-events cost money to create; hence somebody has an interest in disseminating, magnifying, advertising, and extolling them as events worth watching or worth believing. They are therefore advertised in advance, and rerun in order to get money's worth.

(5) Pseudo-events, being planned for intelligibility, are more intelligible and hence more reassuring. Even if we cannot discuss intelligently the qualifications of the candidates or the complicated issues, we can at

least judge the effectiveness of a television performance. How comforting to have some political matter we can grasp!

(6) Pseudo-events are more sociable, more conversable, and more convenient to witness. Their occurrence is planned for our convenience. The Sunday newspaper appears when we have a lazy morning for it. Television programs appear when we are ready with our glass of beer. In the office the next morning, Jack Paar's (or any other star performer's) regular late-night show at the usual hour will overshadow in conversation a casual event that suddenly came up and had to find its way into the news.

(7) Knowledge of pseudo-events—of what has been reported, or what has been staged, and how—becomes the test of being "informed." News magazines provide us regularly with quiz questions concerning not what has happened but concerning "names in the news"—what has been reported in the news magazines. Pseudo-events begin to provide that "common discourse" which some of my old-fashioned friends have hoped to find in the Great Books.

(8) Finally, pseudo-events spawn other pseudo-events in geometric progression. They dominate our consciousness simply because there are more of them, and ever more.

By this new Gresham's law of American public life, counterfeit happenings tend to drive spontaneous happenings out of circulation. The rise in the power and prestige of the Presidency is due not only to the broadening powers of the office and the need for quick decisions, but also to the rise of centralized news gathering and broadcasting, and the increase of the Washington press corps. The President has an ever more ready, more frequent, and more centralized access to the world of pseudo-events. A similar explanation helps account for the rising prominence in recent years of the Congressional investigating committees. In many cases these committees have virtually no legislative impulse, and sometimes no intelligible legislative assignment. But they do have an almost unprecedented power, possessed now by no one else in the Federal government except the President, to make news. Newsmen support the committees because the committees feed the newsmen: they live together in happy symbiosis. The battle for power among Washington agencies becomes a contest to dominate the citizen's information of the government. This can most easily be done by fabricating pseudo-events.

A perfect example of how pseudo-events can dominate is the recent popularity of the quiz show format. Its original appeal came less from the fact that such shows were tests of intelligence (or of dissimulation) than from the fact that the situations were elaborately contrived—with isolation booths, armed bank guards, and all the rest—and they purported to inform the public.

The application of the quiz show format to the so-called "Great Debates" between Presidential candidates in the election of 1960 is only another example. These four campaign programs, pompously and self-righteously advertised by the broadcasting networks, were remarkably successful in reducing great national issues to trivial dimensions. With appropriate vulgarity, they might have been called the $400,000 Question (Prize: a $100,000-a-year job for four years). They were a clinical example of the pseudo-event, of how it is made, why it appeals, and of its consequences for democracy in America.

In origin the Great Debates were confusedly collaborative between politicians and news makers. Public interest centered around the pseudo-event itself: the lighting, make-up, ground rules, whether notes would be allowed, etc. Far more interest was shown in the performance than in what was said. The pseudo-events spawned in turn by the Great Debates were numberless. People who had seen the shows read about them the more avidly, and listened eagerly for interpretations by news commentators. Representatives of both parties made "statements" on the probable effects of the debates. Numerous interviews and discussion programs were broadcast exploring their meaning. Opinion polls kept us informed on the nuances of our own and other people's reactions. Topics of speculation multiplied. Even the question whether there should be a fifth debate became for a while a lively "issue."

The drama of the situation was mostly specious, or at least had an extremely ambiguous relevance to the main (but forgotten) issue: which participant was better qualified for the Presidency. Of course, a man's ability, while standing under klieg lights, without notes, to answer in two and a half minutes a question kept secret until that moment, had only the most dubious relevance—if any at all—to his real qualifications to make deliberate Presidential decisions on long-standing public questions after being instructed by a corps of advisers. The great Presidents in our history (with the possible exception of F.D.R.) would have done miserably; but our most notorious demagogues would have shone. A number of exciting pseudo-events were created—for example, the Quemoy-Matsu issue. But that, too, was a good example of a pseudo-event: it was created to be reported, it concerned a then-quiescent problem, and it put into the most factitious and trivial terms the great and real issue of our relation to Communist China.

The television medium shapes this new kind of political quiz-show spectacular in many crucial ways. Theodore H. White has proven this with copious detail in his *The Making of the President: 1960* (1961). All the circumstances of this particular competition for votes were far more novel than the old word "debate" and the comparisons with the Lincoln-Douglas Debates suggested. Kennedy's great strength in the critical first debate, according to White, was that he was in fact not "debating" at all, but was seizing the opportunity to address the whole nation; while Nixon stuck close to the issues raised by his opponent, rebutting them one by one.

Nixon, moreover, suffered a handicap that was serious only on television: he has a light, naturally transparent skin. On an ordinary camera that takes pictures by optical projection, this skin photographs well. But a television camera projects electronically, by an "image-orthicon tube" which has an x-ray effect. This camera penetrates Nixon's transparent skin and brings out (even just after a shave) the tiniest hair growing in the follicles beneath the surface. For the decisive first program Nixon wore a make-up called "Lazy Shave" which was ineffective under these conditions. He therefore looked haggard and heavy-bearded by contrast to Kennedy, who looked pert and clean-cut.

This greatest opportunity in American history to educate the voters by debating the large issues of the campaign failed. The main reason, as White points out, was the compulsions of the medium. "The nature of both TV and radio is that they abhor silence and 'dead time.' All TV and radio discussion programs are compelled to snap question and answer back and forth as if the contestants were adversaries in an intellectual tennis match. Although every experienced newspaperman and inquirer knows that the most thoughtful and responsive answers to any difficult question come after long pause, and that the longer the pause the more illuminating the thought that follows it, nonetheless the electronic media cannot bear to suffer a pause of more than five seconds; a pause of thirty seconds of dead time on air seems interminable. Thus, snapping their two-and-a-half-minute answers back and forth, both candidates could only react for the cameras and the people, they could not think." Whenever either candidate found himself touching a thought too large for two-minute exploration, he quickly retreated. Finally the television-watching voter was left to judge, not on issues explored by thoughtful men, but on the relative capacity of the two candidates to perform under television stress.

Pseudo-events thus lead to emphasis on pseudo-qualifications. Again the self-fulfilling prophecy. If we test Presidential candidates by their talents on TV quiz performances, we will, of course, choose presidents for precisely these qualifications. In a democracy, reality tends to conform to the pseudo-event. Nature imitates art.

We are frustrated by our very efforts publicly to unmask the pseudo-event. Whenever we describe the lighting, the make-up, the studio setting, the rehearsals, etc., we simply arouse more interest. One newsman's interpretation makes us more eager to hear another's. One commentator's speculation that the debates may have little significance makes us curious to hear whether another commentator disagrees.

Pseudo-events do, of course, increase our illusion of grasp on the world, what some have called the American illusion of omnipotence. Perhaps, we come to think, the world's problems can really be settled by "statements," by "Summit" meetings, by a competition of "prestige," by overshadowing images, and by political quiz shows.

Once we have tasted the charm of pseudo-events, we are tempted to believe they are the only important events. Our progress poisons the sources of our experience. And the poison tastes so sweet that it spoils our appetite for plain fact. Our seeming ability to satisfy our exaggerated expectations makes us forget that they are exaggerated.

2

From Hero to Celebrity:
The Human Pseudo-Event

"He's the greatest!"
ANONYMOUS (BECOMING UNANIMOUS)

IN THE last half century we have misled ourselves, not only about how much novelty the world contains, but about men themselves, and how much greatness can be found among them. One of the oldest of man's visions was the flash of divinity in the great man. He seemed to appear for reasons men could not understand, and the secret of his greatness was God's secret. His generation thanked God for him as for the rain, for the Grand Canyon or the Matterhorn, or for being saved from wreck at sea.

Since the Graphic Revolution, however, much of our thinking about human greatness has changed. Two centuries ago when a great man appeared, people looked for God's purpose in him; today we look for his press agent. Shakespeare, in the familiar lines, divided great men into three classes: those born great, those who achieved greatness, and those who had greatness thrust upon them. It never occurred to him to mention those who hired public relations experts and press secretaries to make themselves look great. Now it is hard even to remember the time when the "Hall of Fame" was only a metaphor, whose inhabitants were selected by

45

the inscrutable processes of history instead of by an *ad hoc* committee appointed to select the best-known names from the media.

The root of our problem, the social source of these exaggerated expectations, is in our novel power to make men famous. Of course, there never was a time when "fame" was precisely the same thing as "greatness." But, until very recently, famous men and great men were pretty nearly the same group. "Fame," wrote Milton, "is the spur the clear spirit doth raise. . . . Fame is no plant that grows on mortal soil." A man's name was not apt to become a household word unless he exemplified greatness in some way or other. He might be a Napoleon, great in power, a J. P. Morgan, great in wealth, a St. Francis, great in virtue, or a Bluebeard, great in evil. To become known to a whole people a man usually had to be something of a hero: as the dictionary tells us, a man "admired for his courage, nobility, or exploits." The war hero was the prototype, because the battle tested character and offered a stage for daring deeds.

Before the Graphic Revolution, the slow, the "natural," way of becoming well known was the usual way. Of course, there were a few men like the Pharaohs and Augustus and the Shah Jahan, who built monuments in their own day to advertise themselves to posterity. But a monument to command the admiration of a whole people was not quickly built. Thus great men, like famous men, came into a nation's consciousness only slowly. The processes by which their fame was made were as mysterious as those by which God ruled the generations. The past became the natural habitat of great men. The universal lament of aging men in all epochs, then, is that greatness has become obsolete.

So it has been commonly believed, in the words of Genesis, that "there were giants in the earth in those days"—in the days before the Flood. Each successive age has believed that heroes—great men- -dwelt mostly before its own time. Thomas Carlyle, in his classic *Heroes, Hero-Worship, and the Heroic in History* (1841), lamented that Napoleon was "our last great man!" Arthur M. Schlesinger, Jr., at the age of 40, has noted with alarm in our day (1958) that while "great men seemed to dominate our lives and shape our destiny" when he was young, "Today no one bestrides our narrow world like a colossus; we have no giants. . . ." This traditional belief in the decline of greatness has expressed the simple social fact that greatness has been equated with fame, and fame could not be made overnight.

Within the last century, and especially since about 1900, we seem to have discovered the processes by which fame is manufactured. Now, at least in the United States, a man's name can become a household word overnight. The Graphic Revolution suddenly gave us, among other things, the means of fabricating well-knownness. Discovering that we (the television watchers, the movie goers, radio listeners, and newspaper and magazine readers) and our servants (the television, movie, and radio producers, newspaper and magazine editors, and ad writers) can so quickly and so effectively give a man "fame," we have willingly been misled into believing that fame—well-knownness—is still a hallmark of greatness. Our power to fill our minds with more and more "big names" has increased our demand for Big Names and our willingness to confuse the Big Name with the Big Man. Again mistaking our powers for our necessities, we have filled our world with artificial fame.

Of course we do not like to believe that our admiration is focused on a largely synthetic product. Having manufactured our celebrities, having willy-nilly made them our cynosures—the guiding stars of our interest—we are tempted to believe that they are not synthetic at all, that they are somehow still God-made heroes who now abound with a marvelous modern prodigality.

The folklore of Great Men survives. We still believe, with Sydney Smith, who wrote in the early nineteenth century, that "Great men hallow a whole people, and lift up all who live in their time." We still agree with Carlyle that "No sadder proof can be given by a man of his own littleness than disbelief in great men. . . . Does not every true man feel that he is himself made higher by doing reverence to that which is really above him?" We still are told from the pulpit, from Congress, from television screen and editorial page, that the lives of great men "all remind us, we can make our lives sublime." Even in our twentieth-century age of doubt, when morality itself has been in ill repute, we have desperately held on to our belief in human greatness. For human models are more vivid and more persuasive than explicit moral commands. Cynics and intellectuals, too, are quicker to doubt moral theories than to question the greatness of their heroes. Agnostics and atheists may deny God, but they are slow to deny divinity to the great agnostics and atheists.

While the folklore of hero-worship, the zestful search for heroes, and the pleasure in reverence for heroes remain, the heroes themselves dissolve. The household names, the famous men, who populate our consciousness are with few exceptions not heroes at all, but an artificial new product— a product of the Graphic Revolution in response to our exaggerated expectations. The more readily we make them and the more numerous they become, the less are they worthy of our admiration. We can fabricate fame, we can at will (though usually at considerable expense) make a man or woman well known; but we cannot make him great. We can make a celebrity, but we can never make a hero. In a now-almost-forgotten sense, all heroes are self-made.

Celebrity-worship and hero-worship should not be confused. Yet we confuse them every day, and by doing so we come dangerously close to depriving ourselves of all real models. We lose sight of the men and women who do not simply seem great because they are famous but who are famous because they are great. We come closer and closer to degrading all fame into notoriety.

In the last half century the old heroic human mold has been broken. A new mold has been made. We have actually demanded that this mold be made, so that marketable human models—modern "heroes"—could be mass-produced, to satisfy the market, and without any hitches. The qualities which now commonly make a man or woman into a "nationally advertised" brand are in fact a new category of human emptiness. Our new mold is shaped not of the stuff of our familiar morality, nor even of the old familiar reality. How has this happened?

I

THE TRADITIONAL heroic type included figures as diverse as Moses, Ulysses, Aeneas, Jesus, Caesar, Mohammed, Joan of Arc, Shakespeare, Washington, Napoleon, and Lincoln. For our purposes it is sufficient to define a hero as a human figure—real or imaginary or both—who has shown greatness in some achievement. He is a man or woman of great deeds.

Of course, many such figures remain. But if we took a census of the names which populate the national consciousness—of all those who mysteriously dwell at the same time in the minds of all, or nearly all Americans—we would now find the truly heroic figures in the old-fashioned mold to be a smaller proportion than ever before. There are many reasons for this.

In the first place, of course, our democratic beliefs and our new scientific insights into human behavior have nibbled away at the heroes we have inherited from the past. Belief in the power of the common people to govern themselves, which has brought with it a passion for human equality, has carried a distrust, or at least a suspicion of individual heroic greatness. A democratic people are understandably wary of finding too much virtue in their leaders, or of attributing too much of their success to their leaders. In the twentieth century the rise of Mussoliniism, Hitlerism, Stalinism, and of totalitarianism in general, has dramatized the perils of any people's credulity in the power of the Great Leader. We have even come erroneously to believe that because tyranny in our time has flourished in the name of the Duce, the Führer, the omniscient, all-virtuous Commissar, or the Dictatorship of the Proletariat, democracy must therefore survive without Great Leaders.

Yet, long before Hitler or Stalin, the cult of the individual hero carried with it contempt for democracy. Hero-worship, from Plato to Carlyle, was often a dogma of anti-democracy. Aristocracy, even in the mild and decadent form in which it survives in Great Britain today, is naturally more favorable to belief in heroes. If one is accustomed to a Royal Family, a Queen, and a House of Lords, one is less apt to feel himself debased by bending the knee before any embodiment of human greatness. Most forms of government depend on a belief in a divine spark possessed by a favored few; but American democracy is embarrassed in the charismatic presence. We fear the man on horseback, the demigod, or the dictator. And if we have had fewer Great Men than have other peoples, it is perhaps because we have wanted, or would allow ourselves to have, fewer. Our most admired national heroes—Franklin, Washington, and Lincoln—are generally supposed to possess the "common touch." We revere them, not because they possess charisma, divine favor, a grace or talent granted them by God, but because they embody popular virtues. We admire them, not because they reveal God, but because they reveal and elevate ourselves.

While these democratic ideas have been arising, and while popular government has flourished in the United States, the growth of the social sciences has given us additional reasons to be sophisticated about the hero and to doubt his essential greatness. We now look on the hero as a common phenomenon of all societies. We learn, as Lord Raglan, a recent president of the Royal Anthropological Institute, pointed out in *The Hero* (1936), that "tradition is never historical." Having examined a number of well-known heroes of tradition, he concludes that "there is no justification for believing that any of these heroes were real persons, or that any of the stories of their exploits had any historical foundation. . . . these heroes, if they were genuinely heroes of tradition, were originally not men but gods . . . the stories were accounts not of fact but of ritual—that is, myths." Or we learn from Joseph Campbell's *The Hero with a Thousand Faces* (1949) that all heroes—Oriental and Occidental, modern, ancient, and primitive—are the multiform expression of "truths disguised for us under the figures of religion and mythology." Following Freud, Campbell explains all heroes as embodiments of a great "monomyth." There are always the stages of (1) separation or departure, (2) trials and victories of initiation, and finally, (3) return and reintegration with society. Nowadays it matters little whether we see the hero exemplifying a universal falsehood or a universal truth. In either case we now stand outside ourselves. We see greatness as an illusion; or, if it does exist, we suspect we know its secret. We look with knowing disillusionment on our admiration for historical figures who used to embody greatness.

Just as the Bible is now widely viewed in enlightened churches and synagogues as a composite document of outmoded folk beliefs, which can nevertheless be appreciated for its "spiritual inspiration" and "literary value"—so with the folk hero. He is no longer naively seen as our champion. We have become self-conscious about our admiration for all models of human greatness. We know that somehow they were not what they seem. They simply illustrate the laws of social illusion.

The rise of "scientific" critical history and its handmaid, critical biography, has had the same effect. In Japan, by contrast, the divine virtue of the Emperors has been preserved by declaring them off-limits for the critical biographer. Even the Meiji Emperor—the "Enlightened" Emperor, founder of modern Japan, who kept detailed journals and left materials to delight a Western biographer—remains unportrayed in an accurate critical account. In the United States until the twentieth century it was usual for biographies of public figures to be written by their admirers. These works were commonly literary memorials, tokens of friendship, of family devotion, or of political piety. This was true even of the better biographies. It was Henry Cabot Lodge, Sr., who wrote the biography of Alexander Hamilton, Albert J. Beveridge who wrote the life of John Marshall, Douglas Southall Freeman who enshrined Robert E. Lee, and Carl Sandburg who wrote a monument to Lincoln. This has ceased to be the rule. Nor is this due only to the new schools of debunking biography (represented by Van Wyck Brooks' *Mark Twain* (1920) and *Henry James* (1925), W. E. Woodward's *George Washington* (1926) and *General Grant* (1928)) which grew in the jaundiced 'twenties. The appearance of American history as a recognized learned specialty in the early twentieth century has produced a new flood of biographical works which are only rarely inspired by personal admiration. Instead they are often merely professional exercises; scholars ply their tools and the chips fall where they may. We have thus learned a great deal more about our national heroes than earlier generations cared to know.

Meanwhile, the influence of Karl Marx, the rise of economic determinism, a growing knowledge of economic and social history, and an increased emphasis on social forces have made the individual leader seem less crucial. The Pilgrim Fathers, we now are told, were simply representatives of the restless, upheaving middle classes; their ideas expressed the rising "Protestant Ethic," which was the true prophet of modern capitalism. The Founding Fathers of the Constitution, Charles A. Beard and others have pointed out, were little more than spokesmen of certain property interests. Andrew Jackson became only one of many possible expressions of a rising West. The Frontier itself became the hero instead of the men. "Isms," "forces," and "classes" have spelled the death of the hero in our historical literature.

Under the hot glare of psychology and sociology the heroes' heroic qualities have been dissolved into a blur of environmental influences and internal maladjustments. For example, Charles Sumner (1811–1874), the aggressive abolitionist Senator from Massachusetts, who was beaten over the head with a cane by Representative Preston S. Brooks of South Carolina, had long been a hero of the abolitionists, a martyr for the Northern cause. From the excellent scholarly biography by David Donald in 1960, Sumner emerges with barely a shred of nobility. He becomes a refugee from an unhappy youth. His ambition now seems to have stemmed from his early insecurity as the son of an illegitimate father, a half-outcast from Cambridge society. His principles in his later years (and his refusal to sit in the Senate for many months after his beating) no longer express a true Crusader's passion. Henry Wadsworth Longfellow once eulogized Sumner:

> So when a great man dies,
> For years beyond our ken,
> The light he leaves behind him lies
> Upon the paths of men.

But now, in David Donald's technical phrase, Sumner's conduct in his late years becomes a "post-traumatic syndrome."

In these middle decades of the twentieth century the hero has almost disappeared from our fiction as well. The central figure in any serious book is more likely to be a victim. In the plays of Tennessee Williams and Arthur Miller, in the novels of Ernest Hemingway, William Faulkner, and John O'Hara, the leading roles are played by men who suffer from circumstances. Even the novelist's imagination is now staggered by the effort to conjure up human greatness.

Today every American, child or adult, encounters a vastly larger number of names, faces, and voices than at any earlier period or in any other country. Newspapers, magazines, second-class mail, books, radio, television, telephone, phonograph records—these and other vehicles confront us with thousands of names, people, or fragments of people. In our always more overpopulated consciousness, the hero every year becomes less significant. Not only does the newspaper or magazine reader or television watcher see the face

and hear the voice of his President and the President's wife
and family; he also sees the faces and hears the voices of his
cabinet members, undersecretaries, Senators, Congressmen,
and of their wives and children as well. Improvements in
public education, with the always increasing emphasis on
recent events, dilute the consciousness. The titanic figure is
now only one of thousands. This is ever more true as we
secure a smaller proportion of our information from books.
The hero, like the spontaneous event, gets lost in the con-
gested traffic of pseudo-events.

II

THE HEROES of the past, then, are dissolved before our eyes
or buried from our view. Except perhaps in wartime, we
find it hard to produce new heroes to replace the old.

We have made peculiar difficulties for ourselves by our
fantastic rate of progress in science, technology, and the
social sciences. The great deeds of our time are now accomplished on *unintelligible frontiers*. When heroism appeared as it once did mostly on the battlefield or in personal
combat, everybody could understand the heroic act. The
claim of the martyr or the Bluebeard to our admiration or
horror was easy enough to grasp. When the dramatic ac-
complishment was an incandescent lamp, a steam engine, a
telegraph, or an automobile, everybody could understand
what the great man had accomplished. This is no longer
true. The heroic thrusts now occur in the laboratory, among
cyclotrons and betatrons, whose very names are popular
symbols of scientific mystery. Even the most dramatic, best-
publicized adventures into space are on the edges of our
comprehension. There are still, of course, rare exceptions—
a Dr. Albert Schweitzer or a Dr. Tom Dooley—whose
heroism is intelligible. But these only illustrate that intelligible heroism now occurs almost exclusively on the field
of sainthood or martyrdom. There no progress has been
made for millennia. In the great areas of human progress,

in science, technology, and the social sciences, our brave twentieth-century innovators work in the twilight just beyond our understanding. This has obviously always been true to some extent; the work of profound thinkers has seldom been more than half-intelligible to the lay public. But never so much as today.

Despite the best efforts of ingenious and conscientious science reporters (now a profession all their own) our inventors and discoverers remain in the penumbra. With every decade popular education falls farther behind technology. Sir Isaac Newton's *Principia Mathematica* was popularized "for ladies and gentlemen" who glimpsed the crude gist of his ideas. But how many "popular" lecturers—even so crudely—have explained Einstein's theory of relativity? Nowadays our interest lies primarily in the mystery of the new findings. Fantastic possibilities engage our imagination without taxing our understanding. We acclaim the flights of Yuri Gagarin and Alan Shepard without quite grasping what they mean.

Not only in science are the frontiers less intelligible. Perhaps most worshipers in Florence could grasp the beauty of a painting by Cimabue or Giotto. How many New Yorkers today can understand a Jackson Pollock or a Rothko?

Our idolized writers are esoteric. How many can find their way in Joyce's *Ulysses* or *Finnegans Wake?* Our most honored literati are only half-intelligible to nearly all the educated community. How many understand a T. S. Eliot, a William Faulkner, a St. John Perse, a Quasimodo? Our great artists battle on a landscape we cannot chart, with weapons we do not comprehend, against adversaries we find unreal. How can we make them our heroes?

As collaborative work increases in science, literature, and social sciences, we find it ever harder to isolate the individual hero for our admiration. The first nuclear chain reaction (which made the atom bomb and atomic power possible) was the product of a huge organization dispersed over the country. Who was the hero of the enterprise? Einstein, without whose theoretical boldness it would not have been conceivable? Or General Grove? Or Enrico Fermi? The social scientists' research enterprises have also become projects. *An American Dilemma,* the monumental study of the Negro and American democracy that was sponsored by the Carnegie Corporation, was the combined product of dozens of individual and collaborative studies. Gunnar Myrdal, director of the project and principal author of the book, played much the same role that the chairman of the board of directors does in a large corporation. The written works which reach the largest number of people in the United States today—advertisements and political speeches—are generally assumed to be collaborative work. The candidate making an eloquent campaign speech is admired for his administrative ingenuity in collecting a good team of speech writers. We cannot read books by our public figures, even their autobiographies and most private memoirs, without being haunted by their ghost writers.

In the United States we have, in a word, witnessed the decline of the "folk" and the rise of the "mass." The usually illiterate folk, while unself-conscious, was creative in its own special ways. Its characteristic products were the spoken word, the gesture, the song: folklore, folk dance, folk song. The folk expressed itself. Its products are still gathered by scholars, antiquarians, and patriots; it was a voice. But the mass, in our world of mass media and mass circulation, is the target and not the arrow. It is the ear and not the voice. The mass is what others aim to reach—by print, photograph, image, and sound. While the folk created heroes, the mass can only look and listen for them. It is waiting to be shown and to be told. Our society, to which the Soviet notion of "the masses" is so irrelevant, still is governed by our own idea of the mass. The folk had a universe of its own creation, its own world of giants and dwarfs, magicians and witches. The mass lives in the very different fantasy world of pseudo-events. The words and images which reach the mass disenchant big names in the very process of conjuring them up.

III

OUR AGE has produced a new kind of eminence. This is as characteristic of our culture and our century as was the divinity of Greek gods in the sixth century B.C. or the chivalry of knights and courtly lovers in the middle ages. It has not yet driven heroism, sainthood, or martyrdom completely out of our consciousness. But with every decade it overshadows them more. All older forms of greatness now survive only in the shadow of this new form. This new kind of eminence is "celebrity."

The word "celebrity" (from the Latin *celebritas* for "multitude" or "fame" and *celeber* meaning "frequented," "populous," or "famous") originally meant not a person but a condition—as the Oxford English Dictionary says, "the condition of being much talked about; famousness, notoriety." In this sense its use dates from at least the early seventeenth century. Even then it had a weaker meaning than "fame" or "renown." Matthew Arnold, for example, remarked in the nineteenth century that while the philosopher Spinoza's followers had "celebrity," Spinoza himself had "fame."

For us, however, "celebrity" means primarily a person —"a person of celebrity." This usage of the word significantly dates from the early years of the Graphic Revolution, the first example being about 1850. Emerson spoke of "the celebrities of wealth and fashion" (1848). Now American dictionaries define a celebrity as "a famous or well-publicized person."

The celebrity in the distinctive modern sense could not have existed in any earlier age, or in America before the Graphic Revolution. *The celebrity is a person who is known for his well-knownness.*

His qualities—or rather his lack of qualities—illustrate our peculiar problems. He is neither good nor bad, great nor petty. He is the human pseudo-event. He has been fabricated on purpose to satisfy our exaggerated expectations of human greatness. He is morally neutral. The product of no conspiracy, of no group promoting vice or emptiness, he is made by honest, industrious men of high professional ethics doing their job, "informing" and educating us. He is made by all of us who willingly read about him, who like to see him on television, who buy recordings of his voice, and talk about him to our friends. His relation to morality and even to reality is highly ambiguous. He is like the woman *in* an Elinor Glyn novel who describes another by saying, "She is like a figure in an Elinor Glyn novel."

The massive *Celebrity Register* (1959), compiled by Earl Blackwell and Cleveland Amory, now gives us a well-documented definition of the word, illustrated by over 2,200 biographies. "We think we have a better yardstick than the *Social Register,* or *Who's Who,* or any such book," they explain. "Our point is that it is impossible to be accurate in listing a man's social standing—even if anyone cared; and it's impossible to list accurately the success or value of men; but you *can* judge a man as a celebrity—all you have to do is weigh his press clippings." The *Celebrity Register*'s alphabetical order shows Mortimer Adler followed by Polly Adler, the Dalai Lama listed beside TV comedienne Dagmar, Dwight Eisenhower preceding Anita Ekberg, ex-President Herbert Hoover following ex-torch singer Libby Holman, Pope John XXIII coming after Mr. John the hat designer, and Bertrand Russell followed by Jane Russell. They are all celebrities. The well-knownness which they have in common overshadows everything else.

The advertising world has proved the market appeal of celebrities. In trade jargon celebrities are "big names." Endorsement advertising not only uses celebrities; it helps make them. Anything that makes a well-known name still better known automatically raises its status as a celebrity. The old practice, well established before the nineteenth century, of declaring the prestige of a product by the phrase "By Appointment to His Majesty" was, of course, a kind of use of the testimonial endorsement. But the King was in fact a great person, one of illustrious lineage and with impressive actual and symbolic powers. The King was not a venal endorser, and he was likely to use only superior products. He was not a mere celebrity. For the test of celebrity is nothing more than well-knownness.

Studies of biographies in popular magazines suggest that editors, and supposedly also readers, of such magazines not long ago shifted their attention away from the old-fashioned hero. From the person known for some serious achievement, they have turned their biographical interests to the new-fashioned celebrity. Of the subjects of biographical articles appearing in the *Saturday Evening Post* and the now-defunct *Collier's* in five sample years between 1901 and 1914, 74 per cent came from politics, business, and the professions. But after about 1922 well over half of them came from the world of entertainment. Even among the entertainers an ever decreasing proportion has come from the serious arts—literature, fine arts, music, dance, and theater. An ever increasing proportion (in recent years nearly all) comes from the fields of light entertainment, sports, and the night club circuit. In the earlier period, say before World War I, the larger group included figures like the President of the United States, a Senator, a State Governor, the Secretary of the Treasury, the banker J. P. Morgan, the railroad magnate James J. Hill, a pioneer in aviation, the inventor of the torpedo, a Negro educator, an immigrant scientist, an opera singer, a famous poet, and a popular fiction writer. By the 1940's the larger group included figures like the boxer Jack Johnson, Clark Gable, Bobby Jones, the movie actresses Brenda Joyce and Brenda Marshall, William Powell, the woman matador Conchita Cintron, the night club entertainer Adelaide Moffett, and the gorilla Toto. Some analysts say the shift is primarily the sign of a new focus of popular attention away from production and toward consumption. But this is oversubtle.

A simpler explanation is that the machinery of information

has brought into being a new substitute for the hero, who is the celebrity, and whose main characteristic is his well-knownness. In the democracy of pseudo-events, anyone can become a celebrity, if only he can get into the news and stay there. Figures from the world of entertainment and sports are most apt to be well known. If they are successful enough, they actually overshadow the real figures they portray. George Arliss overshadowed Disraeli, Vivian Leigh overshadowed Scarlett O'Hara, Fess Parker overshadowed Davy Crockett. Since their stock in trade is their well-knownness, they are most apt to have energetic press agents keeping them in the public eye.

It is hardly surprising then that magazine and newspaper readers no longer find the lives of their heroes instructive. Popular biographies can offer very little in the way of solid information. For the subjects are themselves mere figments of the media. If their lives are empty of drama or achievement, it is only as we might have expected, for they are not known for drama or achievement. They are celebrities. Their chief claim to fame is their fame itself. They are notorious for their notoriety. If this is puzzling or fantastic, if it is mere tautology, it is no more puzzling or fantastic or tautologous than much of the rest of our experience. Our experience tends more and more to become tautology—needless repetition of the same in different words and images. Perhaps what ails us is not so much a vice as a "nothingness." The vacuum of our experience is actually made emptier by our anxious straining with mechanical devices to fill it artificially. What is remarkable is not only that we manage to fill experience with so much emptiness, but that we manage to give the emptiness such appealing variety.

We can hear ourselves straining. "He's the greatest!" Our descriptions of celebrities overflow with superlatives. In popular magazine biographies we learn that a Dr. Brinkley is the "best-advertised doctor in the United States"; an actor is the "luckiest man in the movies today"; a Ringling is "not only the greatest, but the first real showman in the Ringling family"; a general is "one of the best mathematicians this side of Einstein"; a columnist has "one of the strangest of courtships"; a statesman has "the world's most exciting job"; a sportsman is "the loudest and by all odds the most abusive"; a newsman is "one of the most consistently resentful men in the country"; a certain ex-King's mistress is "one of the unhappiest women that ever lived." But, despite the "supercolossal" on the label, the contents are very ordinary. The lives of celebrities which we like to read, as Leo Lowenthal remarks, are a mere catalogue of "hardships" and "breaks." These men and women are "the proved specimens of the average."

No longer external sources which fill us with purpose, these new-model "heroes" are receptacles into which we pour our own purposelessness. They are nothing but ourselves seen in a magnifying mirror. Therefore the lives of entertainer-celebrities cannot extend our horizon. Celebrities populate our horizon with men and women we already know. Or, as an advertisement for the *Celebrity Register* cogently puts it, celebrities are "the 'names' who, once made by news, now make news by themselves." Celebrity is made by simple familiarity, induced and re-enforced by public means. The celebrity therefore is the perfect embodiment of tautology: the most familiar is the most familiar.

IV

THE HERO was distinguished by his achievement; the celebrity by his image or trademark. The hero created himself; the celebrity is created by the media. The hero was a big man; the celebrity is a big name.

Formerly, a public man needed a *private* secretary for a barrier between himself and the public. Nowadays he has a *press* secretary, to keep him properly in the public eye. Before the Graphic Revolution (and still in countries which have not undergone that revolution) it was a mark of solid distinction in a man or a family to keep out of the news. A lady of aristocratic pretensions was supposed to get her name in the papers only three times: when she was born, when she married, and when she died. Now the families who are Society are by definition those always appearing in the papers. The man of truly heroic stature was once supposed to be marked by scorn for publicity. He quietly relied on the power of his character or his achievement.

In the South, where the media developed more slowly than elsewhere in the country, where cities appeared later, and where life was dominated by rural ways, the celebrity grew more slowly. The old-fashioned hero was romanticized. In this as in many other ways, the Confederate General Robert E. Lee was one of the last surviving American models of the older type. Among his many admirable qualities, Southern compatriots admired none more than his retirement from public view. He had the reputation for never having given a newspaper interview. He steadfastly refused to write his memoirs. "I should be trading on the blood of my men," he said. General George C. Marshall (1880–1959) is a more recent and more anachronistic example. He, too, shunned publicity and refused to write his memoirs, even while other generals were serializing theirs in the newspapers. But by his time, few people any longer considered this reticence a virtue. His old-fashioned unwillingness to enter the publicity arena finally left him a victim of the slanders of Senator Joseph McCarthy and others.

The hero was born of time: his gestation required at least a generation. As the saying went, he had "stood the test of time." A maker of tradition, he was himself made by tradition. He grew over the generations as people found new virtues in him and attributed to him new exploits. Receding into the misty past he became more, and not less, heroic. It was not necessary that his face or figure have a sharp, well-delineated outline, nor that his life be footnoted. Of course there could not have been any photographs of him, and often there was not even a likeness. Men of the last century were more heroic than those of today; men of antiquity were still more heroic; and those of pre-history became demigods. The hero was always somehow ranked among the ancients.

The celebrity, on the contrary, is always a contemporary. The hero is made by folklore, sacred texts, and history books, but the celebrity is the creature of gossip, of public opinion, of magazines, newspapers, and the ephemeral images of movie and television screen. The passage of time, which creates and establishes the hero, destroys the celebrity. One is made, the other unmade, by repetition. The celebrity is born in the daily papers and never loses the mark of his fleeting origin.

The very agency which first makes the celebrity in the long run inevitably destroys him. He will be destroyed, as he was made, by publicity. The newspapers make him, and they unmake him—not by murder but by suffocation or starvation. No one is more forgotten than the last generation's celebrity. This fact explains the newspaper feature "Whatever Became Of . . . ?" which amuses us by accounts of the present obscurity of former celebrities. One can always get a laugh by referring knowingly to the once-household names which have lost their celebrity in the last few decades: Mae Bush, William S. Hart, Clara Bow. A woman reveals her age by the celebrities she knows.

There is not even any tragedy in the celebrity's fall, for he is a man returned to his proper anonymous station. The tragic hero, in Aristotle's familiar definition, was a man fallen from great estate, a great man with a tragic flaw. He had somehow become the victim of his own greatness. Yesterday's celebrity, however, is a commonplace man who has been fitted back into his proper commonplaceness not by any fault of his own, but by time itself.

The dead hero becomes immortal. He becomes more vital with the passage of time. The celebrity even in his lifetime becomes passé: he passes out of the picture. The white glare of publicity, which first gave him his specious brilliance, soon melts him away. This was so even when the

only vehicles of publicity were the magazine and the newspaper. Still more now with our vivid round-the-clock media,
with radio and television. Now when it is possible, by bringing their voices and images daily into our living rooms, to
make celebrities more quickly than ever before, they die
more quickly than ever. This has been widely recognized by
entertainment celebrities and politicians. President Franklin
Delano Roosevelt was careful to space out his fireside chats
so the citizenry would not tire of him. Some comedians (for
example, Jackie Gleason in the mid-1950's) have found that
when they have weekly programs they reap quick and
remunerative notoriety, but that they soon wear out their
images. To extend their celebrity-lives, they offer their
images more sparingly—once a month or once every two
months instead of once a week.

There is a subtler difference between the personality of
the hero and that of the celebrity. The figures in each of the
two classes become assimilated to one another, but in two
rather different ways. Heroes standing for greatness in the
traditional mold tend to become colorless and cliché. The
greatest heroes have the least distinctiveness of face or figure.
We may show our reverence for them, as we do for God, by
giving them beards. Yet we find it hard to imagine that Moses
or Jesus could have had other special facial characteristics.
The hero while being thus idealized and generalized loses
his individuality. The fact that George Washington is not a
vivid personality actually helps him serve as the heroic
Father of Our Country. Perhaps Emerson meant just this
when he said that finally every great hero becomes a great
bore. To be a great hero is actually to become lifeless; to
become a face on a coin or a postage stamp. It is to become
a Gilbert Stuart's Washington. Contemporaries, however,
and the celebrities made of them, suffer from idiosyncrasy.
They are too vivid, too individual to be polished into a
symmetrical Greek statue. The Graphic Revolution, with
its klieg lights on face and figure, makes the images of different men more distinctive. This itself disqualifies them

from becoming heroes or demigods.

While heroes are assimilated to one another by the great simple virtues of their character, celebrities are differentiated mainly by trivia of personality. To be known for your personality actually proves you a celebrity. Thus a synonym for "a celebrity" is "a personality." Entertainers, then, are best qualified to become celebrities because they are skilled in the marginal differentiation of their personalities. They succeed by skillfully distinguishing themselves from others essentially like them. They do this by minutiae of grimace, gesture, language, and voice. We identify Jimmy ("Schnozzola") Durante by his nose, Bob Hope by his fixed smile, Jack Benny by his stinginess, Jack Paar by his rudeness, Jackie Gleason by his waddle, Imogene Coca by her bangs.

With the mushroom-fertility of all pseudo-events, celebrities tend to breed more celebrities. They help make and celebrate and publicize one another. Being known primarily for their well-knownness, celebrities intensify their celebrity images simply by becoming widely known for relations among themselves. By a kind of symbiosis, celebrities live off one another. One becomes better known by being the habitual butt of another's jokes, by being another's paramour or ex-wife, by being the subject of another's gossip, or even by being ignored by another celebrity. Elizabeth Taylor's celebrity appeal has consisted less perhaps in her own talents as an actress than in her connections with other celebrities—Nick Hilton, Mike Todd, and Eddie Fisher. Arthur Miller, the playwright, became a "real" celebrity by his marriage to Marilyn Monroe. When we talk or read or write about celebrities, our emphasis on their marital relations and sexual habits, on their tastes in smoking, drinking, dress, sports cars, and interior decoration is our desperate effort to distinguish among the indistinguishable. How can those commonplace people like us (who, by the grace of the media, happened to become celebrities) be made to seem more interesting or bolder than we are?

V

AS OTHER PSEUDO-EVENTS in our day tend to overshadow spontaneous events, so celebrities (who are human pseudo-events) tend to overshadow heroes. They are more up-to-date, more nationally advertised, and more apt to have press agents. And there are far more of them. Celebrities die quickly but they are still more quickly replaced. Every year we experience a larger number than the year before.

Just as real events tend to be cast in the mold of pseudo-events, so in our society heroes survive by acquiring the qualities of celebrities. The best-publicized seems the most authentic experience. If someone does a heroic deed in our time, all the machinery of public information—press, pulpit, radio, and television—soon transform him into a celebrity. If they cannot succeed in this, the would-be hero disappears from public view.

A dramatic, a tragic, example is the career of Charles A. Lindbergh. He performed singlehanded one of the heroic deeds of this century. His deed was heroic in the best epic mold. But he became degraded into a celebrity. He then ceased to symbolize the virtues to which his heroic deed gave him a proper claim. He became filled with emptiness; then he disappeared from view. How did this happen?

On May 21, 1927, Charles A. Lindbergh made the first nonstop solo flight from Roosevelt Field, New York, to Le Bourget Air Field, Paris, in a monoplane, "The Spirit of St. Louis." This was plainly a heroic deed in the classic sense; it was a deed of valor—alone against the elements. In a dreary, unheroic decade Lindbergh's flight was a lightning flash of individual courage. Except for the fact of his flight, Lindbergh was a commonplace person. Twenty-five years old at the time, he had been born in Detroit and raised in Minnesota. He was not a great inventor or a leader of men. He was not extraordinarily intelligent, eloquent, or ingenious. Like many another young man in those years, he had a fanatical love of flying. The air was his element. There he showed superlative skill and extraordinary courage—even to foolhardiness.

He was an authentic hero. Yet this was not enough. Or perhaps it was too much. For he was destined to be made into a mere celebrity; and he was to be the American celebrity par excellence. His rise and fall as a hero, his tribulations, his transformation, and his rise and decline as a celebrity are beautifully told in Kenneth S. Davis' biography.

Lindbergh himself had not failed to predict that his exploit would put him in the news. Before leaving New York he had sold to *The New York Times* the exclusive story of his flight. A supposedly naive and diffident boy, on his arrival in Paris he was confronted by a crowd of newspaper reporters at a press conference in Ambassador Myron T. Herrick's residence. But he would not give out any statement until he had clearance from the *Times* representative. He had actually subscribed to a newspaper clipping service, the clippings to be sent to his mother, who was then teaching school in Minnesota. With uncanny foresight, however, he had limited his subscriptions to clippings to the value of $50. (This did not prevent the company, doubtless seeking publicity as well as money, from suing him for not paying them for clippings beyond the specified amount.) Otherwise he might have had to spend the rest of his life earning the money to pay for clippings about himself.

Lindbergh's newspaper success was unprecedented. The morning after his flight *The New York Times,* a model of journalistic sobriety, gave him the whole of its first five pages, except for a few ads on page five. Other papers gave as much or more. Radio commentators talked of him by the hour. But there was not much hard news available. The flight was a relatively simple operation, lasting only thirty-three and a half hours. Lindbergh had told reporters in Paris just about all there was to tell. During his twenty-five years he had led a relatively uneventful life. He had few quirks of face, of figure, or of personality; little was known about his character.

Some young women called him "tall and handsome," but his physical averageness was striking. He was the boy next door. To tell about this young man on the day after his flight, the nation's newspapers used 25,000 tons of newsprint more than usual. In many places sales were two to five times normal, and might have been higher if the presses could have turned out more papers.

When Lindbergh returned to New York on June 13, 1927, *The New York Times* gave its first sixteen pages the next morning almost exclusively to news about him. At the testimonial dinner in Lindbergh's honor at the Hotel Commodore (reputed to be the largest for an individual "in modern history") Charles Evans Hughes, former Secretary of State, and about to become Chief Justice of the United States, delivered an extravagant eulogy. With unwitting precision he characterized the American hero-turned-celebrity: "We measure heroes as we do ships, by their displacement. Colonel Lindbergh has displaced everything."

Lindbergh was by now the biggest human pseudo-event of modern times. His achievement, actually because it had been accomplished so neatly and with such spectacular simplicity, offered little spontaneous news. The biggest news about Lindbergh was that he was such big news. Pseudo-events multiplied in more than the usual geometric progression, for Lindbergh's well-knownness was so sudden and so overwhelming. It was easy to make stories about what a big celebrity he was; how this youth, unknown a few days before, was now a household word; how he was received by Presidents and Kings and Bishops. There was little else one could say about him. Lindbergh's singularly impressive heroic deed was soon far overshadowed by his even more impressive publicity. If well-knownness made a celebrity, here was the greatest. Of course it was remarkable to fly the ocean by oneself, but far more remarkable thus to dominate the news. His stature as hero was nothing compared with his stature as celebrity. All the more because it had happened, literally, overnight.

A large proportion of the news soon consisted of stories

of how Lindbergh reacted to the "news" and to the publicity about himself. People focused their admiration on how admirably Lindbergh responded to publicity, how gracefully he accepted his role of celebrity. "Quickie" biographies appeared. These were little more than digests of newspaper accounts of the publicity jags during Lindbergh's ceremonial visits to the capitals of Europe and the United States. This was the celebrity after-life of the heroic Lindbergh. This was the tautology of celebrity.

During the next few years Lindbergh stayed in the public eye and remained a celebrity primarily because of two events. One was his marriage on May 27, 1929, to the cultivated and pretty Anne Morrow, daughter of Dwight Morrow, a Morgan partner, then Ambassador to Mexico. Now it was "The Lone Eagle and His Mate." As a newlywed he was more than ever attractive raw material for news. The maudlin pseudo-events of romance were added to all the rest. His newsworthiness was revived. There was no escape. Undaunted newsmen, thwarted in efforts to secure interviews and lacking solid facts, now made columns of copy from Lindbergh's efforts to keep out of the news! Some newspapermen, lacking other material for speculation, cynically suggested that Lindbergh's attempts to dodge reporters were motivated by a devious plan to increase his news-interest. When Lindbergh said he would co-operate with sober, respectable papers, but not with others, those left out pyramided his rebuffs into more news than his own statements would have made.

The second event which kept Lindbergh alive as a celebrity was the kidnaping of his infant son. This occurred at his new country house at Hopewell, New Jersey, on the night of March 1, 1932. For almost five years "Lindbergh" had been an empty receptacle into which news makers had poured their concoctions—saccharine, maudlin, legendary, slanderous, adulatory, or only fantastic. Now, when all other news-making possibilities seemed exhausted, his family was physically consumed. There was a good story in it. Here was "blood sacrifice," as Kenneth S. Davis calls it, to the gods of publicity. Since the case was never fully solved, despite the execution of the supposed kidnaper, no one can know whether the child would have been returned unharmed if the press and the public had behaved differently. But the press (with the collaboration of the bungling police) who had unwittingly destroyed real clues, then garnered and publicized innumerable false clues, and did nothing solid to help. They exploited Lindbergh's personal catastrophe with more than their usual energy.

In its way the kidnaping of Lindbergh's son was as spectacular as Lindbergh's transatlantic flight. In neither case was there much hard news, but this did not prevent the filling of newspaper columns. City editors now gave orders for no space limit on the kidnaping story. "I can't think of any story that would compare with it," observed the general news manager of the United Press, "unless America should enter a war." Hearst's INS photo service assigned its whole staff. They chartered two ambulances which, with sirens screaming, shuttled between Hopewell and New York City carrying photographic equipment out to the Lindbergh estate, and on the way back to the city served as mobile darkrooms in which pictures were developed and printed for delivery on arrival. For on-the-spot reporting at Hopewell, INS had an additional five men with three automobiles. United Press had six men and three cars; the Associated Press had four men, two women, and four cars. By midnight of March 1 the New York *Daily News* had nine reporters at Hopewell, and three more arrived the next day; the New York *American* had a dozen (including William Randolph Hearst, Jr., the paper's president); the New York *Herald Tribune,* four; the New York *World-Telegram, The New York Times,* and the Philadelphia *Ledger,* each about ten. This was only a beginning.

The next day the press agreed to Lindbergh's request to stay off the Hopewell grounds in order to encourage the kidnaper to return the child. The torrent of news did not stop. Within twenty-four hours INS sent over its wires

50,000 words (enough to fill a small volume) about the crime, 30,000 words the following day, and for some time thereafter 10,000 or more words a day. The Associated Press and United Press served their subscribers just as well. Many papers gave the story the whole of the front page, plus inside carry-overs, for a full week. There were virtually no new facts available. Still the news poured forth—pseudo-events by the score—clues, rumors, local color features, and what the trade calls "think" pieces.

Soon there was almost nothing more to be done journalistically with the crime itself. There was little more to be reported, invented, or conjectured. Interest then focused on a number of sub-dramas created largely by newsmen themselves. These were stories about how the original event was being reported, about the mix-up among the different police that had entered the case, and about who would or should be Lindbergh's spokesman to the press world and his go-between with the kidnaper. Much news interest still centered on what a big story all the news added up to, and on how Mr. and Mrs. Lindbergh reacted to the publicity.

At this point the prohibition era crime celebrities came into the picture. "Salvy" Spitale and Irving Bitz, New York speakeasy owners, briefly held the spotlight. They had been suggested by Morris Rosner, who, because he had underworld connections, soon became a kind of personal secretary to the Lindberghs. Spitale and Bitz earned headlines for their effort to make contact with the kidnapers, then suspected to be either the notorious Purple Gang of Detroit or Al Capone's mob in Chicago. The two go-betweens became big names, until Spitale bowed out, appropriately enough, at a press conference. There he explained: "If it was someone I knew, I'll be God-damned if I wouldn't name him. I been in touch all around, and I come to the conclusion that this one was pulled by an independent." Al Capone himself, more a celebrity than ever, since he was about to begin a Federal prison term for income-tax evasion, increased his own newsworthiness by trying to lend a hand. In an interview with the "serious" columnist Arthur Brisbane of the

Hearst papers, Capone offered $10,000 for information lead-
ing to the recovery of the child unharmed and to the capture
of the kidnapers. It was even hinted that to free Capone
might help recover the child.

The case itself produced a spate of new celebrities, whose
significance no one quite understood but whose newsworthiness itself made them important. These included Colonel H.
Norman Schwarzkopf, commander of the New Jersey State
Police; Harry Wolf, Chief of Police in Hopewell; Betty Gow,
the baby's nurse; Colonel Breckenridge, Lindbergh's personal counsel; Dr. J. F. ("Jafsie") Condon, a retired Bronx
schoolteacher who was a volunteer go-between (he offered
to add to the ransom money his own $1,000 life savings "so
a loving mother may again have her child and Colonel Lindbergh may know that the American people are grateful for
the honor bestowed on them by his pluck and daring");
John Hughes Curtis, a half-demented Norfolk, Virginia, boat-
builder who pretended to reach the kidnapers; Gaston B.
Means (author of *The Strange Death of President Harding*),
later convicted of swindling Mrs. Evalyn Walsh McLean out
of $104,000 by posing as a negotiator with the kidnapers;
Violet Sharpe, a waitress in the Morrow home, who married
the Morrow butler and who had had a date with a young
man not her husband on the night of the kidnaping (she
committed suicide on threat of being questioned by the
police); and countless others.

Only a few years later the spotlight was turned off Lindbergh as suddenly as it had been turned on him. *The New
York Times Index*—a thick volume published yearly which
lists all references to a given subject in the pages of the newspaper during the previous twelve months—records this fact
with statistical precision. Each volume of the index for the
years 1927 to 1940 contains several columns of fine print
merely itemizing the different news stories which referred to
Lindbergh. The 1941 volume shows over three columns of
such listings. Then suddenly the news stream dries up, first to
a mere trickle, then to nothing at all. The total listings for all
seventeen years from 1942 through 1958 amount to less than

two columns—only about half that found in the single year 1941. In 1951 and 1958 there was not even a single mention of Lindbergh. In 1957 when the movie *The Spirit of St. Louis,* starring James Stewart, was released, it did poorly at the box office. A poll of the preview audiences showed that few viewers under forty years of age knew about Lindbergh.

A *New Yorker* cartoon gave the gist of the matter. A father and his young son are leaving a movie house where they have just seen *The Spirit of St. Louis.* "If everyone thought what he did was so marvelous," the boy asks his father, "how come he never got famous?"

The hero thus died a celebrity's sudden death. In his fourteen years he had already long outlasted the celebrity's usual life span. An incidental explanation of this quick demise of Charles A. Lindbergh was his response to the pressure to be "all-around." Democratic faith was not satisfied that its hero be only a dauntless flier. He had to become a scientist, an outspoken citizen, and a leader of men. His celebrity status unfortunately had persuaded him to become a public spokesman. When Lindbergh gave in to these temptations, he offended. But his offenses (unlike those, for example, of Al Capone and his henchmen, who used to be applauded when they took their seats in a ball park) were not in themselves dramatic or newsworthy enough to create a new notoriety. His pronouncements were dull, petulant, and vicious. He acquired a reputation as a pro-Nazi and a crude racist; he accepted a decoration from Hitler. Very soon the celebrity was being uncelebrated. The "Lindbergh Beacon" atop a Chicago skyscraper was renamed the "Palmolive Beacon," and high in the Colorado Rockies "Lindbergh Peak" was rechristened the noncommital, "Lone Eagle Peak."

VI

SINCE THE GRAPHIC REVOLUTION, the celebrity overshadows the hero by the same relentless law which gives other kinds of pseudo-events an overshadowing power. When a man appears as hero and/or celebrity, his role as celebrity obscures and is apt to destroy his role as hero. The reasons, too, are those which tend to make all pseudo-events predominate. In the creation of a celebrity somebody always has an interest—newsmen needing stories, press agents paid to make celebrities, and the celebrity himself. But dead heroes have no such interest in their publicity, nor can they hire agents to keep them in the public eye. Celebrities, because they are made to order, can be made to please, comfort, fascinate, and flatter us. They can be produced and displaced in rapid succession.

The people once felt themselves made by their heroes. "The idol," said James Russell Lowell, "is the measure of the worshiper." Celebrities are made by the people. The hero stood for outside standards. The celebrity is a tautology. We still try to make our celebrities stand in for the heroes we no longer have, or for those who have been pushed out of our view. We forget that celebrities are known primarily for their well-knownness. And we imitate them as if they were cast in the mold of greatness. Yet the celebrity is usually nothing greater than a more-publicized version of us. In imitating him, in trying to dress like him, talk like him, look like him, think like him, we are simply imitating ourselves. In the words of the Psalmist, "They that make them are like unto them; so is everyone that trusteth in them." By imitating a tautology, we ourselves become a tautology: standing for what we stand for, reaching to become more emphatically what we already are. When we praise our famous men we pretend to look out the window of history. We do not like to confess that we are looking into a mirror. We look for models, and we see our own image.

Inevitably, most of our few remaining heroes hold our attention by being recast in the celebrity mold. We try to become chummy, gossipy, and friendly with our heroes. In the process we make them affable and flattering to us. Jesus, we are told from the pulpit, was "no sissy, but a regular fellow." Andrew Jackson was a "great guy." Instead of inventing heroic exploits for our heroes, we invent common-places about them (for example, in the successful juvenile series "The Childhood of Famous Americans"). It is com-monplaces, and not exploits, which make them celebrities.

Our very efforts to debunk celebrities, to prove (whether by critical journalistic biographies or by vulgar "confidential" magazines) that they are unworthy of our admiration, are like efforts to get "behind the scenes" in the making of other pseudo-events. They are self-defeating. They increase our interest in the fabrication. As much publicity yardage can be created one way as another. Of course most true celebrities have press agents. And these press agents some-times themselves become celebrities. The hat, the rabbit, and the magician are all equally news. It is twice as news-worthy that a charlatan can become a success. His charla-tanry makes him even more of a personality. A celebrity's private news-making apparatus, far frcm disillusioning us, simply proves him authentic and fully equipped. We are re-assured then that we are not mistaking a nobody for a some-body.

It is not surprising that the word "hero" has itself become a slang term of cynical reproach. Critics of the American Legion call it "The Heroes' Union." What better way of deflating or irritating a self-important person than by calling him "Our Hero"? The very word belongs, we think, in the world of pre-literate societies, of comic strip supermen, or of William Steig's Small Fry.

In America today heroes, like fairy tales, are seldom for sophisticated adults. But we multiply our Oscars and Emmies, our awards for the Father of the Year, our crowns for Mrs. America and Miss Photoflash. We have our Hall of Fame for Great Americans, our Agricultural Hall of Fame, our Baseball Hall of Fame, our Rose Bowl Hall of Fame. We strain to reassure ourselves that we admire the admirable and honor the meritorious. But in the very act of straining we confuse and distract ourselves. At first reluc-tantly, then with fascination, we observe the politicking behind every prize and the shenanigans in front of every effort to enshrine a celebrity or to enthrone a Queen for a Day. Despite our best intentions, our contrivance to provide substitute heroes finally produces nothing but celebrities. To publicize is to expose.

With our unprecedented power to magnify the images and popularize the virtues of heroes, our machinery only multiplies and enlarges the shadows of ourselves. Somehow we cannot make ourselves so uncritical that we reverence or respect (however much we may be interested in) the reflected images of our own emptiness. We continue surreptitiously to wonder whether greatness is not a naturally scarce commodity, whether it can ever really be synthesized. Perhaps, then, our ancestors were right in connecting the very idea of human greatness with belief in a God. Perhaps man cannot make himself. Perhaps heroes are born and not made.

Among the ironic frustrations of our age, none is more tantalizing than these efforts of ours to satisfy our extravagant expectations of human greatness. Vainly do we make scores of artificial celebrities grow where nature planted only a single hero. As soon as a hero begins to be sung about today, he evaporates into a celebrity. "No man can be a hero to his valet"—or, Carlyle might have added, "to his *Time* reporter." In our world of big names, curiously, our true heroes tend to be anonymous. In this life of illusion and quasi-illusion, the person with solid virtues who can be admired for something more substantial than his well-knownness often proves to be the unsung hero: the teacher, the nurse, the mother, the honest cop, the hard worker at lonely, underpaid, unglamorous, unpublicized jobs. Topsy-turvily, these can remain heroes precisely because they remain unsung. *Their* virtues are not the product of our effort to fill our void. Their very anonymity protects them from the flashy ephemeral celebrity life. They alone have the mysterious power to deny our mania for more greatness than there is in the world.

3

From Traveler to Tourist:
The Lost Art of Travel

DURING RECENT DECADES we have come to think that our new technology can save us from the inexorable laws of familiarity. By magical modern machinery we hope to clear the world of its commonplaceness—of its omnipresent tree sparrows, starlings, and blue jays—and fill it with rare Sutton's warblers, ivory-billed woodpeckers, whooping cranes, and rufous hummingbirds. Every bird-watcher knows how hard it is to reconcile oneself to the fact that the common birds are the ones most usually seen and that rare birds are really quite uncommon. Now all of us frustrate ourselves by the expectation that we can make the exotic an everyday experience (without its ceasing to be exotic); and can somehow make commonplaceness itself disappear.

The word "adventure" has become one of the blandest and emptiest in the language. The cheap cafeteria at the corner offers us an "adventure in good eating"; a course in self-development ($13.95) in a few weeks will transform our daily conversation into a "great adventure"; to ride in the new Dodge is an "adventure." By continual overuse, we wear out the once-common meaning of "an unusual, stirring, experience, often of romantic nature," and return "adventure" to its original meaning of a mere "happening" (from the Latin, *adventura,* and *advenire*). But while an "adventure" was originally "that which happens without design; chance, hap, luck," now in common usage it is primarily a contrived experience that somebody is trying to sell us. Its changed meaning is both a symptom of the new pervasiveness of pseudo-events and a symbol of how we defeat ourselves by our exaggerated expectations of the amount of unexpectedness—"adventure"—as of everything else in the world.

There is no better illustration of our newly exaggerated expectations than our changed attitude toward travel. One of the most ancient motives for travel, when men had any choice about it, was to see the unfamiliar. Man's incurable desire to go someplace else is a testimony of his incurable optimism and insatiable curiosity. We always expect things to be different over there. "Traveling," Descartes wrote in the early seventeenth century, "is almost like conversing with men of other centuries." Men who move because they are starved or frightened or oppressed expect to be safer, better fed, and more free in the new place. Men who live in a secure, rich, and decent society travel to escape boredom, to elude the familiar, and to discover the exotic.

They have often succeeded. Great stirrings of the mind have frequently followed great ages of travel. Throughout history by going to far places and seeing strange sights men have prodded their imagination. They have found amazement and delight and have reflected that life back home need not always remain what it has been. They have learned that there is more than one way to skin a cat, that there are more things in heaven and earth than was dreamt of in their philosophy, that the possibilities of life are not exhausted on Main Street.

In the fifteenth century the discovery of the Americas, the voyages around Africa and to the Indies opened eyes, enlarged thought, and helped create the Renaissance. The travels of the seventeenth century around Europe, to America, and to the Orient helped awaken men to ways of life different from their own and led to the Enlightenment. The discovery of new worlds has always renewed men's minds. Travel has been the universal catalyst. It has made men think faster, imagine larger, want more passionately. The returning traveler brings home disturbing ideas. Pascal (three centuries before television) said that man's ills came from the fact that he had not yet learned to sit quietly in a room.

In recent decades more Americans than ever before have traveled outside our country. In 1854 about thirty-odd thousand Americans went abroad; a century later in 1954 almost a million American citizens left the United States for foreign parts other than Canada and Mexico. After allowing for the increase in population, there is about five times as much foreign travel by Americans nowadays as there was a hundred years ago. As a nation we are probably the most traveled people of our time, or of any time. What is remarkable, on reflection, is not that our foreign travel has increased so much. But rather that all this travel has made so little difference in our thinking and feeling.

Our travels have not, it seems, made us noticeably more cosmopolitan or more understanding of other peoples. The explanation is not that Americans are any more obtuse or uneducable than they used to be. Rather, the travel experience itself has been transformed. Many Americans now "travel," yet few are travelers in the old sense of the word. The multiplication, improvement, and cheapening of travel facilities have carried many more people to distant places. But the experience of going there, the experience of being there, and what is brought back from there are all very different. The experience has become diluted, contrived, prefabricated.

The modern American tourist now fills his experience with pseudo-events. He has come to expect both more strangeness and more familiarity than the world naturally offers. He has come to believe that he can have a lifetime of adventure in two weeks and all the thrills of risking his life without any real risk at all. He expects that the exotic and the familiar can be made to order: that a nearby vacation spot can give him Old World charm, and also that if he chooses the right accommodations he can have the comforts of home in the heart of Africa. Expecting all this, he demands that it be supplied to him. Having paid for it, he likes to think he has got his money's worth. He has demanded that the whole world be made a stage for pseudo-events. And there has been no lack of honest and enterprising suppliers who try to give him what he wants, to help him inflate his expectations, and to gratify his insatiable appetite for the impossible.

I

UNTIL ALMOST the present century, travel abroad was uncomfortable, difficult, and expensive. The middle-class American did not go for "fun." Foreign capitals offered sophisticated pleasures: conversation with the great and the witty, views of painting, sculpture, and architecture, romantic musings in the ruins of vanished civilizations, pilgrimages to the birthplaces of poets, to the scenes of glory of statesmen and orators. Men seeing the "Wonders of the World" felt a wonderment for which they usually were well prepared. This had long been the pattern of European travel by Europeans. "As soon as we have got hold of a bit of Latin," the French wit Saint-Évremond caricatured in one of his comedies in the seventeenth century, "we prepare to start on our travels. . . . When our travellers are of a literary turn of mind, they invariably take with them a book consisting solely of blank pages nicely bound, which they call an *Album Amicorum*. Armed with this, they make a point of calling on the various learned men of the locality they happen to be visiting, and beg them to inscribe their names in it."

The serious attitude in the late eighteenth century was expressed by an aristocratic scholar, the Comte de Volney, who explained that, having received a small inheritance:

> On reflection, I thought the sum too inconsiderable to make any sensible addition to my income and too great to be dissipated in frivolous expenses. Some fortunate circumstances had habituated me to study; I had acquired a taste, and even a passion for knowledge, and the accession to my fortune appeared to me a fresh means of gratifying my inclination, and opening a new way to improvement. I had read and frequently heard repeated, that of all methods of adorning the mind, and forming the judgment, travelling is the most efficacious; I determined, therefore, on a plan of travelling, but to what part of the world to direct my course remained still to be chosen: I wished the scene of my observations to be new, or at least brilliant.

Volney decided to go to the Middle East, and his journey through Syria and Egypt (1783–85) produced a travel classic. Arthur Young, the English agriculturalist, took three trips to nearby France in 1787, 1788, and 1789, as a self-appointed surveyor of farming ways; his journal (published 1792) helped revolutionize the agronomy of England and reached its influence far out to the young United States. Jefferson, in France and Italy about the same time, earnestly sought out new plants for Virginia and found the architectural models which shaped the University of Virginia.

The young aristocrat went abroad also to grow up and to sow his wild oats. He could enjoy his rakish pleasures at a comfortable distance from home and reputation. Adam Smith, in *The Wealth of Nations* (1776), recorded that in his day it was the custom among those who could afford it "to send young people to travel in foreign countries immediately upon their leaving school, and without sending them to any university. Our young people, it is said, generally return home much improved by their travels. A young man who goes abroad at seventeen or eighteen, and returns home at one-and-twenty, returns three or four years older than he was when he went abroad; and at that age it is very difficult not to improve a good deal in three or four years." Smith objected, however, that this was a risky practice which often corrupted the young; the custom, he said, could not have arisen except for the low state of English universities. The wealth of England had enabled her young people on the continent (as a German observer somewhat enviously remarked in 1760) to "give a loose to their propensities to pleasure, even in Italy . . . having a great deal of money to lavish away, it not only gives them more spirit to engage in adventures, but likewise furnishes them with means for removing impediments, or buying off any ill-consequences." Casanova's amorous *Memoirs* (1826–38), we sometimes forget, were a record of travels which had taken him through the capitals of Europe—to Venice, Paris, Berlin, Warsaw, Madrid, and as far east as Constantinople.

In the seventeenth and eighteenth centuries many European men of culture liked to boast of having made more than one country their own. To travel was to become a man of the world. Unless one was a man of the world, he might not seem cultivated in his own country. The young Italian, Antonio Conti, for example (as Paul Hazard recalls), was born in Padua, lived for a while in Paris, then in London in 1715 joined a discussion of the recently invented infinitesimal calculus, afterwards stopped to pay his respects to Leeuwenhoek, the naturalist and microscope maker, in Holland—all on his way to meet the philosopher Leibniz in Hanover. In the old Grand Tour (recounted, for example, in Laurence Sterne's *Sentimental Journey*) the young gentleman rounded off his education. Locke, Gibbon, and Hume knew France from extended visits. Gibbon did much of his writing in Switzerland. Monarchs often went abroad, and not only when they abdicated or were banished. Prince Hamlet went abroad to study. Christina of Sweden lived for a while in Paris, and died in Rome in 1689. Peter the Great at the end of the seventeenth century traveled in Germany, Holland, England, and Austria. For Europeans foreign travel was an institution of exiled monarchs, adventuring aristocrats, merchant princes, and wandering scholars.

For Americans, too, until nearly the end of the nineteenth century foreign travel (still mostly European travel) was the experience of a privileged few. Franklin's great overseas success was in the committee rooms of the House of Commons and in the salons (and bedrooms) of Paris. Jefferson and other cultivated Americans, who still believed in a world-wide "Republic of Letters," were eager to meet their European fellow citizens. Henry Adams in Berlin, Rome, London, Paris was an idealized American version of the European on Grand Tour. All the success that Adams or his father or grandfather achieved, so Henry said, "was chiefly due to the field that Europe gave them," and it was more than likely that without the help of Europe they would have all remained local politicians or lawyers, like their neighbors, to the end. When a Franklin, a Jefferson, a Charles Sumner, or a Henry Adams arrived in Europe, he was armed with introductions to the great and famous. Henry Adams called the European journey his third or fourth attempt at education. Like other means of education, such travel had its delights, but it was hard work.

The scarcity of postal facilities and the lack of newspapers gave an added incentive to travel. At the same time, the hardships of a virtually roadless landscape restricted the foreign journey to those with a serious or at least earnestly frivolous purpose, who were willing to risk robbers, cutthroats, and disease, and to find their own way through trackless heath, vast swamps, and mud that came up to the carriage axles. "Under the best of conditions," one historian of the eighteenth century records, "six horses were required to drag across country the lumbering coaches of the gentry, and not infrequently the assistance of oxen was required." It was not until nearly 1800—and the work of two Scottish engineers, Thomas Telford and John Macadam—that the modern science of roadbuilding was developed and cheap and effective hard-surfacing became possible.

The travel experience was an adventure, too, simply because so few could afford or would dare its hardships. The modern hotel—the place which George Bernard Shaw later praised as "a refuge from home life"—had not been invented. In the picturesque inn of the travel books every comfort had to be specially negotiated. The luxury of a private bed was hard to come by, not only because of the constant companionship of cockroaches, bedbugs, and fleas, but because innkeepers felt free to assign more than one guest to a bed. Englishmen traveling in France noted how rare it was to encounter fellow travelers, much less fellow countrymen. Arthur Young in the late eighteenth century found "a paucity of travellers that is amazing"; he traveled a whole day on a main road thirty miles outside of Paris and "met but a single gentleman's carriage, nor anything else on the road that looked like a gentleman." Even later, when sleeping accommodations had improved, the traveler on the continent might expect to find "comfortable hotels, but no uncomfortable crowds." As late as the 1860's an English traveler to Holland noted that "tourists were comparatively rare and there were no cheap trippers."

I I

SOMETIME PAST the middle of the nineteenth century, as the Graphic Revolution was getting under way, the character of foreign travel—first by Europeans, and then by Americans—began to change. This change has reached its climax in our day. Formerly travel required long planning, large expense, and great investments of time. It involved risks to health or even to life. The traveler was active. Now he became passive. Instead of an athletic exercise, travel became a spectator sport.

This change can be described in a word. It was the decline

of the traveler and the rise of the tourist. There is a wonderful, but neglected, precision in these words. The old English noun "travel" (in the sense of a journey) was originally the same word as "travail" (meaning "trouble," "work," or "torment"). And the word "travail," in turn, seems to have been derived, through the French, from a popular Latin or Common Romanic word *trepalium,* which meant a three-staked instrument of torture. To journey—to "travail," or (later) to travel—then was to do something laborious or troublesome. The traveler was an active man at work.

In the early nineteenth century a new word came into the English language which gave a clue to the changed character of world travel, especially from the American point of view. This was the word "tourist"—at first hyphenated as "tour-ist." Our American dictionary now defines a tourist as "a person who makes a pleasure trip" or "a person who makes a tour, especially for pleasure." Significantly, too, the word "tour" in "tourist" was derived by back-formation from the Latin *tornus,* which in turn came from the Greek word for a tool describing a circle. The traveler, then, was working at something; the tourist was a pleasure-seeker. The traveler was active; he went strenuously in search of people, of adventure, of experience. The tourist is passive; he expects interesting things to happen to him. He goes "sight-seeing" (a word, by the way, which came in about the same time, with its first use recorded in 1847). He expects everything to be done to him and for him.

Thus foreign travel ceased to be an activity—an experience, an undertaking—and instead became a commodity. The rise of the tourist was possible, and then inevitable, when attractive items of travel were wrapped up and sold in packages (the "package tour"). By buying a tour you could oblige somebody else to make pleasant and interesting things happen to you. You could buy wholesale (by the month or week, or by the country) or retail (by the day or by the individual foreign capital).

The familiar circumstances which had brought this about

are worth recalling. First and most obvious was the easing of transportation. In the latter part of the nineteenth century railroads and ocean steamers began to make travel actually pleasurable. Discomfort and risks were suddenly reduced. For the first time in history, long-distance transportation was industrially mass-produced. It could be sold to lots of people, and it could be sold cheap. For a satisfactory return on investment, it *had* to be sold in large quantities. The capital invested in any of the old vehicles—a stagecoach or the passenger quarters in a sailing ship—was minute compared with that in a railroad (even a single sleeping car) or a luxury liner. This enormous capital investment required that equipment be kept in constant use and that passengers be found by the thousands. Now great numbers of people would be induced to travel for pleasure. Vast ocean steamers could not be filled with diplomats, with people traveling on business, or with aristocratic Henry Adamses who were intent on deepening their education. The consuming public had to be enlarged to include the vacationing middle class, or at least the upper middle class. Foreign travel became democratized.

The obvious next step was the "personally conducted tour." Well-planned group excursions could entice even the more timid stay-at-homes. Of course guided tours of one sort or another had been very old: the Crusades had sometimes taken on this character. We can recall, in Chaucer's *Canterbury Tales,* in the late fourteenth century, the knowledgeable, generous host of the Tabard Inn, who offered

> And for to make yow the moore mury,
> I wol myselven goodly with yow ryde,
> Right at myn owene cost, and be youre gyde. . . .

But later guides seldom offered their services free. The guided tour itself actually became a commodity. Adventure would be sold in packages and guaranteed to be consumed without risk. In England, with its short distances, its rising middle classes, and its early-developed railroads, came the first organized tours. According to legend the very first of them was arranged in 1838 to take the people of Wadebridge by special train to the nearby town of Bodmin. There they witnessed the hanging of two murderers. Since the Bodmin gallows were in clear sight of the uncovered station, excursionists had their fun without even leaving the open railway carriages.

The real pioneer in the making and marketing of conducted tours was of course Thomas Cook (1808–1892). He began in the early 1840's by arranging special-rate railroad excursions within England. His first planned tour took nearly 600 people the eleven miles from Leicester to Loughborough for a temperance convention—at a reduced round-trip third-class fare of one shilling a head. Soon Cook was sending hundreds to Scotland (1846) and Ireland (1848), and for thousands was arranging tours of the Crystal Palace Exposition in London in 1851. In 1856 he advertised his first "grand circular tour of the Continent," visiting Antwerp, Brussels, the Field of Waterloo, Cologne, the Rhine and its borders, Mayence, Frankfort, Heidelberg, Baden-Baden, Strasbourg, Paris, Le Havre, and back to London. Then, with the help of his enterprising son, he offered Swiss tours, American tours, and finally, in 1869, the first middle-class Conducted Crusade to the Holy Land. He quickly developed all kinds of conveniences: courteous and knowledgeable guides, hotel coupons, room reservations, and protection and advice against disease and thievery.

Sophisticated Englishmen objected. They said that Cook was depriving travelers of initiative and adventure and cluttering the continental landscape with the Philistine middle classes. "Going by railroad," complained John Ruskin, "I do not consider as travelling at all; it is merely being 'sent' to a place, and very little different from becoming a parcel." An article in *Blackwood's Magazine* in February, 1865, by a British consul in Italy, attacked this "new and growing evil . . . of conducting some forty or fifty persons, irrespective of age or sex, from London to Naples and back for a fixed sum." "The Cities of Italy," he lamented, were now "deluged with droves of these creatures, for they never separate, and you see them forty in number pouring along a street with their director—now in front, now at the rear, circling round them like a sheepdog—and really the process is as like herding as may be. I have already met three flocks, and anything so uncouth I never saw before, the men, mostly elderly, dreary, sad-looking; the women, somewhat younger, travel-tossed, but intensely lively, wide-awake, and facetious."

Cook defended his tours, which he called "agencies for the advancement of Human Progress." The attacks on them, he said, were sheer snobbery. The critics belonged in some earlier century. How foolish to "think that places of rare interest should be excluded from the gaze of the common people, and be kept only for the interest of the 'select' of society. But it is too late in this day of progress to talk such exclusive nonsense, God's earth with all its fullness and beauty, is for the people; and railways and steamboats are the result of the common light of science, and are for the people also. . . . The best of men, and the noblest minds, rejoice to see the people follow in their foretrod routes of pleasure."

Still, in the United States, where everything was suddenly available to everybody, it was far more profitable to deal in immigrants than in tourists. Mobile, immigrant-filled, primitive America saw less glamor in travel, whether at home or abroad. Among Americans, even longer than among Englishmen, foreign travel remained close to its aristocratic origins. Until early in the twentieth century, Americans who wanted a planned European excursion still relied on Thomas Cook & Son. President Grant used Cook's. And one of the best testimonials for Cook's new foolproof, carefree travel commodity came from Mark Twain:

Cook has made travel easy and a pleasure. He will sell you a ticket to any place on the globe, or all the places, and give you all the time you need and much more besides. It provides hotels for you everywhere, if you so desire; and you cannot be overcharged, for the coupons show just how much you must pay. Cook's servants at the great stations will attend to your baggage, get you a cab, tell you how much to pay cabmen and porters, procure guides for you, and horses, donkeys, camels, bicycles, or anything else you want, and make life a comfort and satisfaction to you. Cook is your banker everywhere, and his establishment your shelter when you get caught out in the rain. His clerks will answer all the questions you ask and do it courteously. I recommend your Grace to travel on Cook's tickets; and I do this without embarrassment, for I get no commission. I do not know Cook.

Cook's has never lost its early leadership. It is still the largest travel agency in the world.

The principal competitor in the United States was to be the American Express Company. It grew out of the famous Wells, Fargo and other agencies which by the mid-nineteenth century were forwarding goods and money across the vast American spaces. In the nineteenth century these agencies profited from the immigrant influx, by going into the business of arranging remittances from successful, recently arrived Americans to their needy families back in Europe. In 1891 the first American Express Travelers Cheque was copyrighted, and in the years since it has done much to ease the traveler's cares. (By 1960 about two billion dollars' worth were being sold annually.) In 1895 American Express opened its first European office. At first all it offered traveling Americans was a mail-forwarding service, help in securing railroad tickets and hotel reservations, and help in finding lost baggage. President James C. Fargo, in charge until 1914, insisted there was no money in the tourist business. American Express, he said, should deal exclusively in freight and express. But the consolidation of the different express services as part of the war effort in World War I inevitably changed the business. Even before the end of the war American Express had begun to develop an extensive travel service, and after the war its travel department grew spectacularly. By 1961 American Express, serving tourists everywhere, had 279 offices throughout the world.

American Express sent the first postwar escorted tour to Europe in October, 1919. Soon afterwards the first Mediterranean cruise went out in the Cunard liner *Caronia,* under joint control of American Express and Cook's. In 1922 American Express dispatched the first all-water round-the-world pleasure cruise in the *Laconia.* Afterwards a similar cruise was arranged every year. The great backwash had begun. Americans were returning to the Old World in the great tourist invasions of Europe which have fluctuated with our domestic fortunes, but which in recent years have been greater than ever before.

By the middle of the twentieth century, foreign travel had become big business. It was a prominent feature of the American standard of living, an important element in our cultural and financial relations with the rest of the world. In 1957, for example, about ten million American residents spent over two billion dollars on international travel. Of these travelers, 1.5 million went overseas. For the summer of 1961 alone, it was estimated that 800,000 Americans were visiting Europe and were spending there about seven hundred million dollars.

Foreign travel now had, of course, become a commodity. Like any other mass-produced commodity, it could be bought in bargain packages and on the installment plan. It was considered a strange and noteworthy event, a peculiar quirk, when Charles Sumner in early nineteenth-century Boston borrowed money from a couple of old friends who had faith in his future, to finance his tour of Europe. Nowadays more and more travelers take the trip before they can pay for it. "Go Now, Pay Later." Your travel agent will arrange it for you.

When travel is no longer made to order but is an assembly-line, store-boughten commodity, we have less to say about what goes into it. And we know less and less about what we are buying. We buy so many days of vacation pleasure without even knowing what is in the package. Recently on a lecture tour I flew into Hyderabad, a city in central India, of which I had not even heard a year before. Seated beside me on the plane were a tired, elderly American and his wife. He was a real estate broker from Brooklyn. I asked him what was interesting about Hyderabad. He had not the slightest notion. He and his wife were going there because the place was "in the package." Their tour agent had guaranteed to include only places that were "world famous," and so it must be.

A well-packaged tour must include insurance against risks. In this sense the dangers of travel have become obsolete; we buy safety and peace of mind right in the package. Somebody else covers all the risks. In 1954 the suspense-thriller movie *The High and the Mighty* depicted the troubled flight of a luxury air liner from San Francisco to Honolulu. The assorted vacationers aboard were flying to the mid-Pacific for a week or two of relaxation. As the engines failed, the nerves of the passengers began to fray. Finally, in order to keep the plane in the air, the captain ordered the baggage jettisoned. I saw this movie in a suburban theatre outside of Chicago. Beside me sat a mother and her young son. He seemed relatively unperturbed at the mortal risks of the passengers, but when the plane's purser began tossing into the ocean the elegant vacation paraphernalia—fancy suitcases, hatboxes, portable typewriters, golf clubs, tennis rackets— the boy became agitated. "What will they do?" the boy exclaimed. "Don't worry," comforted the mother. "It's all insured."

When the traveler's risks are insurable he has become a tourist.

III

THE TRAVELER used to go about the world to encounter the natives. A function of travel agencies now is to prevent this encounter. They are always devising efficient new ways of insulating the tourist from the travel world.

In the old traveler's accounts, the colorful native inn-keeper, full of sage advice and local lore, was a familiar figure. Now he is obsolete. Today on Main Street in your home town you can arrange transportation, food, lodging, and entertainment for Rome, Sydney, Singapore, or Tokyo.

No more chaffering. A well-planned tour saves the tourist from negotiating with the natives when he gets there. One reason why returning tourists nowadays talk so much about and are so irritated by tipping practices is that these are almost their only direct contact with the people. Even this may soon be eliminated. The Travel Plant Commission of the International Union of Official Travel Organizations in 1958 was studying ways of standardizing tipping practices so that eventually all gratuities could be included in the tour package. Shopping, like tipping, is one of the few activities remaining for the tourist. It is a chink in that wall of prearrangements which separates him from the country he visits. No wonder he finds it exciting. When he shops he actually encounters natives, negotiates in their strange language, and discovers their local business etiquette. In a word, he tastes the thrill and "travail" which the old-time traveler once experienced all along the way—with every purchase of transportation, with every night's lodging, with every meal.

A planned excursion insulates the tourist in still another way. From its first invention by Thomas Cook in the early nineteenth century, the fully prearranged group tour promised good-fellowship with one's countrymen in addition to the exotic pleasure of foreign sights. The luxury ocean liner and the all-expense "cruise" (the word in this sense is very recent and is possibly an American invention; originally it meant "to sail from place to place, as for pleasure, *without* a set destination") have made this kind of travel amount to residence in a floating resort hotel.

Shipmates now replace the natives as a source of adventure. Unadvertised risks from pickpockets and bandits are replaced by over-advertised risks of shipboard romance. The sights which disappoint the bachelor or spinster on a cruise are not the Vatican, the Louvre, or the Acropolis but the shipmates. Except for tipping and shopping adventures, returning cruisers have little to report about encounters with the natives, but they have a great deal to say about their countrymen on tour with them. The authorized centennial history of American Express recounts the tribulations of a cruise director on a round-the-world cruise. He was obliged, among other things, "to rescue a susceptible young playboy from the wiles of a cruising adventuress; play cupid to a British baronet and an American actress; guard the widow of an Australian pearl magnate who carried tin cans full of matched pearls loose in her baggage; quietly settle an attempted murder in Calcutta; protect his charges during the pitched battle with which Hindus and Mohammedans celebrated the Harvest Festival in Agra; reason with a passenger who demanded a refund because he lost a day when the ship crossed the international date line; and hold the hand of a lonely old lady as she lay dying in a hotel in Rome." In the old days, an excursion director was called a "guide"; now he is a "social director."

Of course the voyager, even on a planned excursion, is likely to be less insulated on land than on sea, and he is least insulated if he goes alone. But the notion of packaged touring has so prevailed that when a person goes by himself the American Express travel department gives his package a special name, "F.I.T." or "D.I.T."—for "Foreign (or Domestic) Independent Travel." If you want to buy a vacation tour package all for yourself (that is, voyage alone and at will), this is actually offered as a "special feature." It is described as an attractive new departure from the routine group arrangements, much as only a half century ago the group excursion was offered as something special. The individualized package, the American Express chronicler explains, "is for individuals who prefer to travel alone rather than in a conducted group. A tour is planned to meet the particular specifications of the client. The exact cost is reckoned and, on payment of this amount, the traveler is given the familiar American Express package containing tickets and coupons to cover his entire trip."

Today more than ever before the traveler is isolated from the landscape he traverses. The newest and most popular means of passenger transportation to foreign parts is the most insulating known to man. By 1958 about four times as many international travelers from the United States went by air as by sea. Recently I boarded a plane at Idlewild Airport in New York at 6:30 one evening. The next morning at 11:30 I was in Amsterdam. The flight was routine, at an altitude of about 23,000 feet, far above the clouds, too high to observe landmark or seamark. Nothing to see but the weather; since we had no weather, nothing to see at all. I had flown not through space but through time. My only personal sign that we had gone so far was the discovery on arrival in Amsterdam that I had lost six hours. My only problem en route was to pass the time. My passage through space was unnoticeable and effortless. The airplane robbed me of the landscape.

The tourist gets there without the experience of having gone. For him it is all the same: going to one place or to another. Today it is only by going short distances, which we still traverse on land, that we can have the experience of going any place. When I have driven from Chicago to a summer resort in nearby Indiana or Wisconsin, or when I used to commute from a suburb to the University by train or by car, I have had more variety of sensations, have observed more varied scenes, and have met more varied people, than I did when I went from New York to Amsterdam.

For ages the sensations of going there were inseparable from the experience of being there. Nowadays, "Getting there is half the fun." "Rome," announces the British Overseas Airways Corporation, is "A Fun Stop." And there is nothing more homogeneous than fun, wherever it is found. Now we can have plenty en route. United States Lines advertises:

You're just 15 gourmet meals from Europe on the world's fastest ship. Caviar from Iran, pheasant from Scotland . . . you can choose superb food from all over the world, another rewarding experience in gracious living on this ship. There's a pool, gym, 2 theatres, 3 Meyer Davis orchestras. It's a 5-day adventure in the lost art of leisure.

In an accompanying photograph we see how "Mrs. Leonard Kleckner shows off her dogs to Chief Officer Ridington. This great modern ocean liner has dog kennels with a veterinarian and a dog-walking area." Shipboard swimming pools, cocktail lounges, and the latest movies! "One of the World's great Restaurants sails for Europe" whenever a Holland-America liner pushes off from New York. The experience of going there has been erased. For it we have substituted all the pleasures of de luxe relaxation. Even better than at home.

If we go by air, then too we are encompassed in music, and enjoy our cocktail in a lounge with the décor of the best resort hotel. In 1961, TWA began showing first-run movies on a special wide screen in the First Class section of its Super Jet flights. A full-page color advertisement for Lufthansa, German Airlines, portrays the attractive Miss Dietland von Schönfeldt—a typical Lufthansa stewardess, of "gracious background, poise and charm, intelligence and education" who, of course, speaks fluent English. She "Invites You to an Unusual Supper Party. . . . Every flight is a charming, informal Continental supper party, eight jet-smooth miles over the Atlantic."

The airline stewardess, a breed first developed in the United States and now found on all major international airlines, is a new subspecies of womankind. With her standardized impersonal charm she offers us, anywhere in the world, the same kind of pillow for our head and the latest issue of *Look* or *The Reader's Digest*. She is the Madonna of the Airways, a pretty symbol of the new homogenized blandness of the tourist's world. The first airline stewardesses were the eight girls hired by United Airlines on May 15, 1930; their union was organized in 1946. By 1958 there were 8,200 of them employed by American-owned airlines. They were being trained in a program which lasted about six weeks. The general requirements, as a careful reporter summarized them, were that the young lady be twenty-one to twenty-six years old, "unmarried, reasonably pretty and slender, especially around the hips, which will be at eye level for the passengers. She should have been to high school, be poised and tactful, have a good disposition and a pleasant speaking voice." Stewardesses with similar qualifications were later trained for service on trains and long-distance buses.

Cabral's company, which went from Portugal to India in 1500, did not, of course, have the advantage of slender-hipped, smooth-voiced stewardesses. They spent over six months at sea. They could not help knowing they had really gone somewhere. In the days before refrigeration or canning the passenger cuisine was not for gourmets. Fresh water was rationed, and fresh fruits and vegetables were not to be had. Scurvy was the plague of seafarers. Typhoid, typhus, and malaria were rife.

The *Mayflower* passengers were at sea for nearly two months, from mid-September to early November, 1620. On arrival William Bradford reported, "They fell upon their knees and blessed the God of heaven, who had brought them over the vast and furious ocean, and delivered them from all the periles and miseries thereof, againe to set their feete on the firme and stable earth, their proper elemente. . . . Being thus passed the vast ocean, and a sea of troubles." Knowledge that they had come so far stayed with them even into the second generation. Increase Mather gave over the first chapter of his catalogue of divine providences to "remarkable sea-deliverances." These were as important in the American experience as were the forests or the Indians.

For Americans moving westward in the nineteenth century, their ways of living together en route shaped their lives on arrival, just as the proverbial forty years during which Moses led the children of Israel from Egypt through the wilderness to the promised land shaped them into a nation. As westering Americans organized against the perils of the trip they framed constitutions and by-laws which prepared them to organize new communities at their destinations.

Now, when one risks so little and experiences so little on the voyage, the experience of being there somehow becomes emptier and more trivial. When getting there was more troublesome, being there was more vivid. When getting there is "fun," arriving there somehow seems not to be arriving any place.

The tourist who arrives at his destination, where tourist facilities have been "improved," remains almost as insulated as he was en route. Today the ideal tourist hotel abroad is as much as possible like the best accommodations back home. Beds, lighting facilities, ventilation, air conditioning, central heating, plumbing are all American style, although a shrewd hotel management will, of course, have made a special effort to retain some "local atmosphere."

Stirred by air travel, international hotel chains have grown phenomenally since World War II. In 1942 Conrad Hilton took over his first hotel outside the United States, the Chihuahua Hilton, just over the border in northern Mexico. "I felt," he later recalled "that by organizing week-end bus excursions with guides, large-scale entertainment at the hotel, an all-expenses-paid holiday, we could make a very good thing of it—which we did." At the end of the war Hilton Hotels International, Inc., was founded. "What used to be a month-long vacation trip," Hilton explained, "is now almost a week-end possibility. . . , The airplane is here to stay. Americans not only can but want to travel farther, see more, do more, in less time. . . . Father Junipero Serra set his California missions a day's journey apart. Today you can fly over the whole string in a few hours. If we were to set our hotels a day's journey apart, we'd be around the world in no time. So perfectly sound business is in line with national idealism."

Hilton changed his slogan from "Across the Nation" to "Around the World." The Caribe Hilton in San Juan, Puerto Rico, opened in 1947, the Castellana Hilton in Madrid in 1953, the Istanbul Hilton in 1955—and these were only a beginning. By 1961 Hilton Hotels were also operating in Mexico City and Acapulco, Panama City, Montreal, Cairo, West Berlin, St. Thomas (Virgin Islands), Santiago, and Honolulu. There were associated hotels in Sydney, Melbourne, and Queensland. Hotels were under construction in Port-of-Spain (Trinidad), Athens, Amsterdam and Rotterdam, London, Teheran, and Rome, and projected in Paris, Mayaguez (Puerto Rico), Tokyo, Addis Ababa, Bogotá, Dorval (Quebec), and Tunis.

The spirit of these new hotels was well expressed in Conrad Hilton's own account of the Istanbul Hilton opening in 1955, to which he brought a planeload of American celebrities and news makers. "When we flew into Istanbul for the opening with our guests from America, Carol Channing, Irene Dunne and her husband, Dr. Francis Griffin, Mona Freeman, Sonja Henie, Diana Lynn, Merle Oberon, Ann Miller, representatives of the American press, John Cameron Swazey, Bob Considine, Horace Sutton, Louella Parsons, Hedda Hopper, and Cobina Wright, not to mention my very old friend, Leo Carillo, who once owned a deer named Sequoia, there is no question but that we all felt the antiquity, romance and mystery of this ancient city. . . . I felt this 'City of the Golden Horn' was a tremendous place to plant a little bit of America." "Each of our hotels," Hilton announced at the opening, "is a 'little America.' "

I have been in both the Caribe Hilton and the Istanbul Hilton and can testify that both are models of American modernity and antisepsis. They are as indistinguishable in interior feeling and design as two planes of the American Airlines. Except for the views from the picture windows, you do not know where you are. You have the comforting feeling of not really being there. Even the measured admixture of carefully filtered local atmosphere proves that you are still in the U.S.A.

IV

THE SELF-CONSCIOUS effort to provide local atmosphere is itself thoroughly American. And an effective insulation from the place where you have gone. Out-of-doors the real Turkey surrounds the Istanbul Hilton. But inside it is only an imitation of the Turkish style. The hotel achieves the subtle effect, right in the heart of Turkey, of making the experience of Turkey quite secondhand.

A similar insulation comes from all the efforts of different countries which are or hope to become "Tourist Meccas" to provide attractions for tourists. These "attractions" offer an elaborately contrived indirect experience, an artificial product to be consumed in the very places where the real thing is free as air. They are ways for the traveler to remain out of contact with foreign peoples in the very act of "sight-seeing" them. They keep the natives in quarantine while the tourist in air-conditioned comfort views them through a picture window. They are the cultural mirages now found at tourist oases everywhere.

Oddly enough, many of these attractions came into being, rather accidentally, as by-products of democratic revolutions. But soon they were being carefully designed, planned in large numbers and on a grand scale by national tourist agencies eager to attract visitors from far away.

The modern museum, like the modern tourist himself, is a symptom of the rise of democracy. Both signal the diffusion of scientific knowledge, the popularization of the arts, the decline of private patronage of artists, and the spread of literacy among the middle classes. Collections of valuable, curious, and beautiful objects had always been gathered by men of wealth and power. There had long been private museums, but these were seldom open to the public. In ancient days, and especially before the printed book, museums and libraries had been closely allied, as in Alexandria, for example. Of course, there had always been some works of art especially designed for public display, as in the Pinacotheca (a marble hall of the propylaeum on the Athenian Acropolis) or in the forum of Augustus in Rome. At least since Roman times, the best collections of the works of art and of learning were privately owned. And the first modern public museum was the British Museum, established by Act of Parliament in 1753. It had been inspired by the will of Sir Hans Sloane, who on his death that year left the nation his remarkable collection of books, manuscripts, and curiosities. On the European continent most of the great art museums are part of the booty which the rising middle classes have captured for themselves in the revolutions since the late eighteenth century. The Louvre, which had been a royal palace, became a public art museum after the French Revolution of 1789.

Nowadays a visit to the best art museums in Europe is often a tour of the vacated residences of magnates, noblemen, and monarchs of the pre-democratic age: in Florence, the Uffizi and Pitti Palaces; in Venice, the Doge's Palace; in Paris, the Louvre; in Vienna, Schönbrunn. Beautiful objects, taken from scores of princely residences, are crowded together for public display in the grandest of defunct palaces. Painting, sculpture, tapestries, tableware, and other *objets d'art* (once part of the interior decoration or household equipment of a working aristocracy) were thus "liberated" by and for the people. Now they were to be shown to the nation and to all comers. Common people could now see treasures from the inner sanctums of palaces, treasures originally designed to adorn the intimate dining tables, bedrooms, and bathrooms of a well-guarded aristocracy. At last everyone could take a Cook's Tour of the art of the ages for a nominal admission fee or free of charge. Statesmen saw these new museums as symbols of wide-spreading education and culture, as monuments and catalysts of national pride. So they were. Today they remain the destination of tourist-pilgrims from afar.

To bring the paintings of Botticelli, Rubens, and Titian into a room where one could see them in a few minutes, to gather together the sculpture of Donatello and Cellini from widely dispersed churches, monasteries, and drawing rooms for chronological display in a single hall, to remove the tapestries designed for wall-covering in remote mansions and hunting lodges, and spread them in the halls of centrally located museums—this was a great convenience. But there was one unavoidable consequence. All these things were being removed from their context. In a sense, therefore, they were all being misrepresented. Perhaps more was gained in the quantity of people who could see them at all than was lost in the quality of the experience. This is not the question. The effect on experience is plain and undeniable.

Inevitably these museums—and others made later on the defunct-palace model—become major tourist attractions. They still are. It remains true, however, that, almost without exception, whatever one sees in a museum is seen out of its proper surroundings. The impression of individual works of art or of a country's past culture as a whole, whenever it is formed from museum visits, is inevitably factitious. It has been put together for your and my convenience, instruction, amusement, and delight. But to put it together the art commissioners have had to take apart the very environment, the culture which was once real, and which actually created and enjoyed these very works. The museum visitor tours a warehouse of cultural artifacts; he does not see vital organs of living culture. Even where (as in the Prado in Madrid or the Hermitage in Leningrad) one visits what was once a private museum, the original collection has been so diluted or expanded and the atmosphere so changed that the experience is itself a new artifact. Only the museum itself is quite real—a functioning part of a going concern. The ribbon across the chair, the ancestral portrait no longer viewed by its descendant, is a symbol of the change. Each living art object, taken out of its native habitat so we can conveniently gaze at it, is like an animal in a zoo. Something about it has died in the removal.

Of course, there remain sites all over the world—Windsor Castle, the Medici Palace in Florence, the Hindu rock carvings at Elefanta, Japanese Imperial Palaces, and countless churches, shrines and temples—where works of art remain in their original sites. But in nearly all Tourist Meccas much of the tourist's sight-seeing is museum-seeing. And most museums have this unreal, misrepresentative character.

The museum is only one example of the tourist attraction. All tourist attractions share this factitious, pseudo-eventful quality. Formerly when the old-time traveler visited a country whatever he saw was apt to be what really went on there. A Titian, a Rubens or a Gobelin tapestry would be seen on a palace wall as background to a princely party or a public function. Folk song and folk dance were for the natives themselves. Now, however, the tourist sees less of the country than of its tourist attractions. Today what he sees is seldom the living culture, but usually specimens collected and embalmed especially for him, or attractions specially staged for him: proved specimens of the artificial.

Since the mid-nineteenth century, international expositions have increased in number and grown in prominence. They usually have some solid purposes—to promote trade, to strengthen world peace, to exchange technological information. But when expositions become tourist attractions they acquire an artificial character. From the London Crystal Palace Exposition of 1851 and the Exposition on the Champs Elysées in 1855 down to Chicago's Century of Progress Exposition in 1933–34, the New York World's Fair of 1939–40, the Brussels World's Fair of 1958, and the annual Cinema Festivals in Venice, modern expositions have been designed for propaganda, to attract foreign tourists and their currency. An exposition planned for tourists is a self-conscious and contrived national image. It is a pseudo-event for foreign consumption.

The rise of tourist traffic has brought the relatively recent phenomenon of the tourist attraction pure and simple. It often has no purpose but to attract in the interest of the owner or of the nation. As we might expect, this use of the word "attraction" as "a thing or feature which 'draws' people; especially, any interesting or amusing exhibition" dates only from about 1862. It is a new species: the most attenuated form of a nation's culture. All over the world now we find these "attractions"—of little significance for the inward life of a people, but wonderfully salable as tourist commodity. Examples are Madame Tussaud's exhibition of wax figures in London (she first became known for her modeled heads of the leaders and victims of the French Revolution) and the Tiger Balm Gardens in Hong Kong. Disneyland in California—the American "attraction" which tourist Khrushchev most wanted to see—is the example to end all examples. Here indeed Nature imitates Art. The visitor to Disneyland encounters not the two-dimensional comic strip or movie originals, but only their three-dimensional facsimiles.

Tourist attractions serve their purpose best when they are pseudo-events. To be repeatable at will they must be factitious. Emphasis on the artificial comes from the ruthless truthfulness of tourist agents. What they can really guarantee you are not spontaneous cultural products but only those made especially for tourist consumption, for foreign cash customers. Not only in Mexico City and Montreal, but also in the remote Guatemalan Tourist Mecca of Chichecastenango and in far-off villages of Japan, earnest honest natives embellish their ancient rites, change, enlarge, and spectacularize their festivals, so that tourists will not be disappointed. In order to satisfy the exaggerated expectations of tour agents and tourists, people everywhere obligingly become dishonest mimics of themselves. To provide a full schedule of events at the best seasons and at convenient hours, they travesty their most solemn rituals, holidays, and folk celebrations—all for the benefit of tourists.

In Berlin, in the days before the First World War, legend

tells us that precisely at the stroke of noon, just as the imperial military band would begin its daily concert in front of the Imperial Palace, Kaiser Wilhelm used to interrupt whatever he was doing inside the palace. If he was in a council of state he would say, "With your kind forbearance, gentlemen, I must excuse myself now to appear in the window. You see, it says in Baedeker that at this hour I always do."

Modern tourist guidebooks have helped raise tourist expectations. And they have provided the natives—from Kaiser Wilhelm down to the villagers of Chichecastenango—with a detailed and itemized list of what is expected of them and when. These are the up-to-date scripts for actors on the tourists' stage. The pioneer, of course, was Karl Baedeker (1801–1859) of Leipzig, whose name long since has entered our language as a synonym for his product. He began offering his packaged tours in print at the same time that Thomas Cook in England was perfecting the personally conducted packaged tour. Baedeker issued a guidebook to Coblenz in 1829, first in German; then in 1846 came his first foreign-language edition (in French); in 1861 appeared his first English-language edition. By the beginning of World War II the Baedeker firm had sold more than two million copies of about a hundred different guides in English, French, and German, the languages that reached those nations with rising middle classes who were now strenuously adapting the Grand Tour to their more meager budgets and more limited education. Despite the setback of the war and the destruction of the Baedeker plant in Leipzig by the Royal Air Force, fifty new editions were published in the decade after 1950. In the single year 1958 about 80,000 Baedeker guides were sold at a price of nearly five dollars apiece. At this rate, within twenty-five years as many Baedekers would be sold as in the whole previous century.

Karl Baedeker himself was a relentless sight-seer. In the beginning he refused to describe anything he had not personally seen. His guidebooks have held a reputation for scrupulous accuracy, leading many tourists to share A. P. Herbert's faith:

> For kings and governments may err
> But never Mr. Baedeker.

A testimony to Baedeker's incorruptibility was his statement in an early edition that "Hotels which cannot be accurately characterized without exposing the editor to the risk of legal proceedings are left unmentioned." Baedeker saved his readers from unnecessary encounters with the natives, warned against mosquitoes, bedbugs, and fleas, advised wariness of unwashed fruit and uncooked salads, told the price of a postage stamp, and indicated how much to tip (overtipping was a cardinal sin in Baedeker's book).

Eventually Baedeker actually instructed the tourist how to dress and how to act the role of a decent, respectable, tolerant member of his own country, so as not to disappoint or shock the native spectators in the country he was visiting. By the early years of the twentieth century Baedeker was prompting the English reader to play this role "by his tact and reserve, and by refraining from noisy behaviour and contemptuous remarks (in public buildings, hotels, etc.), and especially from airing his political views." "The Englishman's customary holiday attire of rough tweeds, 'plus fours,' etc., is unsuitable for town wear in Italy." "The traveller should refrain from taking photographs of beggars, etc."

Baedeker's most powerful invention was the "star system," which soon had as much charm over sight-seers as its namesake later came to have over movie-goers. His system of rating gave two stars (**) to sights that were extraordinary (the Louvre, Yellowstone Park, Windsor Castle, St. Peter's, the Uffizi, the Pyramids, the Colosseum), one star (*) to sights of lesser rank (merely noteworthy), and no stars at all to the mine-run tourist attractions. This scheme, later copied or adapted by Baedeker's successors (Russell Muirhead of the successful *Blue Guides* and *Penguin Guides,* and nu-

merous American authors of guides), has dominated the uneasy, half-cultivated modern tourist. Hermann Göring, instructing his *Luftwaffe* in 1942, is said to have directed them
to destroy "every historical building and landmark in Britain
that is marked with an asterisk in Baedeker." These were
sometimes called the "Baedeker raids."

Anyone who has toured with Baedeker knows the com-
placent feeling of having checked off all the starred attractions in any given place, or the frustration of having gone to
great trouble and expense to see a sight only to discover after-
ward that it had not even rated a single asterisk. Tourists
versed in one-upmanship who visit some frequented place
like Paris or Florence have been known to concentrate their
sight-seeing on unstarred items, so that in conversation back
home they can face-down their plodding acquaintances who
go by the book. But the star system, like the public museums
and the whole phenomenon of middle-class touring, has been
a by-product of the democratic revolutions. It, too, has
helped blaze "an easy path to cultural sophistication for millions." As Ivor Brown shrewdly observes, this star system has
tended to produce star-gazers rather than explorers.

The tourist looks for caricature; travel agents at home and
national tourist bureaus abroad are quick to oblige. The tourist seldom likes the authentic (to him often unintelligible)
product of the foreign culture; he prefers his own provincial
expectations. The French chanteuse singing English with a
French accent seems more charmingly French than one who
simply sings in French. The American tourist in Japan looks
less for what is Japanese than for what is Japanesey. He
wants to believe that geishas are only quaint oriental prosti-
tutes; it is nearly impossible for him to imagine they can be
anything else. After all, he hasn't spent all that money and
gone all the way over there to be made a fool of. The Noh or
Kabuki or Bunraku (which have long entertained the Japanese in their distinctive theatrical idiom) bore him, but he
can grasp the Takarazuka girlie show, a Japanesey musical
extravaganza on the Ziegfeld-Billy Rose model, distin-

guished from its American counterparts mainly by the fact that all the performers are women. The out-of-dateness of its manner he mistakes for an oriental flavor. Even the official Japanese Tourist Bureau guidebook, anxiously reminding the American that in Japan he will not fail to find what he wants, notes that "strip tease . . . performances are advancing somewhat artistically." The Takarazuka extravaganza is described at length as "an opera peculiar to Japan, known as the girls' opera." Like its Frenchy counterpart, the Folies Bergères which is sometimes featured in Las Vegas, a Takarazuka-type show from any country will be a box-office success in the United States.

As the obliging foreign producers work harder to give Americans just what they expect, American tourists, in turn, oblige by becoming more and more naive, to the point of gullibility. Tourists, however, are willing gulls, if only because they are always secretly fearful their extravagant (and expensive) expectations may not be fulfilled. They are determined to have their money's worth. Wherever in the world the American tourist goes, then, he is prepared to be ruled by the law of pseudo-events, by which the image, the well-contrived imitation, outshines the original.

Everywhere, picturesque natives fashion papier-maché images of themselves. Yet all this earnest picturesqueness too often produces only a pallid imitation of the technicolor motion picture which the tourist goes to verify. The Eternal City becomes the site of the box-office hit *Roman Holiday;* tourist-pilgrims are eager to visit the "actual" scenes where famous movies like *Ben Hur* and *Spartacus* were really photographed. Mount Sinai becomes well-known as the site about which *The Ten Commandments* was filmed. In 1960 a highly successful packaged tour was organized which traced the route of events in Leon Uris' novel *Exodus;* the next year El Al Israel Airlines announced a new sixteen-day tour which promised to cover the very places where Otto Preminger and his film crew had shot scenes for the movie version.

The problems of satisfying the tourist expectations of a great middle-class market were summarized in a government study (1936) under the auspices of the Union of South Africa and the South African Railways and Harbours:

Supply of Tourist Attractions

In the wake of advertising and demand, creation must ordinarily follow an organized and systematic supply. If publicity has been given in foreign countries to the national tourist attractions of a country and if a demand has been created therefor, then it is imperative not only that that which has been advertised should come up to reasonable expectations but that it should also be ordinarily available and normally accessible. So, for example, if animal or native life is made to feature in foreign publicity then as such it must be ordinarily available to tourists. Under no circumstances should any aspect of animal or native life which is not ordinarily present be made to feature in a country's tourist publicity. Thus it is wrong to make a feature of native initiation ceremonies or native dances which are only seen on rare occasions since in their true character they have ritual significance.

The sight-seeing items which can be confidently guaranteed and conveniently and quickly delivered to tourists on arrival have these merchandisable qualities precisely because they are *not* naive expressions of the country. They cannot be the real ritual or the real festival; that was never originally planned for tourists. Like the hula dances now staged for photographer-tourists in Hawaii (courtesy of the Eastman Kodak Company), the widely appealing tourist attractions are apt to be those specially made for tourist consumption.

And the tourist demands more and more pseudo-events. The most popular of these must be easily photographed (plenty of daylight) and inoffensive—suitable for family viewing. By the mirror-effect law of pseudo-events, they tend to become bland and unsurprising reproductions of what the image-flooded tourist knew was there all the time. The tourist's appetite for strangeness thus seems best satisfied when the pictures in his own mind are verified in some far country.

V

So far I have been writing about foreign travel—tours to distant places. I have shown how Americans going to remote parts of the world have been transformed from travelers into tourists by the very same advances which have made travel cheap, safe, and available. A similar transformation has been going on here at home. Even within the United States to go from one place to another is no longer to travel in the old sense of the word. Not only because, as we often hear, the culture of different parts of the country has been homogenized—so that wherever you go in the United States you see the same motion pictures, hear the same radio programs, watch the same television shows, eat the same packaged foods, select from the same ice cream flavors. We all know how desperately Chambers of Commerce work to create local color, how auto license plates advertise unreal distinctions. Alabama is the "Heart of Dixie," Arkansas is the "Land of Opportunity," Illinois is the "Land of Lincoln," Maine is "Vacationland," Minnesota has "10,000 Lakes," North Dakota is "Peace Garden State." All this is obvious.

But in addition to this, the democratizing of travel, the lowering cost, increased organization, and improved means of long-distance transportation within our country have themselves helped dilute the experience. Even here at home we are little more than tourists. "Traveling," the Swiss novelist Max Frisch observes, ". . . is medieval, today we have means of communication, not to speak of tomorrow and the day after, means of communication that bring the world into our homes, to travel from one place to another is atavistic. You laugh, gentlemen, but it's true, travel is atavistic, the day

will come when there will be no more traffic at all and only
newlyweds will travel." That day has almost arrived. Not because we no longer move about the earth. But because the
more we move about, the more difficult it becomes not to remain in the same place. Nearly all the changes in foreign
travel have appeared with equal or greater effect in domestic
travel.

Organized domestic conducted tours have grown only recently. In 1927 what is claimed to be the first escorted tour
by air was planned by Thomas Cook & Son. It was an excursion from New York to Chicago to see the Dempsey-Tunney
fight in which the famous "long count" occurred. Since this
was even before any regular passenger air service between
the cities, the trip was made by chartered plane. In recent
decades the multiplying conventions of professional organizations, trade associations, unions, fraternal groups, and of the
employees of large firms have supported the domestic travel
business.

As late as 1928 the travel department of American Express was sending only five or six tours out West each year,
and for each tour eighteen people were considered a good
crowd. Then an enterprising new manager of the Chicago office sent 120 members of the Chicago Athletic Club on a
tour to Alaska; a special train took Chicago doctors to the annual convention of the American Hospital Association in
California; two shiploads of Spanish-American War veterans
were sent to Cuba; and 300 electrical workers went to
Miami. A new program of packaged Western tours was
then developed. Even during the depression these tours
somehow stayed in demand. In the depression summer of
1933 at the opening of the Chicago World's Fair, American
Express did over a million dollars' worth of business within
a single month, and handled nearly a quarter-million visitors
to the Fair during the season. At the close of the Fair in 1934,
American Express organized the annual Rotary Club convention in Mexico City; a Pullman city was brought down to
house Rotarians taken there to see Mexico. In 1936 Ameri-

can Express expanded its "Banner Tours," and in the summer of 1939, it sent out West twenty-two special trains on all-expense tours.

Since 1928 the domestic excursion business of American Express has increased a hundredfold. The items have ranged from expensive "Grand Tours" of the West and the Canadian Rockies, priced at nearly $1,000 apiece, to a bargain package three-day tour of New York at $19.95, "in the course of which the traveler stays at a well-known midtown hotel and does the metropolitan area from Bear Mountain to the Battery, including seeing the Hudson from an excursion steamer, Chinatown, Greenwich Village, a baseball game at Yankee Stadium, and an evening at Billy Rose's Diamond Horseshoe. . . . It rather makes a native New Yorker believe in miracles."

The growth of tourist attractions—or the better baiting of tourist traps—has been unprecedented in recent years. From the grandiose Disneyland, which we have already noted, and its smaller imitators (Freedomland, Frontierland, etc.) to the plaster-of-paris "Covered Wagon" and "Indian Tepee" filling stations and "museums" now lining highways in Kansas and Nebraska. The pre-eminence of Yellowstone National Park as a tourist attraction is doubtless due to the fact that its natural phenomena—its geysers and "paintpots" which erupt and boil on schedule—come closest to the artificiality of "regular" tourist performances. They are Nature imitating the pseudo-event.

The automobile itself has been one of the chief insulating agencies. And the insulation has become more effective as we have improved body design from the old open touring car to the new moving "picture window" through which we can look out from air-conditioned comfort while we hear our familiar radio program. The whizzing cross-country motorist stops at his familiar trademark, refueling at gas stations of uniform design. His speed makes him reluctant to stop at all. On a train it used to be possible to make a casual acquaintance; the Pullman smoker was a traditionally fertile source of jokes and folklore. Now the train is dying out as a means of long-distance travel. And if we travel by air we are seldom aloft long enough to strike up new acquaintances. But for meeting new people the private automobile is the least promising of all. Even hitchhikers are slowly becoming obsolete as well as illegal.

The nation-wide route numbering system, with its standardized signs of the new era, was adopted in 1925 by the Joint Board of State and Federal Highways, supposedly to eliminate "confusion" from the "motley array" of signs which differed from place to place. Even before our new transcontinental super highways it was not necessary to know where you were (provided you could remember the number of your route) or where you had to go to reach your destination. To-day when we ask directions we usually inquire not for a place but for a number.

Super highways have been the climax in homogenizing the motorist's landscape. A friend of mine recently drove his family from Chicago to New York on one of these tollways. His boy had heard about the prosperous Ohio farms and wanted to visit one. But this proved too difficult. Once on the super highway (with not a traffic light to stop them), they seemed more remote than ever from the environing farms. Where would one leave the toll road? How and where could one return?

As late as the early years of this century in the United States the general demand was for roads extending only two to five miles from railroad stations. Then the Federal Highway Act of 1921 began to co-ordinate state highways and to standardize road-building practice. The Federal Aid Highway Act of 1944 established the new National System of Interstate Highways, an arterial network of 40,000 miles planned to reach forty-two state capitals, and to serve 182 of the 199 cities in the country having populations over 50,-000. There has been an increasing tendency to concentrate road improvements on these most-used roads, which become more and more like one another in every respect. The seven-hundred-odd thousand miles of Federal Aid roads (primary and secondary) make up only a quarter of the total rural road mileage in the United States. Yet they serve almost 90 per cent of the total rural highway travel. An increasing proportion of passengers go over well-traveled roads. The better traveled the roads, the more they become assimilated to one another. Economy and good engineering require that they traverse the dullest expanses of the landscape.

Increase in motor travel, both for business and pleasure, has changed the character of lodgings en route. Formerly the motorist seeking good lodging en route had to detour through the heart of the city. There he could not avoid a view of the courthouse, the shops, the industrial, commercial, and residential districts. Now the motel makes all this unnecessary. Meanwhile, city planners and traffic engineers, hoping to reduce congestion in urban centers, spend large sums on bypasses and super highways to prevent the long-distance motorist from becoming entangled in the daily life of their community.

Motor courts sprang up during the depression of the 1930's. The earliest tourist cabins were simply a cheaper alternative to the hotel, resembling camping facilities. But within a decade motor courts were improved and standardized. In 1935, the first year for which the Department of Commerce reported statistics, there were about ten thousand motels or tourist courts; after twenty years there were some thirty thousand. The new chains and associations of motels soon enabled a motorist to use the same brand of soap, the same cellophane-covered drinking glasses, and the same "sanitized" toilet seats all the way across the country. The long-distance motorist, usually anxious to avoid the "business route," then needed to wander no more than a few hundred yards off the super highway for his food and lodging. What he secures in one place is indistinguishable from that in another. One thing motels everywhere have in common is the effort of their managers to fabricate an inoffensive bit of "local atmosphere."

The next development has been the luxury motel. With its stateroom-sized sleeping rooms, "fabulous" bar, and deck-sized swimming pool, it now resembles nothing so much as the luxury ocean liner. "Getting there is half the fun." Tourists and business travelers "relax in luxurious surroundings." The motel passenger, too, is now always in mid-ocean, comfortably out of touch with the landscape.

On the new interstate speedways we see the thorough dilution of travel experience. The motels, which Vladimir Nabokov has brilliantly caricatured in *Lolita,* are the appropriate symbol of homogenized American experience. Although (perhaps *because*) no place is less any place than a motel, people nowadays vacation in motels for a week or more as they used to relax in luxury liners. They prefer to be no place in particular—in limbo, en route. Some new tourist restaurants on super highways (Fred Harvey has a large chain of these of uniform design, appropriately called "oases") are actually built on top of the highway, on a bridge, to which speeding motorists have equally easy access, regardless of the direction in which they are going. There people can eat without having to look out on an individualized, localized landscape. The disposable paper mat on which they are served shows no local scenes, but a map of numbered super highways with the location of other "oases." They feel most at home above the highway itself, soothed by the auto stream to which they belong.

Now it is the very "improvements" in interstate super highways (at expense to the Federal government alone of a half billion dollars a year) that enable us as we travel along to see nothing but the road. Motor touring has been nearly reduced to the emptiness of air travel. On land, too, we now calculate distances in hours, rather than in miles. We never know quite where we are. At home, as well as abroad, travel itself has become a pseudo-event. It is hard to imagine how further improvements could subtract anything more from the travel experience.

VI

NOT so many years ago there was no simpler or more intelligible notion than that of going on a journey. Travel—movement through space—provided the universal metaphor for change. When men died they went on a journey to that land from which no traveler returns. Or, in our cliché, when a man dies he "passes away." Philosophers observed that we took refuge from the mystery of time in the concreteness of space. Bergson, for example, once argued that measurements of time had to be expressed in metaphors of space: time was "long" or "short"; another epoch was "remote" or "near."

One of the subtle confusions—perhaps one of the secret terrors—of modern life is that we have lost this refuge. No longer do we move through space as we once did. Moving only through time, measuring our distances in homogeneous ticks of the clock, we are at a loss to explain to ourselves what we are doing, where, or even whether, we are going.

As there comes to be less and less difference between the time it takes to reach one place rather than another, time itself dissolves as a measure of space. The new supersonic transports, already in the design stage, will take passengers across our continent in less than two hours, from Europe to America in two hours and a half. We are moving toward "Instant Travel." It is then, I suppose, thoroughly appropriate in this age of tautological experience that we should eventually find ourselves measuring time against itself.

We call ours the "Space Age," but to us space has less meaning than ever before. Perhaps we should call ours the "Spaceless Age." Having lost the art of travel on this earth, having homogenized earthly space, we take refuge in the homogeneity (or in the hope for variety) of outer space. To travel through outer space can hardly give us less landscape experience than we find on our new American super highways. We are already encapsulated, already overcome by the tourist problems of fueling, eating, sleeping, and sight-seeing.

Will we enlarge our experience on the moon? Only until tourist attractions have been prepared for us there.

Even our travel literature has shown a noticeable change. Formerly these books brought us information about the conduct of life in foreign courts, about burial rites and marriage customs, about the strange ways of beggars, craftsmen, tavern hosts, and shopkeepers. Most travel literature long remained on the pattern of Marco Polo. Since the mid-nineteenth century, however, and especially in the twentieth century, travel books have increasingly become a record not of new information but of personal "reactions." From "Life in Italy," they become "The American in Italy." People go to see what they already know is there. The only thing to record, the only possible source of surprise, is their own reaction.

The foreign country, like the celebrity, is the confirmation of a pseudo-event. Much of our interest comes from our curiosity about whether our impression resembles the images found in the newspapers, in movies, and on television. Is the Trevi Fountain in Rome really like its portrayal in the movie *Three Coins in the Fountain?* Is Hong Kong really like *Love is a Many-Splendored Thing?* Is it full of Suzie Wongs? We go not to test the image by the reality, but to test reality by the image.

Of course travel adventure is still possible. Nowadays, however, it is seldom the by-product of people going places. We must scheme, and contrive, and plan long in advance (at great expense) to be assured that when we arrive there we will encounter something other than the antiseptic, pleasant, relaxing, comfortable experience of the hundreds of thousands of other tourists. We must fabricate risks and dangers, or hunt them out. The writings of Richard Halliburton (*The Royal Road to Romance,* 1925; *The Glorious Adventure,* 1927; *New World to Conquer,* 1929; *The Flying Carpet,* 1932; and *Seven League Boots,* 1935), became popular at the very time when travel for thousands of Americans was becoming a bland and riskless commodity. To make a glorious adventure out of travel, Halliburton had to relive ancient adventures. Like Leander he swam the Hellespont; he retraced the routes of Ulysses, Cortés, Balboa, Alexander, and Hannibal. Even "Mysterious Tibet"—one of the few remaining places on earth which physically challenge the traveler—has had its mystery abolished. Recently, Justice William O. Douglas has shown ingenuity in seeking out travel adventures; his books are understandably popular. But they too are only a blander version of Richard Halliburton. Pierre and Peg Streit ingeniously make adventure by motoring by English Land Rover from Paris to Katmandu in Nepal: "A Jouncing Tour of Kipling's Wild Land" (*Life,* September 2, 1957).

Nowadays it costs more and takes greater ingenuity, imagination and enterprise to fabricate travel risks than it once required to avoid them. Almost as much effort goes into designing the adventure as into surviving it. For this the tourist millions have not the time or the money. Travel adventure today thus inevitably acquires a factitious, make-believe, unreal quality. And only the dull travel experience seems genuine. Both for the few adventuring travelers who still exist and for the larger number of travelers-turned-tourists, voyaging becomes a pseudo-event.

Here again, the pseudo-event overshadows the spontaneous. And for the usual reasons. Planned tours, attractions, fairs, expositions "especially for tourists," and all their prefabricated adventures can be persuasively advertised in advance. They can be made convenient, comfortable, risk-free, trouble-free, as spontaneous travel never was and never is. We go more and more where we expect to go. We get money-back guarantees that we will see what we expect to see. Anyway, we go more and more, not to see at all, but only to take pictures. Like the rest of our experience, travel becomes a tautology. The more strenuously and self-consciously we work at enlarging our experience, the more pervasive the tautology becomes. Whether we seek models of greatness, or experience elsewhere on the earth, we look into a mirror instead of out a window, and we see only ourselves.

4

From Shapes to Shadows:
Dissolving Forms

FIRST YOUNG LADY: *"Have you seen* Omnibook? *It takes five or six books and boils them down. That way you can read them all in one evening."*
SECOND YOUNG LADY: *"I wouldn't like it. Seems to me it would just spoil the movie for you."*

IT IS ONLY a short step from exaggerating what we can find in the world to exaggerating our power to remake the world. Expecting more novelty than there is, more greatness than there is, and more strangeness than there is, we imagine ourselves masters of a plastic universe. But a world we can shape to our will—or to our extravagant expectations—is a shapeless world.

When Michelangelo in the traditional story explained that he carved his statue of David simply by taking away the superfluous marble, he meant that his peculiar vision dwelt somehow in that particular block of stone. Sculptors always, of course, choose a piece of marble because it is well suited to the figure they have in mind; and they often shape the figure to the marble's flaws. Every artist marries form to matter: he sees his poem in words, his painting in oils on canvas, his statue in stone, his building in some specific material.

Art has often been identified with divinity, precisely be-

cause the artist gives his work a unique, inimitable embodiment. Like a man, a work of art has a soul, a life all its own.
It used to be taken for granted that every work of art possessed a mysterious individuality. A picture could not be
made into a poem, a play was not to be found in a novel. Until recently there were surprisingly few dramatizations of
novels. Abridgment was an art not much practiced in literature. Of course there were legends and folk tales which were
transformed by different minstrels or different generations,
and so were variously embodied, but the great work of art
was that which had the power somehow to remain uniquely
itself, and itself alone.

The "original" had a priceless and ineffable uniqueness.
Men spent fortunes and risked lives to possess the Elgin mar-
bles or a Mona Lisa, to save a particular painting by Do-
menico Veneziano, or to secure a treasure by Benvenuto Cellini. Approximation was never enough. Every work of art
had the fixity, the precise boundaries, which until recently
were attributed to God's work in the Creation. The idea of
fixity of species, which possessed the minds of European and
American men until the mid-nineteenth century, was a way
of extending to all creation the simple notion that the world
was not infinitely malleable. God's artistry had made fixed,
definite forms, so that, in Lucretius' words, "Where each
thing can grow and abide is fixed and ordained."

I

THE DEMOCRATIC REVOLUTIONS of the eighteenth and nineteenth centuries and the Graphic Revolution of the nineteenth and twentieth centuries have done much to change
this. If art and literature were to be made accessible to all,
they had to be made intelligible (and inoffensive) to all.
Popularity was then often bought at the cost of the integrity
of the individual work. With the rise of liberalism came the
rise of the vernacular languages and literatures. Now the

common people could read great works in their own market-
place English, French, German, Spanish, or Italian, instead
of having to know the learned languages of Hebrew, Greek,
and Latin in which classical authors had written. Popular government, bringing with it universal literacy and education for
everybody, brought also the popularizing of works of art and
literature.

The age of the rising middle class in Victorian England
was, of course, the age of the fig leaf. "The fig leaves of decent reticence" which Charles Kingsley described were applied not only to statuary but to literature as well. In order
to make works of art a national resource available to all, so
that anybody of either sex could without embarrassment be
taken on an edifying conducted tour of the greatness of the
past, the works of art themselves were garbled, emended, wa-
tered down, and taken out of context—all in order to make
them bland and digestible to uncultivated palates. The Age
of Education thus ironically became the Age of Expurgation.
The New Expurgation, unlike the Old (of the days of the li-
censing of printed matter), aimed less to expunge offensive
doctrine than to hide offensive facts of life. All this had its
effect on literature. Charles and Mary Lamb's *Tales from
Shakespeare* (1807) were designed to make the bard familiar to the young. Thomas Bowdler (1754–1825), from whose
name we derive the word "bowdlerize," meaning to expur-
gate by removing offensive passages, in 1818 published his
ten-volume *Family Shakespeare,* "in which nothing is added
to the original text; but those words and expressions are
omitted which cannot with propriety be read aloud in a family." It went through four editions in six years, and numerous
others thereafter. Encouraged by his success, he prepared a
similar six-volume edition of Gibbon's *Decline and Fall of
the Roman Empire,* "for the use of Families and Young Persons, reprinted from the original text with the careful omis-
sions of all passages of an irreligious or immoral tendency."

What the new public museums were to works of art, the
new popularizations were to works of literature. The precious

literary objects, once enjoyed almost exclusively by the aristocrats of birth, wealth, or learning, were now to be put on
display for the millions. Some, of course, went into tolerably
accurate cheap editions. But while sculpture, painting, tapestries, and *objets d'art* were taken out of context by being
removed from monastery and palace to the public museums,
much of the best literature was taken out of context by being
abridged, expurgated, simplified, and popularized.

How to make the esoteric, difficult, lengthy, archaic, and
subtle classics of an aristocratic society "interesting" and
"edifying" (the eighteenth-century phrase was "amusing
and instructive") for everyone? In England and elsewhere
the age of the Protestant Reformation, the seedtime of modern liberalism, was of course an age of translations—for example, Sir John North's Plutarch (1579), John Florio's Montaigne (1603), and above all, the great King James version
of the Bible (1611).

In the United States in the nineteenth century popular education and popularization tended to become synonymous. A
stigma, the odium of an outdated priestly aristocracy, was
put on anything that could not be made universally intelligible. Equalitarian America attached a new, disproportionate
importance to the knowledge which all could get and to techniques which all could master. In England, for example, rules
of spelling had been slow to develop; Shakespeare himself
had been illiterate by the standards of the American school-
marm. But in the United States, where the people were desperately in search of a cultural standard that any able-bodied
citizen could meet with reasonable effort and modest opportunities, the spelling fetish established itself quite rapidly.
Noah Webster's *American Spelling Book* (1789) and his
American Dictionary of the English Language (1828) sold
by the millions. Americans were inclined to overvalue whatever could be made intelligible to all: the work of the journalist (Benjamin Franklin) or of the popular humorist
(Mark Twain). Popularity became confused with universal-
ity. If the Bible was truly an inspired Great Book, it must

have something to say to everyone; by a quaint reversal, it then became axiomatic that anyone could understand the Bible. In the twentieth century our highest praise is to call the Bible "The World's Best Seller." And it has come to be more and more difficult to say whether we think it is a best seller because it is great, or vice versa.

The Graphic Revolution accentuated all these tendencies. It brought new forces toward popularizing, toward reshaping —and toward disembodying—works of art. This it did in several ways.

First came the cheapening of printed matter. In the United States until about 1830 books were sturdily made, but expensive to manufacture. The cheap book came in the 1840's. It had been made possible by the new paper-making machines and cylinder presses, which could turn out large quantities at low cost. What historians of the subject call the "Great Revolution in Publishing" had arrived when, in 1841, two New York weeklies, the *New World* and *Brother Jonathan,* entered into cutthroat competition. These weeklies, printed like newspapers to secure a cheap postal rate, were actually devoted to printing serialized novels which had been pirated from England or written by Americans. When readers objected that they could elsewhere buy some of these novels complete before the serials were finished, the competing weeklies began to issue "supplements" and "extras." Each of these was a whole novel, printed on newspaper presses, and commonly unbound. Competition became intense and prices came down. In 1842 Bulwer's *Zanoni,* issued almost simultaneously by the two weeklies (and also by the more reputable *Harper's*), could be bought for as little as six cents a copy. This intense competition did not last. In April, 1843, the United States Post Office ruled that supplements had to be mailed under book rates; then these weeklies, and with them the appeal of shoddy books, declined. The rise of copyrights laws, and the gradual enforcement of international copyright regulations (not generally effective till the Berne Convention of 1886) later made pirating difficult and reduced the supply of widely salable, royalty-free books. But never again was the American book trade quite the same. Cheap books were here to stay.

Well before the Civil War book publishing and book selling in the United States had become a highly profitable, highly organized business, offering its wares through retail bookshops, subscription agents, peddlers, and auctioneers. One of the most famous of the early subscription salesmen was Parson Mason Weems. An author as well as a salesman, he wrote the best-selling life of George Washington in which appears the earliest version of the story of the cherry tree. By the time Weems died, in 1825, he had sold for Caleb P. Wayne, a Philadelphia publisher, nearly 4,000 sets of Marshall's five-volume *Life of Washington* and had collected for him on that book alone the sum of $40,000.

Apart from improvements in paper making and printing, the industrialization of bookbinding was perhaps the most important step in the democratization of the book in America. The crucial change was the departure from the old hand-binding method, by which each book and its own binding were made together. By the new "casing-in" method, the printed sheets were sewn in one operation and then attached to a standard binding that had been made separately. This method came into the United States about 1832. Another important innovation was the introduction of cloth for binding (vellum, calf, or paper-covered cardboard had been the common materials before). Machines were then developed for pressing the pages together, for stamping design and lettering on bookbinding cloth, for folding paper, for sewing the pages; and, finally (an ingenious American invention of the 1890's) for making the case of the book by machine, and for putting the sheets into the case. All this, of course, brought down the price of hardbound books. Mark Twain's *Innocents Abroad* (1869) for some time after publication was being sold by subscription agents to about 4,000 purchasers a month.

When Shakespeare had been available only in expensive

leather-bound folios for noble mansions, there was of course little pressure to abridge, bowdlerize, or popularize. But as rising literacy created a demand for cheaper books the industrialization of book making was an incentive to wider sales. A significant, but seldom-noticed, change has taken place in the United States in the subscription sale of books (by book agents who come to the door and sell sets on the installment plan) during the twentieth century. Subscription books of this kind have always had at least as much the character of home furnishings as of reading matter. Before about 1900 the staples of these salesmen were complete sets of authors like Shakespeare, Dickens, Bulwer-Lytton, and Thackeray. Since then the staples have come to be the multi-volumed encyclopedias (The Britannica, Americana, Child-craft, World Book, Book of Knowledge, Collier's, International, for example), which give you the gist of anything you want (including the writings of Shakespeare, Dickens, Bulwer-Lytton, and Thackeray). One large seller has been a twenty-volume encyclopedia of book digests. Copious photographs and illustrations, many in full color, are the most advertised, and perhaps the most used, features of these works.

Cheap "de luxe" editions (both of books and of magazines) also have had spectacular success. The Limited Editions Club, organized by subscription in 1929, limited its editions to 1,500 in order to give its members only books printed direct from type and from the original illustration plates. The success of the venture led its director, George Macy, to found The Heritage Press for a larger audience. This produced the novel phenomenon of books supposed to have most of the typographical virtues of "limited" editions, but now in almost unlimited numbers. Many imitators have produced books which purport to offer the hand-crafted beauties of small editions at bargain prices to a mass market.

The same newer and cheaper techniques of printing and book making which widened the audience also varied the forms in which literature reached the public. A comparable change took place in the graphic arts, and especially in the fine arts of painting and sculpture. Well before the middle of the twentieth century an American could buy for a few dollars a full-color copy of the "Mona Lisa" or of Van Gogh's "Sunflowers" which, properly framed and viewed at a decent distance, was hardly distinguishable from its original. This was a new development. A few connoisseurs looked down their noses at these "vulgar misrepresentations" of a unique original. Was the old-fashioned traveler in the world of art now to be made into a mere tourist? Was he to be seduced into being satisfied with quick looks at handy copies which, at best, would be no more than a "bicycle ride through the Louvre"? The new techniques provided means for popularizing the original and transforming its general idea into a thousand forms: in cheap books, on lampshades, serving platters, and pencil boxes.

The first reproduction of a photograph in a newspaper appeared as recently as March 4, 1880, when a picture entitled "Shanty-Town" was printed in the New York *Daily Graphic*. This was made by a new process and was called a "halftone." An object is photographed through a fine screen, and then the shadings are represented in print by the dots on the photographic plate. The technique, still in use, was developed by Stephen Horgan and Frederick Eugene Ives. Horgan had tried without success to persuade James Gordon Bennett to use it in the New York *Herald*. He finally managed to introduce it in the New York *Tribune,* where the first halftones were printed on power presses in 1897.

Improvements in color printing made possible the colored comic strip. Now the "yellow press" could appear in a full range of colors. In the fall of 1896 Hearst issued a comic supplement all in color, which he advertised, with characteristic reticence, as "eight pages of iridescent polychromous effulgence that makes the rainbow look like a lead pipe." The new collotype presses (first imported to this country from Germany in 1890) soon made possible nuances of color reproduction for fine medical and art books. Henry

Watson Kent, who had lately been with the Metropolitan Museum of Art in New York, joined Max Jaffé's pioneer color printing establishment in Vienna in 1926. There high-grade art reproductions were made for the Museum, for other institutions, and for book publishers. Jaffé's son Arthur established his own presses in New York in 1938. Since then the quality of cheap color reproductions has been much improved. This has been reflected in book and magazine illustration, and in the admirable color prints of great paintings now to be found in private homes, hotel rooms, and restaurants throughout the country.

Similar improvements have still more recently appeared in the processes of casting and in the making of metallic and plastic reproductions of sculpture. At the reception desks of museums, in gift shops, and in bookstores it is now possible to purchase cheap reproductions of classic pieces of Egyptian, Greek, or Roman sculpture which only an expert can distinguish from the originals.

The Graphic Revolution, in one area after another, has provided us with mass-produced "originals." Inevitably, then, we come to think that the "original" is to be distinguished from its technically precise (and often more durable) copy only by its price. Respect for the original comes close to pure snobbery. What is more natural in a democratic age than that we should begin to measure the stature of a work of art—especially of a painting—by how widely and how well it is reproduced? Van Gogh's "Sunflowers," which challenged the techniques of color reproduction and which could be tolerably and brightly reproduced at low cost, began to overshadow the drabber classics of the Italian Renaissance. As never before in art it has become easy for the great, the famous, and the cliché to be synonymous.

The original then somehow loses its originality. The copy is far more familiar. Indeed it is only the copy which is _really_ popular. It often gives us more pleasure. At the Gauguin show at the Chicago Art Institute in 1959 visitors complained that the original paintings were less brilliant than the familiar reproductions.

The original itself acquires a technical, esoteric status. It becomes nothing more than a kind of prototype, like the type-castings for our books, or the dies from which other mass-produced items are made. We begin to wonder whether the primary purpose of a great work of art may not be to provide an original matrix from which copies can be produced. From our point of view it is more and more the copy, and not the original, which seems to fulfill the artist's true democratic-humanitarian-"life-enriching" purpose. It is the Van Gogh "Sunflowers" that hung in our college room, and not that which hangs in the Museum, that is full of meaning for us.

In the world of dramatic arts, the Graphic Revolution has produced a still subtler and more widespread confusion of forms. The English novel, we must remember, did not arrive as a popular literary form until the eighteenth century. English drama was, of course, much older, reaching back to the medieval mystery and morality plays, and coming to a climax with Shakespeare and the other Elizabethan dramatists. For a number of reasons, however, the two forms—the novel and the play—long remained quite distinct in English literature. It was not usual for a successful novel to be put into dramatic form, much less for a play to be cast into a novel. The obvious limitations of the stage had something to do with this.

The sweep of landscape and the panoramas of violent action seen in the pages of novels could not be convincingly transferred to the stage. How could you make sets for *War and Peace?* With the rise of motion pictures, however, these limits were almost destroyed. The new technique made it possible to change scenery in the flash of an eye, to bring vast landscapes and wild action into the theater—now on the screen. The new possibilities of the movie camera (especially in the early days before sound) tempted movie makers to exploit the peculiar capacity of the movie screen to depict what could not have been physically represented on the stage. The first great box-office success (still a record-holder) was D. W. Griffith's *Birth of a Nation* (1915), which attracted millions by its expansive battle scenes, its torrential action, and its close-ups of the faces of leering villains and of dead soldiers. This was the first movie ever shown in the White House. After seeing it, President Wilson is said to have remarked, "It is like writing history with lightning." The man-made lightning was important not only because it had created a new dramatic form. Equally significant, if less noted, was the simple fact that scenes which before could be vividly depicted only in the pages of a book (but not on the stage) now for the first time could appear in another form: on the movie screen. This new apparent interchangeableness of dramatic forms was seductive. Before long it helped produce a new amorphousness and elusiveness of all literary-dramatic form. From the point of view of the individual's experience, too, this was epoch-making. It made the world of literary forms blurry as it had never been before.

Now, for the first time, you *could* dramatize almost any scene from any novel. The grander the expanses of scenery, the more violent and wide-sweeping the action, the more rapid the changes of scene—in other words, the more ill-suited any drama was to the narrowly confining stage, with its real men and women and its real stage sets physically present in the theater—the more appealing was the story for movie purposes. It was now only a rare novel (which depended on unique and intricate literary devices) that could *not* be made into a movie. Often the movie was more widely appealing, as it was of course more visually vivid, than its literary original. There were few plays and (after the addition of sound, signalized by Al Jolson's *Jazz Singer* in 1927) few musicals which could not better attract the public from the screen.

One consequence of the movie form was to make it possible (or even common) for a spectator to arrive in the middle of one performance, and then to see the beginning afterwards. The fragmentation of experience was increased by the invention of television, when a viewer could turn the knob at will and enter programs one after another free of charge, seeing only a piece of each. The distracting possibilities of television reached a climax when, during the much-publicized quarrel between Jack Paar and Ed Sullivan, De Forest Television advertised in the Chicago *Sun-Times* on March 12, 1961 sets with two or three screens in the same cabinet:

> The great networks are sharpening their weapons—competitive performances at the same hour—you simply can't jump all round the dial and take a small bite—there's too much to miss. But De Forest double or triple screen TV lets you see all—all the time—when you like what you see better on one, you touch your remote button and switch sound only, or flick the super magic infra-red remote for channel changing: head phones for the stubborn. It's more fun than you dreamed about—try it tonight. Enjoy it up to 1 year if you like without paying anything.

The increasing technical possibilities of movies and television did have the effect of leaving the novel with an entirely new role. It was now a kind of residuary legatee: of radio, of movies, of television. Some of the ablest literary artists (like James Joyce, William Faulkner, and Henry Miller) more and more now explored the inner world—the world of eroticism, obscenity, blasphemy, symbolism, stream of consciousness, and introspection—which could not be acceptably displayed on the movie screen. The novelist, then, has been encouraged to explore the boundless non-visual world, as the movie maker has taken over much of his former jurisdiction over the fantasy world of sight, sound, and action.

A clue to the new interchangeability of dramatic forms appeared in America in the emergence of a new meaning for the phrase "legitimate theater." In England the word "legitimate" had long been used in this phrase to distinguish the body of plays, Shakespearean and other, which had a recognized theatrical and literary merit, as contrasted, for example, with light musical entertainment, farce, and melodrama. In the United States after the rise of movies, "legitimate theater" expressed a distinction not of quality but of technology. "Legitimate theater" here came to mean any drama, including musicals, farces, and melodramas, performed by live actors on a stage, as opposed to performances in movies, on radio, or television.

Before I explore these subtler influences of the Graphic Revolution on our expectations and our experience, I will begin by recalling one of the most elementary and widespread symptoms of dissolving literary forms. This is the rise and popularization of the abridgment and the digest.

II

IN EARLIER times in Europe the "abridgment" or "digest" was a highly specialized literary form. It was used for technical (usually legal) materials. The most famous was the "Digests" (533 A.D.) of the Byzantine-Roman Emperor Justinian, who selected the writings of earlier Roman jurists and so preserved Roman Law for future ages. English lawyers in the eighteenth and nineteenth centuries made comparable digests of the common law. The pioneer American work was Nathan Dane's *General Abridgment and Digest of American Law* (eight volumes, 1823). It has been followed by still more elaborate abridgments and digests. Prosperous American law publishers (for example, the West Publishing Company of St. Paul, Minnesota) have made big business out of reducing to accessible form our ever-multiplying statutes and judicial precedents.

In the past it was usually for the student of some special subject matter (needing, for professional reasons, to be informed about essential points in a vast literature) that publishers prepared abridgments or digests. The general reader, whether reading for pleasure or for instruction, selected his book for its total character and content. He chose a novel—his Cooper, Dickens, or Thackeray—because he liked what the author put in, what he left out, and how he told the story. In a work of nonfiction—in Jared Sparks, George Bancroft, Francis Parkman, Ralph Waldo Emerson, William Hickling Prescott—he liked what the author told him and he was attracted by the author's peculiar way of expanding, compressing, and discoursing. Since the later nineteenth century much of this has changed. The popular abridgment is the great symptom of the change.

With the spread of literacy and the cheapening of books since the Graphic Revolution, the printed matter available to the citizen has multiplied. The same technological advances which account for modern journalism and for the flood of political pseudo-events also account for the flood of magazines and books. The rising American standard of living has enabled more people to buy them at the same time that improvements in paper making and printing have made them cheaper to buy. The diffusion of secondary and higher education has made more people want to buy printed matter. Improvements in merchandising have made books and magazines handier. Advertising has supported more and more magazines. Democratic faith in an informed, participating citizenry has persuaded people they ought to read more and more.

The intimate impact of world events, the ever-present threats of depression and war, the spectacular pace of scientific advance—all these remind the citizen of more things he should know about. Magazines themselves, trading on the duty to be informed, prick the citizen's conscience. He must be up on the latest book, conversational about the most recently notorious magazine article, "informed" about the world in which he lives. James Bryant Conant, former president of Harvard, said in October 1960 that the minimum goal in reading skill for almost all pupils at the end of Grade 9 is "that these future voters should be able to read with comprehension the front page of a newspaper at the rate of about 200 words a minute." Everybody must know more and more about more and more. How to do it?

Today, therefore, everybody feels the need for "abridgment," for digests and summaries of the world's culture, the world's opinions, and the world's happenings. Not merely the specialist, the lawyer or the doctor, but the common citizen needs help. In twentieth-century America—a literate, prosperous, earnest democracy—the digest has become the citizen's tool.

Digests have taken many different forms. One of the earliest and most straightforward was the *Literary Digest* (1890–1938). Its first issue, in March 1890, abridged notable articles from leading magazines, summarized stories and editorials from newspapers, offered "Book Digests," an "Index of Current Literature," and a "Chronicle of Current Events." The emphasis was emphatically highbrow: the opening sections were entitled "Sociological," "Industrial," and "Political." The lead article in Volume I, Number 1, by Professor Thomas H. Huxley, "On the Natural Inequality of Men," was taken from the issue of an English review, *The Nineteenth Century,* which had appeared two months before. There followed heavy selections from French, German, Italian, and Russian reviews. "The articles in the Review and Press Departments," the editors explained, "are condensations or summaries of the original articles, or of salient points in those articles. In no case do they represent the personal opinions of the editors of the *Literary Digest,* whose constant endeavor is to present the thought of the author from his own standpoint." *The Review of Reviews,* begun in England in the same year, within a few months was being separately edited and published in America. It professed a more grandiose purpose. Expressly adapting Matthew Arnold's definition of culture, the editors aimed "to make the best thoughts of the best writers in our periodicals universally accessible. To enable the busiest and the poorest in the community to know the best thoughts of the wisest;

to follow with intelligent interest the movement of contemporary history."

Digests of books and magazines would not long remain so highfalutin. By the early twentieth century the *Literary Digest* had come down to the level of the newspaper reader. It was then read mostly for its summaries of journalistic reactions to current events, and for its items of popular interest discovered in the less popular magazines.

With the founding of *The Reader's Digest* by De Witt Wallace, in February 1922, a new era of abridgments began. Wallace, son of a Presbyterian preacher-professor in a small midwestern denominational college, proved to be an editorial genius. His *Digest* was soon far more popular than any of the magazines it digested. It became the publishing phenomenon of the twentieth century. During the year 1959, for example, when the American Bible Society distributed a total of seventeen and a half million volumes of Scripture, *The Reader's Digest* was published in some thirty editions (including Braille) and in thirteen languages, totaling a world circulation of about twenty-one million copies a month. In the United States alone its monthly circulation was then well over twelve million, which was almost twice the circulation of the next most popular American magazine. A reliable survey estimated that *The Reader's Digest* was read every month by at least thirty-two million Americans—one of every four adults in the nation.

There is no better clue than the rise of *The Reader's Digest* to the dissolution of forms and to the increasing secondhandness of our experience in twentieth-century America. This, the most popular magazine in the United States, has offered itself not as an "original," but as a digest. The shadow outsells the substance. Abridging and digesting is no longer a device to lead the reader to an original which will give him what he really wants. The digest itself is what he wants. The shadow has become the substance.

The story of *The Reader's Digest* is an epic (perhaps we should say a "pseudo-epic") of the production of pseudo-events, of the dilution and tautologizing of American experience. Since 1939, when the *Digest* moved into a specially designed one-and-a-half-million-dollar Georgian-style office building, its headquarters have been an eighty-acre estate of park and wooded hills outside of Chappaqua, New York, employing about 100 editors and 2,500 clerical workers. It has offices also in New York, London, Paris, Copenhagen, Havana, Helsinki, Quebec, Madrid, Milan, Oslo, Rio de Janeiro, Stockholm, Stuttgart, Sydney, Toronto, and Tokyo. Its writers are constantly traveling the world. But the magazine had modest beginnings. The first issue was prepared in a one-room basement office under a Greenwich Village speakeasy, by De Witt Wallace and his wife, Lila Acheson Wallace, a former English teacher and social worker. They put it together with their own scissors and paste and carried the mail sacks to the post office. It was an immediate success.

The venture could be started on a shoestring precisely because it required no authors or editors. Wallace simply went to The New York Public Library, and copied out by hand from other magazines his own abridged, adapted version of articles he thought would interest readers. The editors of the original magazines considered the circulation of these brief versions to be free advertising. With few exceptions, they gladly allowed Wallace to reprint them without charge. The first issue, setting a pattern which has changed very little, consisted of sixty-two pages (exclusive of the covers) and offered thirty-one articles. A legend on the cover of an early issue announced: " 'An Article a Day' from leading Magazines—each article of enduring value and interest, in condensed permanent booklet form." True to its factitious character, the *Digest* represented itself not as a commercial enterprise, but as an "Association." The issue of August, 1923, explained, *"The Reader's Digest* is not a magazine in the usual sense, but rather a co-operative means of rendering a timesaving service. Our Association is serving you; it should also be serving your friends." There was indeed a Reader's Digest Association. De Witt Wallace owned 52 per cent of the stock, Lila Acheson Wallace owned 48 per cent; subscribers automatically became "members," but were not encumbered with any ownership or control.

The essence of the idea—"De Witt Wallace's basic discovery"—as the official history of the magazine explains, was that this magazine would, by a mirror magic, actually express the reader himself. This is why it was called a *reader's* digest. "Magazine articles could be written to please the reader, to give him the nub of the matter in the new fast-moving world of the 1920's, instead of being written at length and with literary embellishments to please the author or the editor."

For about ten years the *Digest* followed Wallace's simple, original procedure, searching other magazines for articles and stories to be adapted for its readers. Then, by the inexorable law of pseudo-events, *The Reader's Digest* began to spawn other pseudo-events. Wallace himself later described this innovation as "an inevitable development, perhaps the most important in the *Digest's* history." Like all great inventions, the idea was beautifully simple. It was merely to "plant" a full-length article (prepared under *Reader's Digest* direction) in some other magazine, so it could afterwards be digested in *The Reader's Digest*. The editors of the *Digest* would conceive a two-page piece for their own magazine. Instead of directly writing the two-page article themselves, they would commission an author to prepare on this topic a "full-length" article—say five times the length of the predestined *Digest* abridgment. This proposed article (sometimes even before it was written) was then accepted by some other magazine, which would print it among its regular contents. The *Digest* paid for the whole process, including the full-length original. Here, of course, was a perfect example of a literary pseudo-event. The article was made to appear in the *Saturday Evening Post, Ladies' Home Journal, Holiday,* the *American Legionnaire,* or the *Rotarian,* primarily in order that it might afterwards be reported in the *Digest*.

The motives behind this *Reader's Digest* innovation are not clear. Perhaps the energetic Wallace, now restless at remaining a dealer in secondhand articles, simply wanted to try manufacturing the original commodity. The magazine's official historian says it had become necessary. Many of the leading magazines which had been fruitful sources of *Digest* material in the 1920's (*The North American Review, Scribner's, The Century, Review of Reviews, Hearst's International, The Forum, World's Work, McClure's, The American, Collier's, Current History, Judge,* the old *Life, The Delineator, Pictorial Review, Woman's Home Companion*) were now dead. Therefore, material which in condensed form would be suitable for the peculiar tone and character of *The Reader's Digest* was harder to find.

The new *Digest* formula required certain ideas in the originals which could not always be found in adequate supply. The very success of the *Digest* had created a need which could be satisfied only by insuring a steady flow of such articles (pseudo-articles, if necessary) written for the purpose of being digested. Anyway, the difference between a pseudo-article and a spontaneous article would not appear in the skillfully digested product—just as the walls of Babylon on a movie set did not need to be solid so long as the photographed version made them look so.

Whatever the motives, the effect was plain enough. The magazine whose initial appeal was its ability to survey the scene, was now itself making the scene to be surveyed. Like the political interview or the tourist attraction, the planted article was produced in the honest effort to do a job, to give people what they paid for and what they expected. It was the determination of *Digest* editors to be honest that actually accounted for the misrepresentation. The planted article, when it was digested in *The Reader's Digest,* could, of course, honestly be described as "Condensed from the *American Legionnaire.*"

Editors of the *Digest* for a while were understandably reticent about this development. The practice grew up only gradually. In the April 1930 *Digest* appeared the first article not attributed to any source publication. The article, "Music and Work," was unsigned. Avoiding any damagingly clear admission of originality, it was labeled "a special compilation for *The Reader's Digest*." Three years later appeared the first signed original article, "Insanity—the Modern Menace," by Henry Morton Robinson. It was followed that year by a number of others, including "The Burning Question," an article on cremation.

At about the same time there appeared in the *Digest* the first planted article. Sensitivity on this subject has made it hard to gather precise statistics. An independent study by George W. Bennett of the five years 1939 to 1943, inclusive, discovered the facts on 1,718, or 90 per cent, of the 1,908 articles printed in the *Digest* during this period. Of these, 720 were digests on the original formula (reprinted abridgments of articles initiated by other periodicals), 316 were written expressly for the *Digest* and printed there alone. The remaining 682 were digests of planted articles. In other words, only a little over 40 per cent of *Digest* items in this period were really "digests" of what had spontaneously appeared elsewhere. Almost 60 per cent were either confessed originals or disguised originals, fabricated by a contrived back-formation from a contrived original. Later samplings suggest that about the same proportion continued into the following years. Most of what one read in *The Reader's Digest,* therefore, was not really a "digest" at all.

In the age of the Graphic Revolution people quite naturally prefer a shadow of a shadow to a shadow of an original. The uneasy editors of the most popular magazine of the twentieth century, when they give readers gratis an attenuated piece of authentic literary originality, hardly dare confess it. Not until lately has *The Reader's Digest* openly defended its overshadowing of "real" abridgments by "imitation" abridgments. The practice, it is said, offers "numerous advantages to the writer, the magazine which first publishes the material, and to the *Digest*." Where else but in twentieth-century America could editors have a guilty conscience and feel that somehow they might be cheating their readers when they offer something more original than it seems?

III

THE READER'S DIGEST, while by far the most successful, was, of course, only one of a legion of digests. It produced a host of imitators and disciples. Scores of others sprang up quite independently. There was *Writer's Digest, Catholic Digest, Protestant Digest, Omnibook, Science Digest, Negro Digest, Mystery Digest, Children's Digest, Compact: The Young People's Digest, Quick Digest, New Editions* (a digest of best sellers), and so on. Each commonly had a circulation larger than those of many of the magazines from which its materials were reprinted. Their existence, not to mention their spectacular success, witnessed the decline—even the dissolution —of literary form. When readers received (as the *Digest* might boast) only "the nub of the matter" instead of articles "written at length and with literary embellishments to please the author or the editors," they were receiving idea without form. A piece of printed matter was then believed to exist in a non-literary void. Then a story or article was indeed a nub or essence, for which words were only so much baggage. It was an emanation—a whiff of literary ectoplasm exuding from print, but not really residing in any set of words. The most popular reading matter now offered itself as substance without form. "Literary embellishments" (that is, anything— matter or form—which interested the author but might not interest some particular reader) seemed so much waste. They seemed merely to interfere with the reader.

Magazine digests and abridgments—only one kind of many new dissolutions of form—were a by-product of the multiplication and cheapening of printed matter. Between 1885 and 1905 the number of magazines being published at any one time in the United States, according to Frank Luther Mott's estimate, increased from 3,300 to 6,000. About 7,500 new magazines had been started. Seeing more magazines than anyone could possibly read, seeing a crowd of magazines almost indistinguishable from one another, the reader naturally needed help. He was glad to join an "association" to give him the "nub" of each of them.

Not only in popular writing have we seen a dissolution of form and a search for the essence. The same dissolution has gone on in the world of science. It helps explain the modern divorce between scientist and humanist. The humanist has always been interested in the particular form (the "literary embellishments") in which an idea is cast. He has considered language, rhetoric, vocabulary, and dramatic structure inseparable from idea. But the scientist now more than ever treats a scientific article or book as only a vehicle. He moves further and further away from the literary skills which made John James Audubon on ornithology, Charles Darwin on biology, and William James and Sigmund Freud on psychology, become literary as well as scientific classics.

This is due not only to the fast pace of advance in twentieth-century science, but also to the sheer multiplication (since the Graphic Revolution) of the printed matter in which these advances are diffused. Between 1940 and 1960 the number of scientific and technical articles published each year increased twofold or threefold. In 1960 alone the number of these articles appearing in the sixty-odd major languages of the world was between one and two million. These were published in between 50,000 and 100,000 technical journals.

To collect and digest the information on any subject has therefore become a vast and complex new problem. To help solve it, an IBM inventor, H. Peter Luhn, has developed a computer program for "auto-abstracting." A machine automatically makes a statistical analysis of all the significant words in an article. It is designed to omit the trivial words—the if's, and's, and but's. Having calculated the ten or twenty most frequent words, the machine then picks out sentences with the highest density of these key words. An automatic compilation of these sentences becomes the "auto-abstract" of the article. The pressing need for such a machine comes from the fact that even the abstracts of scientific articles have become so numerous that no scientist can keep up with them. By the middle of the twentieth century there were about 300 journals devoted exclusively to summarizing articles appearing in other journals. "If we do not find some way of abstracting the abstracts," observes Derek J. de Sola Price in his brilliant *Science Since Babylon* (1961), "it may well happen that the printed research paper will be doomed, though it will be difficult to rid ourselves of the obsession that it seems vital to science."

What Thomas J. Watson, Jr., president of International Business Machines Corporation, calls the "Information Explosion" is having an ever wider and deeper effect on the form in which we are willing to have our ideas expressed. And incidentally, it cannot fail to affect the respect we show for literary or any other kind of form. Translation, until recently, has been among the subtlest, most difficult, and most respected of literary arts. Many literary figures (like Chapman, North, Dryden, and Longfellow) earned laurels by translations of Homer, Plutarch, and Dante. Others (like Fitzgerald and Scott-Moncrieff) attained literary fame primarily through their translations. Much of the intellectual finesse which came from a traditional classical education (in England, for example) came from the exercise of translation into and out of Greek, Latin, and English.

The decline of the classics and of foreign language study generally in America has gradually deprived us of this discipline. Now, in order to make available the increasing printed resources in other languages, the new data processing industry has perfected a machine translator. The Mark II machine, developed jointly by IBM and the Air Force, can take a passage of Russian and translate it into what IBM calls "rough but meaningful English." Here is a sample product of the machine when applied to a passage of Russian literary criticism:

> United States appeared new translation immortal novel L. N. Tolstago "war and world / peace." Truth, not all novel, but only several fragments out of it, even so few / little, that they occupy all one typewritten page. But nonetheless this achievement. Nevertheless culture not stands / costs on place. Something translate. Something print. Truth, by opinion certain literature sceptics, translation made enough / fairly "oak." But this, as they say, opinion separate malignant. If however who doubt in qualification translator, that admirer it / its talent can tell / disclose, that it possess store words, equal 600 thousands, at the time when Shakespeare had to satisfy all only some pitiful 24 thousands words. Inflamed discussion literature specialists. Representative American unification translators, obviously, out of competition consideration, attempted defame new celebrity. Indicated, in particular, on that, that certain specific Russian expression translated too much literally, without transmission them / their true meaning. On the other hand, engineer assured, that this shortage will be soon after removed and on light / world will be able to appear even written in verse translation.

With scientific research moving ahead so speedily, scientists dare not wait even the two or three months usually required to secure publication in a technical journal. They cannot wait to secure reprints like those which social scientists and humanists circulate among their colleagues. Instead (by a kind of scientific analogue to *The Reader's Digest* abridgment of the planted article) they now use the device of the "preprint." This is a version of an article made available *before* its "publication." The most important scientific research institutions are coming to be what Derek J. de Sola Price calls the new "Invisible Colleges"—the regular informal meetings of the most advanced scientists where they exchange their latest findings. In the great centers of research, impatient, energetic scientists will not wait till their fellows elsewhere put results in printed form. They commonly use the long-distance telephone to be sure they have not neglected what their enterprising collaborators elsewhere may have discovered only this morning.

IV

THE BOOK, like the magazine article, has suffered a dissolution. This, too, has been a by-product of the Graphic Revolution. In the single year 1901, the number of book titles printed—about 8,000—was more than six times that of all the titles which had been printed in the United States by the year 1804. Such increase, reaching a climax in our own age, has still further intensified the pressures to abridge and to digest books as well as magazines. By far the largest book club in the United States in 1961 actually offered not books but only condensations of them.

The word "condense," which originally meant to make denser or heavier—and which only in the early nineteenth century acquired its figurative literary significance of concentrating ideas into a small compass—by the early twentieth century acquired a nearly contrary meaning. The object of a literary condensation now was to make the work not "heavier," but "lighter," in every sense of the word. To make it more portable and more palatable to the man who reads as he runs, who supposedly is unwilling to "plow through" the thick original. The Reader's Digest Condensed Book Club, founded in 1950, acquired over half a million members within a single year. Within four years it had 2,500,000 members. In 1958 it had more members than the two next-largest book clubs combined. The sales of individual volumes sometimes came near three million. Almost twelve million Reader's Digest Condensed Books were being printed every year.

The rise of the paperback book, with its multiplying reprints of book titles in the public domain, and its need to compete against magazines on the newsstands, has created an ever greater pressure to modify and abridge. Sometimes the abridgment is indicated ambiguously or not at all. More often it is advertised as a superior commodity, precisely because it is abridged. The Bantam Book edition of Lew Wallace's *Ben Hur* describes itself on the cover as "The Definitive Modern Abridgment."

Contrary to highfalutin belief, the gravest problems of literature in the United States today do not come from the small number of books sold. Rather from the contrary fact that books (now including paperbacks as well as hardcovers) are sold in unprecedented large numbers. The narrowing profit margin and the commercial need to put out large runs (100,000 or more in the case of many paperbacks) in order to produce the economies required by the competition have increased pressures against risk-taking. Publishers of paperback books, as Albert Van Nostrand has shown in his admirable *Denatured Novel* (1960), tend to produce books in only a few patterns: the business novel, the war novel, the mystery novel, etc. More and more of these have come to be commissioned by the "reprint" houses themselves. The exhausting of genuine reprint titles from publishers' backlists and the desire to produce a risk-free commodity have in turn led to more and more "reprint" originals. Many of these are planted in advance with a regular hardcover trade publishing house, much as *The Reader's Digest* plants its articles.

By 1960, as many as a third of the books on the lists of "reprint" houses were in fact originals, confessed or disguised, and this percentage was increasing. The relation between many publishers of hardcover books and the "reprinters" had become not far different from that between the magazine publisher and *The Reader's Digest*. The fact that a large reprint edition of any book has been contracted for before the publication date of the hardcover "original" helps reassure the regular bookseller that the book will have wide appeal and encourages him to stock and push the hardcover book. This fact is given the widest possible publicity in the trade through articles and advertisements in *Publishers' Weekly* and by other means. Vice versa, the fact that a hardcover edition has appeared helps the reprint publisher sell his commodity by reassuring potential customers of the paperback that the book has enduring substance. Sometimes a hardcover publisher insists on placing a book with a reprint house before he will publish it himself. He wants to cover his own risks on any uncertain item like a first novel. Sometimes a reprint publisher, having found what he thinks is a salable commodity, will not publish it himself until he has first planted the book for prior publication with a hardcover publisher. In this way he secures respectability and serious reviews—or, in the jargon, he manages to "famous it up."

V

THE MOVIES, which came with the Graphic Revolution, as I have already suggested, made possible a new dissolution of literary forms. Motion pictures offered, for the first time in history, a visual medium for literary work with an audience far exceeding that for the printed work. "Talking" (perhaps they should be called "non-reading") films removed the movies one step further from the printed page. After the invention of movable type and the introduction of vernacular literatures, the movies were the most decisive new influence on popular attitudes toward literature. And especially on the attitude toward imaginative writing. In this era people began to speak of "nonfiction." (The earliest recorded usage is about 1910.) Earlier they had treated "fact" as the norm. It was reserved to our age to find so negative a way of describing the world of fact. "Fiction" (that is, "non-fact") came to seem so real and natural that fact itself had to be described as a departure from it. Surely the movies must have had a large part in bringing us to this way of thinking.

The movies had a still subtler influence. This more vivid, more universal medium into which literary form could be translated did much to dissolve the very concept of literary form. The motion picture industry became the trade publisher's largest customer. The most vivid form in which important literary happenings now reached people was no longer direct. The novelist's product was his novel: a pattern of words with a form all its own. The larger audience, however, now experienced not the novel but a motion picture adaptation of the novel. Of course it was only the printed page that could offer the authentic "original" version of the author's creation. The movie, at best, was an image of it.

While the motion picture version of a novel was not produced primarily to be reported, it did have other features of a pseudo-event. It was synthetic, repeatable at will, wonderfully suited to the comfort, convenience, and indolence of the viewer. And it shared the most momentous characteristic of the pseudo-event: for most people it was actually more vivid and more impressive than the spontaneous original, which in this case was the novel itself. Before very long Americans would come to think of the movie version of any novel as the "original." The literary form would appeal then only as a secondhand printed account. The superior vividness of the motion picture—in sound and technicolor and on the wide screen—made this inevitable. One could buy a paperback version of the "original" movie of *Gone With the Wind* or *War and Peace* with illustrations showing the "real" characters (Clark Gable as Rhett Butler, Vivien Leigh as Scarlett O'Hara). Sometimes the printed version which came after the movie was made more "authentic" by following the story line found in the movie—often quite different from its literary prototype. After the Walt Disney production of *Swiss Family Robinson* (itself a barely recognizable version of Johann Rudolph Wyss's proto-classic) there appeared a "classic" comic book which aimed to educate young people by bringing them a story which scrupulously followed the story in Disney's much-altered movie "original."

This inevitable tendency to view the motion picture as the more authentic inevitably simplified all the dramatic forms which now dominated popular consciousness. For, despite its more elaborate technical apparatus, the movie tends to be dramatically simpler than the novel. Characters or episodes are generally added only to keep the story in a recognized monochromatic pattern: to provide the familiar love interest, to sharpen the distinction between good guys and bad guys, or to insure a happy ending.

Budd Schulberg, who wrote the scenario for the superb movie *Waterfront*—a brilliant box-office success—was not satisfied with what could be said in the movie. The movie was made from a screenplay by Schulberg himself before he had written a novel on the same subject. Having seen the movie (directed by Elia Kazan and starring Marlon Brando), which he found superlatively effective as a movie, Schulberg then determined to write his novel around the same story. He explained his reasons for doing so in an eloquent essay in *The Saturday Review* (September 3, 1955), "Why Write It When You Can't Sell It to the Pictures?" This was a clear statement of the too-often forgotten difference between the movie and the novel. Although in Schulberg's opinion the movie had been well done—it had won every possible recognition, from Academy Award Oscars to the prize at the International Film Festival in Venice—Schulberg still felt he had more to say than could possibly be said even in the best movie.

Here were two ways of storytelling, and, Schulberg argued, one could not substitute for the other.

The screenplay is restricted in form. It is the director who has the opportunity to develop character and background through insight, so that the authorship of a film at best becomes a true director-writer co-creation. To take my *Waterfront* script as an example, its length (after much pruning) was 115 manuscript pages. The novel was five times as long. The film is an art of high points. I think of it as embracing five or six sequences, each one mounting to a climax that rushes the action onward. The novel is an art of high, middle, and low points. . . . The film does best when it concentrates on a single character. It tells the *Informer* superbly. It tends to lose itself in the ramifications of *War and Peace*. It has no time for what I call the essential digression. The "digression" of complicated, contradictory character. The "digression" of social background. The film must go from significant episode to more significant episode in a constantly mounting pattern. It's an exciting form. But it pays a price for this excitement. It cannot wander as life wanders, or pause as life always pauses, to contemplate the incidental or the unexpected.

We may often be unfair, then, in accusing movie directors of being simple-minded. They are working in a medium which, like every other, has its limitations. Even at its best the movie remains a simplifying medium. The great box-office successes, even when they had the panoramic sweep of *Birth of a Nation* or *Gone With the Wind,* had a simple story line and an uncomplicated (therefore often also a misleading) moral. Even the great D. W. Griffith had a hard time (and produced a box-office failure) when he tried a complexly interwoven story in his *Intolerance.* And that challenging model, boldly experimental in its intricacy, has not successfully followed, while the prototypical *Birth of a Nation* has been made again and again.

Our extravagant expectations of our power over the world, illustrated by our belief that we can put the essence of a novel into a movie, have led us to forget that something (and in a good novel it is always a great deal) remains in the novel that cannot be moviefied. Simply because many things could be done visually in a movie which could not be accomplished on the legitimate stage or in a novel, we too easily came to believe that there was nothing—or at least nothing of impor-

tance—which could not be put on film. The ninety-minute
limit (even if doubled or trebled) necessarily includes only a
narrow province of human experience. And, as Schulberg insists, despite all the improvements in sound, technicolor,
wide-angle lenses, Cinerama, and 3-D, there remains a vast,
rich, subtle, world outside the movie-makers' or movie-goers'
ken. The nuance, the perspective, the contradictions of historical development and social interaction were not made for
the camera eye. The real tyrant is not the Hays Office or
local censorship, but the film form itself. To be sure, the film
can "speak-out," vividly and terrifyingly, as did *Waterfront*.
But the novel is able, in Schulberg's phrase, "to speak-*in,* to
search the interior drama in the heart and mind." While the
movie *Waterfront* ended with a dramatic close-up of Marlon
Brando, excellent in its own way, the novel could end "with
the deeper truth of inconclusiveness. . . . A film must act, a
book has time to think and wonder. . . . In the flush of TV
spectaculars, wider and wider screeneramas, and all the rest
of our frightful, fruitful mechanical advancements the book
is still the essential civilizing influence, able to penetrate the
unknowns of human aspiration."

The danger to our sense of reality is not that movies should
be made of novels, and vice versa. But rather that we should
lose our sense that neither can become the other, that the
traditional novel form continues to enlarge our experience in
those very areas where the wide-angle lens and the Cinerama screen tend to narrow it. The danger is not in the interchangeableness of the story, but in our belief in the interchangeableness of the forms. We have lost our grip on reality
when we have let ourselves believe (as we are eager to be
reassured by movie-makers and their press agents) that the
movie can ever give us the nub of the matter.

Yet movie-makers themselves, driven by the needs of the
movie form (as the *Digest* editors are driven by the needs of
their form), inevitably treat the novel itself as nothing but
the wrapping paper and string of "literary embellishment."
This must be removed to reveal a quintessence, a story line.

Thus the multiplying kinds of images—from the printed page to the photograph to the movie to radio and television, to the comic book and back again—make our literary-dramatic experience a limbo. In that limbo there are no forms but only the ghosts of other forms.

VI

THE MOVIES were, of course, the first of the new alternative visual forms for narrative literature which were to come with the Graphic Revolution. Motion pictures became commercially important only around 1910. By 1917 *Publishers' Weekly* was writing about "cinema novels." In the 1920's studios were paying hundreds of thousands of dollars for film rights to novels. In 1931 Cheney's *Economic Survey of the Book Industry* reported that the incredible prices for screen rights had brought on some severe cases of a new occupational disease known as " 'novelist's nystagmus,' caused by keeping one eye on the typewriter and the other on Hollywood. The result has been a feverish production of certain books of 'a certain type.' " In the following years the changing economics of the movie industry made the disease more prevalent than ever. After World War II the cost of movie making became so high that most producers instead of owning studios began to lease facilities. It then became easier to produce a movie on credit. Between 1945 and 1960 there came into being over a hundred new firms of independent producers buying novels for the films.

By 1946 M-G-M had established a contest for novelists which paid the winner $125,000. Twentieth Century-Fox gave Grace Metalious $265,000 to write a sequel to her *Peyton Place* (1956), the box-office success made from her novel that sold eight million copies. The sequel was to be called *Return to Peyton Place*.

When the high price paid for movie rights itself had a publicity value ("It must be good if they paid so much!"), even the business transaction became an elaborately contrived pseudo-event (like the concluding of contracts by movie stars and sports celebrities), with photographs of the signing of the contract, interviews of author, producer, etc. Here was a new kind of advance testimonial whose authenticity actually depended on the fact that big money was paid by the movie producer—the person giving the testimonial.

In *Publishers' Weekly,* the magazine of the book trade, the column "Books into Films" became a regular feature in 1944. By November 15, 1952, the author of the column, Paul S. Nathan, found the title too confining. "Film rights," he explained, "after all, are only one kind of subsidiary rights; there is really no reason why publishers, editors, booksellers, and other interested parties should be more concerned with books being sold to the movies than with books acquired by the *Ladies' Home Journal,* or by *Omnibook* for digest, or by the Broadway theater for adaptation." He added that the advances paid by Hollywood were beginning to be overshadowed by those of the paperback reprint houses; and that television only within the last six years had become "a bigger, more voracious market for subsidiary rights than the movies." Having discarded the more general title, "Books into Money," Nathan renamed his column "Rights and Permissions," and it has remained one of the most widely read features in the magazine.

It became an axiom of the book trade that booksellers were more apt to be interested in a book, and more inclined to stock it and to push its sale, if the movie rights had already been sold for a substantial sum. This was assurance that the book itself would be profitable. Here are a couple of sample items from *Publishers' Weekly* for a single issue (December 12, 1960).

A Broadway pre-production deal of a like never seen before—one which goes the limit—has just been entered into by Columbia Pictures in connection with the new stage version of Vern Sneider's new Putnam novel,

The King from Ashtabula.

The studio will furnish the entire financing for the play, which will open under the banner of Robert Fryer and Lawrence Carr, with Morton Da Costa directing. Columbia also is making a substantial down payment on the screen rights, plus escalator payments relating to the length of the theatrical run, up to a ceiling of $500,-000.

From here it looks as though Da Costa in particular stands to clean up under the terms of the agreement. In addition to directing the play, he is assured of the same job when the cameras start turning. Furthermore, as collaborator on the dramatization with Sneider, he will cut in on the profits from the adaptation; and as an extra wallet stuffer, his own independent outfit, Belgrave Productions, will co-produce the motion picture with Columbia.

These are the highlights of the agreement, which has other details setting it apart from the usual. Abe Lastfogel, the big gun at the William Morris Agency, presided over negotiations, with Claire S. Degener of Curtis Brown, Ltd., co-operating as Sneider's representative.

It is known that other movie companies, visualizing *The King from Ashtabula* as a lucrative successor to the same author's *Teahouse of the August Moon,* were desirous of tying up the rights but boggled at the conditions.

In order to stir interest in the sale of movie rights to a book, the book need not yet have been written. Nor even need the supposed writer of the non-existent book himself be an author.

In this week of the out-of-the-ordinary, the disclosure that Bernard Geis Associates plans to publish the autobiography of entertainer Sammy Davis, Jr., has stirred lively interest which has manifested itself in an extreme form. On hearing the news, one of the major studios

straightway dispatched a messenger to the office of
Scott Meredith, agent for the book, with a sizable offer
for screen rights. The offer has not at the moment been
accepted. For one thing, Davis' own services as a performer are expected to be part of the package, and it is
thought to be too early to make a commitment along
such lines—especially since work on the book itself
won't be starting till January at least.

Davis will have the assistance of a friend, Burt Boyar,
syndicated columnist for the Newhouse papers, in setting his life down on paper.

In an earlier instance the Meredith agency did sell
the picture rights to a book then unwritten. That one,
Evan Hunter's *Mothers and Daughters* (to be published
by Simon and Schuster late this spring), has now been
completed, and German rights have just gone to Kindler
Verlag, in a deal closed with their representative here,
Maximilian Becker, for a record $17,000 advance.
Also, Corgi has just acquired British paperback rights
on a £15,000 advance.

In this world of the shadows of shadows, the very concept
of literary authorship dissolves and disappears. William Wy-
ler's presentation of *Ben Hur* opened on Broadway in 1959
with high-priced reserved seats, a printed program, and all
the familiar paraphernalia of the movie spectacular. The detailed printed program listed everybody from Sam Zimbalist,
the producer, to Joan Bridge who was Color Consultant for
Costumes, and Gabriella Borzelli, the hair stylist. But it nowhere listed the name of Lew Wallace, the author.

Since both Lew Wallace and his copyright had long since
expired, there was nobody to protest. When the author is still
alive, however, he sometimes objects that his work has been
"adapted" out of existence. This has led to a number of law-
suits, which authors have seldom won. One of the most memorable and most ironic occurred in 1931 when Theodore
Dreiser sought a court injunction to prevent a New York the-

ater from presenting the Paramount movie of his *American Tragedy*. The movie (based both on the novel and on a stage play adapted from the novel), according to Dreiser, had reduced his work from a subtle exploration of how a whole society can be responsible for one young man's crime to a "tabloid murder story." Dreiser lost his case.

In the movie world the distilling of novels into films, as Van Nostrand observes, has become a series of standard processes. In Hollywood jargon these include the making of a "treatment" (a narrative based on a synopsis), the development of a "continuity" (translating the treatment into movie scenes), and the concocting of a "shooting script." This is finally elaborated by "cross-cutting" (showing alternate shots of different scenes), by the "gimmick" or "switcheroo" (suddenly cutting to another scene and revealing new facts to heighten suspense), by the "yak" (a funny surprise), and the "bleeder" (a pathetic surprise). A comparable set of transformations takes place whenever a novel, a stage play, or a movie is adapted into a television show. Such multiplication of the media into which a dramatic notion can be cast inevitably divorces the content from literary form.

Compared with the twentieth-century movie adaptations of novels, John Dryden's "adaptations" or Thomas Bowdler's "family" versions of Shakespeare look like literal transcription. The very notion of literary art—"the word one with the thing"—disappears from the popular mind. Each embodiment then competes with all others for the kudos of being the "original." Out of this competition, by the law of pseudo-events, the winner in the viewer's consciousness is the embodiment most remote from the naive, spontaneous product of an author.

VII

OUT OF the Graphic Revolution came still another phenomenon dissolving the traditional forms of dramatic literature.

This was the "star system." It would have been unthinkable without the invention of photography and motion pictures, without the many new means for reproducing stories and faces and images.

"Stars" were the celebrities of the entertainment world. Like other celebrities they were to be distinguished by their well-knownness more than by any other quality. In them, as in other celebrities, fame and notoriety were thoroughly confused. Their hallmark was simply and primarily their prominence in popular consciousness, and it made very little difference how this publicity was secured. They could become well known either by flaunting morality (Mary Pickford) or by flouting it (Mae West). As a species of celebrities, stars, too, were spawned in the world of pseudo-events. And they, too, were fertile of other pseudo-events. It is not surprising, then, that movie stars became our celebrities par excellence. In 1940 about 300 correspondents were assigned to Hollywood, which was the largest single source of news (an estimated 100,000 words a day) in the United States outside of Washington, D.C., and New York City.

Although not born with the movies, the star system emerged within the first decade or so of the commercial life of the motion pictures, and under appropriately pseudo-eventful auspices. Early in 1908 an issue of *Moving Picture World* carried an advertisement showing a photograph of the beautiful movie actress Florence Lawrence, over the word "Imp," and reading as follows:

We Nail a Lie

The blackest and at the same time the silliest lie yet circulated by enemies of the "Imp" was the story foisted on the public of St. Louis last week to the effect that Miss Lawrence (the "Imp" girl, formerly known as the "Biograph" girl) had been killed by a street car. It was a black lie because so cowardly. It was a silly lie because so easily disproved. Miss Lawrence was not even in a street-car accident, is in the best of health, will continue to appear in "Imp" films, and very shortly some of the best work in her career is to be released. We now announce our next films:

"The Broken Bath"
(Released March 14th. Length 950 feet.)

A powerful melodrama dealing with a young chap, his sweetheart and a secret society. There's action from the first foot of film and . . .

This advertisement was purporting to answer a story in the St. Louis newspapers which had said that Florence Lawrence, known to nickelodeon fans as the "Biograph girl" (she made films for the Biograph film company), had been killed in a streetcar accident. In his advertisement Carl Laemmle meant to imply that the newspaper story had been concocted by his competitors, the film trust, to prevent the public from learning that Miss Lawrence had left Biograph for Laemmle's company and that in the future she would be lending her fame and face and figure to his productions. Actually Laemmle had planted the original newspaper story himself, for publicity purposes. The whole episode, including Laemmle's advertised "reply," was only his characteristic way of announcing that Miss Lawrence, then the most popular personality in films, was now his property.

This was not the only such stunt that the ingenious Laemmle used to discredit his competitors and to advertise his own products. It was true that the big General Film Company, sometimes disparagingly called "the trust," for whom Miss Lawrence had worked, had refused to give out the names of actors. This was both because General Film were trying to standardize film manufacture (keeping it uncluttered by individual personalities) and because they foresaw that if individual actors became famous and known by name, the actors would command higher pay. Among some early movie companies this practice had become a strict rule. But the nickelodeon public insisted on individualizing their favorites, and gave them such names as the "Biograph girl," the "little girl with the golden curls," etc. Independent movie-makers like Laemmle, seeing a competitive advantage, and realizing that the public did not like its actors kept anonymous, then began strenuously publicizing their own actors. Incidentally, they were able to lure over to their own studios from the larger companies the actors and actresses who wanted both more publicity and more money. Geraldine Farrar (followed by Mary Garden) signed with Samuel Goldwyn at $10,000 a week. Movie stars became gilded idols. Their salaries soon were the biggest single item in a film budget.

The star system, as Richard Griffith and Arthur Mayer explain in their excellent pictorial history of the movies, was thus in a sense created by the public itself: by movie-goers who would not be satisfied by anonymous idols. They demanded that their idols be named—and be apotheosized by expensive publicity. In a word, that they be made into celebrities with the characteristics described in an earlier chapter. What movie-goers wanted in a star was not a strong character, but a definable, publicizable personality: a figure with some physical idiosyncrasy or personal mannerism which could become a nationally advertised trademark. Among these were John Bunny's jovial bulk, Mary Pickford's golden curls and winsome smile, Douglas Fairbanks' waxed mustache and energetic leap, Maurice Costello's urbanity, Charlie Chaplin's bowed legs and cane, and Clara Kimball Young's calf eyes. Acting ability and symmetry of face or figure became less important than the capacity to be made into a trademark.

Many producers—not only Laemmle, but also Adolf Zukor, with his Famous Players (1912), and Cecil B. De Mille—helped develop the star system. The keynote of the new era was set when Zukor imported Sarah Bernhardt, who had been world-famous for her voice, to act in the silent film of Queen Elizabeth. The film-star legend of the accidentally discovered soda-fountain girl who was quickly elevated to stardom soon took its place alongside the log-cabin-to-White-

House legend as a leitmotif of American democratic folk-lore. And the legend could reflect reality precisely because there really was so much chance and whimsy in the star-selecting process. A former prison guard, a hat-check girl—or anyone else who happened to have "what it takes" (which included a distinctive commonplaceness of personality, but seldom much acting talent)—might get the "breaks" and make it to the top. This helped make the movies a democratic art and made Hollywood the American dream factory in an age when dream and illusion were hardly distinguished.

By about 1920 the star system was well established. It has dominated the screen and much else ever since. Mary Pick-ford—"America's Sweetheart"—was among the first stars. There followed many others: John Barrymore, Minnie Mad-dern Fiske, James K. Hackett, William S. Hart, Pola Negri, Dorothy Gish, Clara Bow, Greta Garbo, Rudolph Valentino, etc., etc., etc. This great innovation has sometimes been de-scribed as a movement from the "star film" (the movie which included a famous actor) to the "film star" (the personality whose mere presence made a film). Producers quickly found that the star system paid. Even if they had no new drama to sell, they could do well by displaying the same star in turn in a variety of new vehicles. The more money the film stars made for their producers, the more money producers were in turn willing to invest in "making" particular stars. Of course producers had to pay well and invest heavily in order to pro-tect their investment and to meet competition. The high cost of making new stars led the producer who had a star with proved box-office appeal to exploit him in every conceivable way before his appeal wore out. Despite spectacular excep-tions like Marlene Dietrich, the artificial celebrity life of a star was apt to be brief. For this very reason some actors were said to prefer to play supporting roles in order to make their careers less ephemeral.

High salaries became news and themselves helped make stars into celebrities. These salaries in turn re-enforced the star system. Producers could not afford to abandon it.

The great significance of the star system for literary and dramatic form was simply that the star came to dominate the form and make it irrelevant. Of course the star had first appeared as an actor—a person skilled at playing assigned roles. Originally it was the play that gave form to the product. But when the system became established, the relation between play and player was reversed. The sign of a true star was in fact that whatever he appeared in was only a "vehicle." The actor himself was no longer tested by his ability to interpret the play. Instead, the play was tested by its ability to display the actor. But the actor himself was an empty vessel. He was no true hero; usually he was a mere celebrity—a human pseudo-event, "the greatest." To exploit a star meant only to show his familiar face and figure and gestures, and always as much as possible in his familiar role. It was less what he could do than how widely he was known, how "popular" he was, that made him, and kept him, a star. Again the self-fulfilling prophecy of the true pseudo-event. Every time an actor appeared in a starring role, that fact itself made him more of a star, and, of course, more of a celebrity.

Each star soon became type-cast. This meant that every one of his appearances had to be more of the same. By definition, then, the star could not offer anything strikingly new. The vehicle would be unacceptable to him unless it reenforced his desired image. A sign of the rise of the star system, noted by historians of the film, was that about 1914 Febo Mari refused to wear a beard as Attila and Alberto Capozzi rejected the role of St. Paul because it would require him to wear a beard. Stars commonly refused roles or costumes which seemed inappropriate to their star personality, or which concealed the face already well known to millions. Occasionally before, a stage play had been written for a particular actor. Now it became standard practice for a screen play to be modified, a new character to be inserted, or a whole plot developed, to meet the box-office proved specifications of the stars.

As the star rose, he became one with his roles. Francis X.

Bushman and Beverly Bayne, who were the first starring movie "love team" (*Romeo and Juliet,* 1916), kept their marriage a secret for fear it would tarnish their romantic appeal. Douglas Fairbanks and Mary Pickford were married (1920; divorced, 1935) by the logic of a world which, as one writer has observed, "existed, really, more through the screen than on the screen." "People say," Jean Gabin once remarked, "I'm the same in real life as I am in my movies, and that's why they like me." Charles Boyer received a letter addressed to him c/o Mayerling, Hollywood, U.S.A. In 1936 the Gary Cooper Fan Club of San Antonio boomed him for President of the United States: they said he had already demonstrated his political acumen in *Mr. Deeds Goes to Town.*

Everyone knows, of course, that a star is not born, but made. The familiar process was well described by Edgar Morin:

> A talent scout is struck by a promising face in the subway. Proposition, test photo, test recording. If the tests are conclusive, the young beauty leaves for Hollywood. Immediately put under contract, she is refashioned by the masseurs, the beauticians, the dentists, even the surgeons. She learns to walk, loses her accent, is taught to sing, to dance, to stand, to sit still, to "hold herself." She is instructed in literature, ideas. The foreign star whom Hollywood cuts back to starlet level sees her beauty transformed, recomposed, Max-Factorized, and she learns American. Then there are more tests: among others a 30-second close-up in technicolor. There is a new winnowing-out. She is noticed, approved, and given a minor role. Her car, her servants, her dogs, her goldfish, her birds are chosen for her. Her personality grows more complex, becomes enriched. She waits for letters. Nothing. Failure. But one day or the next the Fan Mail Department might notify the Executive Producer that she is receiving 300 letters a day from admirers. The studio decides to launch her, and fabricates

a fairy tale of which she is the heroine. She provides material for the columnists; her private life is already illuminated by the glare of the projectors. At last she is given the lead in a major film. Apotheosis: the day when her fans tear her clothes: she is a star.

Plainly the star is a pseudo-event. He proves it by spawning other pseudo-events. The Fan Club, for example. Although these clubs are generally not fomented by a press agent, they are encouraged by press agents and by the star himself. When the star visits a city, the local fan club becomes a body guard, following the fan about, attracting attention, asking for autographs, and encouraging non-members to do the same. The star sometimes has a series of photographs of himself—posing in his "real" costume in character—with some token of the season, holding lilies or bunnies or holly berries or turkeys, to send to his fan clubs. Nelson Eddy, for example, once sent a Christmas box of chocolates to each of the presidents of his fan clubs in different cities. The Bing Crosby Club of Ramseur, North Carolina (including 40 per cent of the population) once persuaded the city government to rename a thoroughfare Crosby Street. In 1960 Ricky Nelson alone had some 9,000 fan clubs. Early in that year the national secretary of the fan club for the Ozzie Nelson family was receiving every week about 10,000 letters and between 120 and 150 requests to start "official" fan clubs for some member of the family (mostly for Ricky). The Deanna Durbin Club, with higher standards than others, had limited membership to fans who: (1) had seen each of Deanna's movies at least twice, (2) presented an important collection of documents about Deanna, and (3) subscribed to the *Deanna Journal.* Dues of fan clubs are commonly about fifty cents a year.

Fan magazines have been both the products and the multipliers of the fan clubs. About a quarter of all magazine titles on most newsstands were in the fan-romance category, according to a survey reported in *Newsdealer,* a trade publication, in April 1960. Their combined sales then ran to thirty-three million a month, almost 400 million copies a year. In addition there are the so-called "one-shots," which are not serial publications, but each of which usually centers around an entertainer-celebrity. Dick Clark once sold 180,000 copies of one such dollar one-shot by displaying it over his "American Bandstand." An Elvis Presley one-shot sold nearly a million copies.

A pseudo-eventful by-product of the star system is what *Time* magazine has accurately described as "non-books." These are printed matter between covers, usually put together by someone other than the ostensible autobiographer. An energetic new "non-publisher," Bernard Geis Associates (distributing their works through Random House), has specialized in the pseudo-products of the entertainment world. A typical example is *Ustinov's Diplomats,* in which Peter Ustinov, taking advantage of his beard, mimics United Nations representatives; the volume is prefaced by Kirk Douglas' introduction reminding readers that Ustinov appears with him in the movie *Spartacus.* Another is *Zsa Zsa Gabor: My Story Written for Me by Gerold Frank* (World Publishers), which with disarming profundity concludes, "Who knows, in this life of ours, what is really true and what is enchanting make-believe?"

The star is the ultimate American verification of Jean Jacques Rousseau's *Émile.* His mere existence proves the perfectibility of any man or woman. Oh wonderful pliability of human nature, in a society where anyone can become a celebrity! And where any celebrity (boxer "Sugar Ray" Robinson, singer Elvis Presley, lawyer Joseph L. Welch) may become a star! Once the star has been established as a celebrity, or the celebrity established as a star, he can "perform" in almost any kind of piece—a war movie, a musical spectacular, a murder mystery, or a gangster story—provided he is paid enough and he can preserve his "real" personality. The star-celebrity is an undifferentiated entertainer.

VIII

THE STAR system has reached far beyond the movies. Wherever it reaches it confuses traditional forms of achievement. It focuses on the personality rather than on the work. It puts a premium on well-knownness for its own sake. It is a generalized process for transforming hero into celebrity. It leads institutions to employ pseudo-events to "build up" big names. In the United States it has come to dominate even the world of fiction-writing itself. By contrast, in England, for example (where aristocratic survivals and a lower standard of living have retarded the effects of the Graphic Revolution), a good novelist can without difficulty secure publication of a work of high literary quality which promises a sale of only a few thousand—barely enough to cover production costs and a small profit margin. But, as Harvey Swados has observed, the American publishing scene has been dominated by a few stars—Ernest Hemingway, Norman Mailer, J. D. Salinger—who have prospered as authors partly because they could be touted as "personalities."

Columnists for our popular literary reviews and weekly book sections discuss star-authors less in the spirit of a Dr. Samuel Johnson than in that of a Louella Parsons. They gossip simultaneously about the star's private life, his work, and his roles. Perhaps as Swados suggests, J. D. Salinger is the Greta Garbo of American letters, and Ernest Hemingway was a kind of Douglas Fairbanks. The host of other good writers who have not achieved star status, whose personalities have not yet become publicly mixed with their works— these writers suffer literary and personal obscurity. Here we see "massive concentration on a handful of writers (for reasons all too often nonliterary)." Publishers then, are less the midwives of literary culture than "drumbeaters for an arbitrarily limited galaxy of stars." The star system prevails, as Norman Mailer explains, because American audiences are "incapable of confronting a book unless it is successful."

Mailer might have added that while the star system may have begun for this reason, it has in turn made its own reasons. American bigotry in favor of success (and intolerance of failure) itself expresses a star-dominated world.

Best-sellerism is the star system of the book world. A "best seller" is a celebrity among books. It is a book known primarily (sometimes exclusively) for its well-knownness. And it is a relatively new phenomenon. Until the present century no one would have thought of revering the Bible for being the World's Best Seller. On the contrary, in pre-democratic ages, before the invention of movable type, the text viewed with awe was not popular but esoteric. Much of the sacredness of holy texts doubtless used to come from their scarcity and inaccessibility, from the fact that the few existing copies were in the custody of holy priests. To this day the Torah (the Pentateuch, or first five books of the Bible, the sacred texts of Judaism) enshrined in the ark of synagogues is a text laboriously hand-written on parchment. The Holy Book, the revered book, which had been slowly and reverently written down and handed as an heirloom from generation to generation, was guarded from the vulgar eye, to be shown to the populace only on the sanctified occasions of prayer, of the Sabbath, of religious holidays, etc. It was in almost every way the antithesis of our distinctive writings, our newspapers, our mass-circulation magazines, and our best sellers. The popular book, the best seller, which holds the highest status among contemporary texts, is that which is universally in the public eye. Everybody has it on his living room table, the commuter carries it on the train, the secretary reads it at her typewriter, it is featured in the windows of department stores, bookstores, now even in drugstores and on newsstands.

The expression "best seller" is, of course, another by-product of the Graphic Revolution. It is an Americanism (still not found in some of the best English dictionaries) which first came into use in the United States at the beginning of the present century. In 1895 *The Bookman,* a conservative monthly literary review edited by Harry Thurston Peck, published in its first issue a list of retail booksellers' reports of the six new books most in demand in nineteen cities. In 1897 the same magazine published the first national survey of "Best-Selling Books." The word "seller" in England had originally meant a person who sold; only around 1900 did the word come to mean a book (later any other item) that sold well. This subtle transference of ideas was itself interesting, for the very expression "best seller" or "seller" now implied that a book somehow sold itself: that sales bred more sales. This was closely related to the idea that this kind of book would continue to sell well simply because it was already a seller, and thus there was a kind of tautology in the very notion. A best seller was a book which somehow sold well simply because it was selling well.

The expression soon became firmly established and entered common American usage. By 1902 "best seller" had become a term denoting not any commodity which sold, but specifically a book which outsold most others. About 1903 *The Bookman* set the number of its monthly titles at six and called the list "the six best sellers." There had, of course, been occasional earlier lists, but *The Bookman* was responsible for making them into an institution. The imprimatur of the book trade itself was given in January 1911, when *Publishers' Weekly* printed its first annual consensus, "Best Sellers of 1910," and later used *The Bookman*'s lists for its retrospective surveys of the years 1895–1912. Since then *Publishers' Weekly, The New York Times,* many local newspapers, literary reviews, and news magazines have published their own lists as news items of general interest. In recent years the biggest and most widespread news of the world of books has not been who is writing what, but what are the best sellers. Newspaper, magazine, and television quizzes ask us about them. As a celebrity of the book world, a best seller has all the dignity and appeal of other pseudo-events.

Best-sellerism has thus come to dominate the book world. Leaders in the book trade have themselves often attacked it.

In his *Economic Survey of the Book Industry* in 1931, O. H. Cheney called best-sellerism "an intolerable curse on the industry." But, he explained, there was (and there remains) a substantial commercial basis for the institution: one way to make a book a best seller is to call it one. Then many potential book buyers "want to join the thousands—or hundreds of thousands—of the inner circle of the readers of the book. As soon as everybody thinks that everybody else has read it—or should read it—a best seller gets talked about—and talk leads to the ringing of the cash register." A buyer going into a bookstore is apt to ask for the best seller; even if he doesn't, he is apt to be urged to buy a book because it is one. If booksellers can be convinced before publication that a book is bound to be a best seller, they are apt to place large orders so as not to be caught short; if, after publication, they can be convinced that a book actually is a best seller, they will more readily reorder. According to Cheney, the substantial accuracy of this pattern had given best-sellerism its strangle hold on the book trade.

One of the most interesting features of the institution is how flimsy is the factual basis for calling any particular book a best seller. To speak of *a* best seller—to use the superlative to apply not to one item but to a score of items—is, of course, a logical contradiction. But the bookstores are full of "best sellers," just as the media world of celebrities is full of "the biggest," "the best," and "the greatest." The factual basis for calling any book a best seller is not so much a statistic as an amalgam including a small ingredient of fact along with much larger ingredients of hope, intention, frustration, ballyhoo, and pure hokum. Trade practices (hardly changed since Cheney noted them in 1931) are as follows:

> A bookseller, asked to report on sales, begins by trying to remember or he asks the friendly traveler what he thinks is the best-seller. Or else he sees a stack of a title which has been decreasing—and at the next step he sees a stack which he wishes would disappear—and then he

remembers a title on which he ordered too many. The title becomes one of his best-sellers.

Publishers' figures are hardly a better index, because publishers do not compare sales and seldom reveal them. Therefore, any statement about which books are having the best sales cannot possibly be based on fact—even if the sales on publishers' records represented actual sales to readers (which they do not). Inevitably, then, best seller lists are a tissue of falsehood, if not always in what they say, always in what they imply. The publishing industry thus deludes not only the booksellers and readers, but even itself. The art of promoting books, then, like the art of government administration and some others, has increasingly become a technique of telling attractive untruths without actually lying.

It is not only the moral and aesthetic effects of best-sellerism that have plagued the book trade. The commercial side-effects have been serious. In May 1961 *Publishers' Weekly* noted that bookstores in the metropolitan New York area, in their struggle to maintain Fair Trade prices, were selling fewer and fewer best sellers. This was because as soon as a book appeared on one of the more publicized best seller lists, it was customarily selected by Macy's and Gimbel's to be offered as a loss-leader and was then sold by them at cost or below. Under these circumstances regular bookstores could not afford to compete; they could not find buyers for the book at its list price, and hence did not order it. One bookseller proposed, therefore, that the Best Seller List be called instead a "Worst Seller List"—"this cutthroat list no bookseller wants except the outlets that football a few titles as traffic builders. If there were no best seller lists, all booksellers would sell more books at a profit." But the public demands its best sellers and its best seller lists as it demands its celebrities and all its other pseudo-events. The synthetic character of all of them bothers most people very little. The quality of being a best seller, despite everything, still remains the most

advertised and advertisable fact—the biggest "news"—
about a book.

The increasing popularity of the "popular" book (or best
seller)—like our increasing tendency to motor over the most-
traveled roads—re-enforces the mirror effect and makes it
increasingly difficult to learn from our literary experience.
As James D. Hart shrewdly observes in his study *The Popular Book,* the most popular book in the short run is apt to be
that which most effectively tells us what we already know. It
is a kind of literary tourist attraction guaranteed to give us
an adventure which we know all about in advance: it is nothing but the projection of our own expectations. The reason
why Maria Cummins' *The Lamplighter* or T. S. Arthur's *Ten
Nights in a Bar-Room* (both best sellers in their day) tell us
more about what most Americans were thinking in 1854 than
does Thoreau's *Walden,* or why Gertrude Atherton's *Black
Oxen* tells us more than Wallace Stevens' *Harmonium* about
popular feelings in 1923, is precisely that Cummins and Arthur and Atherton reflected, rather than amplified, the experience of their readers. "The book that time judges to be
great," remarks Hart, "is occasionally also the book popular
in its own period; but, by and large, the longer-lived work
reflects the demands of the moment only in the most general
sense. Usually the book that is popular pleases the reader because it is shaped by the same forces that mold his non-
reading hours, so that its dispositions and convictions, its language and subject, re-create the sense of the present, to die
away as soon as that present becomes the past. Books of that
sort generally are unreadable for succeeding ages."

The star system thus reaches out into one field after another of American life. What the book trade promotes is, in
Van Nostrand's telling phrase, "not an art form but an artifact." Reading a book becomes less a way of looking out at
the world than a way of looking at ourselves. The best seller
may promise to take us to "the mysterious East," but that
also becomes a "fun stop," and we find ourselves back in the

sanitary, air-conditioned facilities of another Hilton Hotel.

What the entertainment trade sells is not a talent, but a name. The quest for celebrity, the pressure for well-known-ness, everywhere makes the worker overshadow the work. And in some cases, if what there is to become well known is attractive enough, there need be no work at all. For example, the Gabor sisters in the 'fifties became "film personalities" even though they had made almost no films at all. How thoroughly appropriate, too, that one of them should have become "author" of a best selling "book"!

In science, too, the increasing pressures to secure foundation and government support, the increasing unintelligibility of the task, and the widespread pressure to devise news, make us concentrate on big names. This leads to increasing emphasis on all sorts of prizes—Oscars, Nobels, National Book Awards, Critics' Circle Awards, Pulitzers, and others less known and more factitious. Universities, the traditional refuge of timelessness, nowadays look for big names, and enlarge their public relations and press relations departments to make the university itself a celebrity, known for its well-knownness. National politics (with the full paraphernalia of make-up, rehearsals, and klieg lights) has adopted the star system which dominates it more with every election.

Yet anyone—or almost anyone—can be transformed into a star. Originally a person destined for stardom is chosen less for his intrinsic value than for his capacity to be "built up." How good a receptacle is he for what the public wants to see in him? A star, then, must allow his personality to dominate his work; he is judged by his personality in place of his achievement. In a world of dissolving moral and artistic forms, man the self-maker displaces them all. But his figure, too, is only a figment.

IX

IN PAINTING and sculpture we find similar dissolutions—from our exaggerated expectations of how plastic is our world. A photograph of the tiny Sumerian cylinder seal makes it appear the same size as an Egyptian colossus. André Malraux, in his *Voices of Silence,* shows how photography tends to destroy our sense of scale. When we can photograph any work and make an accurate reproduction of any size we please, we lose our feeling for the distinctiveness of every work.

Many problems of the modern artist, as Malraux observes, come actually from improvements in techniques of reproduction. In other words, from the Graphic Revolution. When it is so easy mechanically to make a precise color reproduction direct from nature, much of the age-old challenge which nature offered the artist is destroyed. Aggressively "modern" artists insist that only now (when they are finally freed from the need to represent) can their work become truly interesting and expressive. But the force of their argument is reduced by one simple fact. They now have a vested interest in *non*-representation (much as for centuries they once had a vested interest in representation). Formerly the artist was the only instrument which could make a representation of a man or a landscape. Now the artist is the only instrument which can make a "non-representation." We need only walk through the Guggenheim Museum or visit the Art Institute of Chicago during its annual exhibit of local artists, to sense the dissolution of forms—the limbo in which the American artist now floats.

Meanwhile, as I have observed, the feeling for any original declines as it becomes easier and cheaper to make color reproductions—of works of art as well as of nature. The Metropolitan Museum of Art sells blurry postage-stamp-sized reproductions of paintings, supposedly to "heighten" our appreciation by allowing us to have them at our fingertips right in our own home. Formerly a competent copy (say of a Giotto by a member of his school) had an authentic and dignified originality all its own. Now, when mechanical reproductions offer items precisely like the original, the uniqueness both of originals and of copies is dissolved. Both move into a limbo something like that between the novelist's typewriter and the movie-maker's camera.

Here is another universal tendency of the graphic age. We have already seen how the pseudo-event derives interest from the process of making it, how citizens become more interested in the performance than in the argument in television debates, how fans enjoy watching the process of celebrity-making. The same is true of works of art. The faithfulness of the reproduction overshadows the quality of what is reproduced. The most refined skills of color printing, the intricate techniques of wide-angle photography, provide us pictures of trivia bigger and more real than life. We forget that we see trivia and notice only that the reproduction is so good.

Man fulfills his dream and by photographic magic produces a precise image of the Grand Canyon. The result is not that he adores nature or beauty the more. Instead he adores his camera—and himself. He is impressed, not by what he sees, nor by the forms that can be made or found. Rather by the extreme and ever-growing cleverness of his way of seeing it. Fidgeting with his camera, he becomes less concerned with what is out there. Photography, as practiced by the millions of do-it-yourself photographers, is not, oddly enough, a way of producing images with a life of their own detached from their maker (which, as T. S. Eliot observes, is a true characteristic of a work of art). Instead photography becomes a form of narcissism. "Have you seen *my* snapshots of the Mona Lisa?"

Photography, by enabling any mechanically adept amateur to produce a kind of "original"—that is, a unique view of an unrepeatable moment of what was really out there—confuses our sense of what is original and what is a copy of experience. The moment is gone, yet somehow the photograph still lives. By the almost forgotten axiom which once made (but now dissolves) art, the image is again more vivid than the original. We live willy-nilly in a world where every man is his own artist. Using a camera, every man can feel somehow that what he has made is "his" image, even though it has almost nothing of him in it.

X

IN MUSIC, too, the Graphic Revolution has worked its dissolutions. The photographer who enjoys fidgeting with his light meters, filters, and electronic flashes, finally takes a picture of nothing at all: his machinery is his activity. So too the hi-fi addict puts together his precision components—woofers, tweeters, pre-amplifiers, and stereophonic speakers—for their own sake. We are quite precise when we describe him as a devotee of hi-fi rather than of music. In the recorded words of "At the Drop of a Hat" (Michael Flanders and Donald Swann):

> With a tone control at a single touch
> I can make Caruso sound like Hutch,
> I never did care for music much—
> It's the high fidelity!

The addict demonstrates his machinery by records of approaching locomotives, of sneezes, coughs, street sounds, and animal calls. His investment in musical records is only a minute fraction of that in his machinery. Of course, this is all obvious.

It is not only, however, in directing attention from the music itself to the machinery of reproduction that the Graphic Revolution has had its effect. In quite another way the new means of reproducing music have dissolved the form of particular musical works.

Until very recently, every performance was unique. Skilled musicians had to be gathered, they had to practice together. Before the invention of the phonograph in 1877 a performance could be heard only if offered by live artists. It was impossible ever to reproduce precisely any particular performance. In the long run, the phonograph had a revolutionary effect, not only on the number of people who could enjoy music, but on the very nature of everybody's musical experience. Thomas A. Edison first perfected the cylindrical wax record in 1888. Within a half century Americans were buying records as casually as they bought books or magazines. Recent American dictionaries define "best seller" as peculiarly applicable to records as well as books. In a single year at the end of World War II over 225,000,000 records were sold. This demand had been created in part by rapid improvements in the techniques of sound reproduction. Until 1924 commercial records were made by the "acoustical" process: sound vibrations were directly inscribed on the disc without intervention of electrical amplifying devices. Record surfaces were scratchy, and all sounds were distorted. After the development of radio, the electric microphone, and high-fidelity electrical transcripts, home hi-fi systems well within a middle-class budget could give out sounds hard to distinguish from those of the original instruments.

An obvious consequence in our musical experience has been to confuse the relationship here, too, between the "original" and its "copy," between the script and the performance. Of course the relationship between a novel and a movie that has been made from the novel is very different from that between the printed musical score and the phonograph recording made from it. But a comparable new confusion has appeared in the American experience. The phonograph record of a composition has become more widely accessible, and is vivid to a far greater number of people, than the musical notations from which it is made or than scattered live performances. People begin, then, to think of certain recordings, say by Leopold Stokowski, which they can play over and over again in their own homes, as being themselves somehow the true "originals," by which other performances of a Beethoven or Brahms symphony are to be judged. The image of Stokowski overshadows the ideal of Beethoven. This inevitably becomes the case among the new music-listening masses of unmusical amateurs. Even though live symphonic performances by orchestras still are very special occasions, a mere flick of the switch brings the recorded symphony into our living rooms. Recording technique itself becomes an art. It is said that some of Stokowski's great influence on listeners of his era was due to his willingness to work closely with engineers to make a product which, mechanically speaking, would be a good recording.

Some professional devotees, like Paul S. Carpenter, have lamented the decline of those whom they call "first-hand consumers" of new music (that is, those who use the composer's notation to perform the music themselves) at the same time that the number of "secondhand consumers" (that is, auditors) through phonograph, radio, and television has vastly increased. Today it is generally more expensive to print a piece of music on paper in musical notation than to put it on records. The record-buying public is, of course, many times the size of the market for printed music (other than popular song sheets). And the record market has been constantly increasing. It is obviously misleading, however, to call the printed notation of music (grasped through the eye) "firsthand" and to stigmatize the recording of an actual performance (grasped through the ear) as "secondhand." The question is much more complicated than that. Our new confusion comes, rather, from the fact that, since the Graphic Revolution, the very notion of an "original" or of a "performance" of music has been transformed.

The phonograph record, in one way at least, does to the musical performance what the motion picture does to the dramatic performance: it makes it infinitely and precisely and conveniently repeatable. But in order to make this product, the wholeness and spontaneity of the actor's or the musician's performance may be shattered. The movie actor in the studio may re-enact a scene a dozen times so that the director or film editor can select the best "take," then to be pieced together with others similarly filmed. The actor himself engaged in this piecemeal repetition finds it difficult to keep his sense of the whole. "The performance" (which exists now only metaphorically) is no longer a unique, spontaneous experience even for the actor. So, too, with the musical performer. For recordings also can be edited. Neither the film actor nor the recording musical performer then does his work in the physical presence and under the responsive stimulus of an audience. Filmed and recorded performances themselves become a species of pseudo-event, with all the attendant characteristics and overshadowing powers of other pseudo-events. The dubbed-in laughter and applause on taped television shows are only the crudest example of the new pseudo-eventfulness which plagues actor and audience alike. Can we any longer speak so confidently of the "original"? Music, like drama and almost all other experience, now reaches us in a new limbo—floating somewhere between the form and the performance.

We have come a long way from the time when music was heard only on unique, formal occasions. When people heard music in concerts by live artists they expected the music itself to make the atmosphere. The event *was* the music. In a concert hall they listened to hear precisely what the composer or the performer had to offer at that particular moment. At home they listened while they themselves, a member of the family, or a friend sang or played an instrument. Nowadays, of course, we still have our occasional home concerts and special performances by particular artists in concert halls and auditoriums. Many of us play instruments. But this is no longer the commonest way music reaches us. Far commoner is the sound from the car radio as we drive along; or from the AM-FM radio while we cook a meal, wash the dishes, or work in our basement; or from the automatic-record-playing hi-fi as we play cards, read a book, or make conversation. A normal feature of upper-middle-class domestic architecture today is the hi-fi radio-phonograph system with a speaker in every room. We are music-soothed and music-encompassed as we go about our business. Now the appropriate music for any occasion is that which need not be followed but can simply be inhaled.

Music, in a word, ceases to be primarily something which comes in individual compositions, each with a form all its own. Instead it becomes an endless homogeneous stream. It is usually subordinate to something else. When actors become "entertainers," drama is only entertainment, and music, too, is "entertainment." We all want "mood music." In the actual titles of a new record series: "Music to Relax By," "Music for Lovers," "Music to Dine By," "Music to Read By," etc., etc. There has grown up a flourishing business which pipes music into offices, factories, and public places. Music has taken its place somewhere between engineering and interior decoration: alongside air conditioning, sound-proof ceilings, indirect lighting, and contour chairs.

The Muzak Company, which became a large business operation between 1940 and 1960, is a spectacular example of these developments. In the early 1930's a scheme was developed for using telephone circuits to pipe music into places which leased the Muzak service. By the mid 1950's "functional" background music could be heard, among other places, in Yankee Stadium, Fenway Park, Slenderella reducing salons, cemeteries in Los Angeles and San Angelo (Texas), a Kansas City puppet factory, a Chicago sausage plant, pet hospitals, the vaults of the Federal Reserve banks, an olive-stuffing plant in Cincinnati, a uranium company in Denver, and under water in the swimming pool at Eaton's Motel, Hamilton, Ohio.

In 1957 the Muzak library consisted of 49,000 selections (about 7,500 of which were in use at any one time), each recorded on a 16-inch disk. In the New York office, housed in the large Muzak Building, these selections were combined and made up into groups of three eight-hour reels of magnetic tape, each group comprising a twenty-four-hour sequence. Sets of reels were shipped to the seven different Muzak central offices around the country. Each central office had about twenty franchisers serving subscribers in their own areas. Reels went from one central office to another. When each area had heard the tapes, they were returned to the New York office to be erased and reused. This vast operation, employing a record library valued at ten million dollars, played approximately two hundred million miles of tape per year. Muzak became the world's largest user of telephone line networks. It was conservatively estimated that in one way or another, music by Muzak was being heard by about fifty million Americans daily.

What these millions of Muzak-listeners heard was not, however, a set of musical compositions in the old sense of the word. "We don't sell music," explained Donald O'Neill, who for over twenty years designed and packaged the Muzak tapings in their New York headquarters, "we sell programming. We believe that the best results are attained when you consider the factors of time, environment and activity. Take restaurants, for example. Breakfast programs usually consist of novelty numbers without too much brass. For lunch, we play a lot of ballads with plenty of strings. During dinnertime, the program calls for standards, usually given concert arrangements. Then, after dinner, we begin to speed things up a bit with some pretty lively tunes." Once individual musical items have been dissolved into different programming streams, the proper stream can be prescribed for any desired purpose.

The most satisfactory offering is not any series of separate, well-rounded musical dramas. These would be too apt to distract the hearer from his main concern, which in each of these cases is anything but the music. The object is instead to bathe an already half-conscious patient in an anesthetic or a tonic aural fluid. In factories or offices, for example, as Mr. O'Neill has explained, the stream must "go counter to the industrial fatigue curve. When the employee shows up in the morning he's usually in good spirits, and, accordingly, the music is relatively calm. By ten-thirty he's getting a little tired and feels a bit of tension, so we hit him with something that will give him a lift. Around noontime he's looking forward to lunch, which calls for melodies in a more relaxed mood. Then toward the middle of the afternoon, fatigue is likely to set in again, and once more we pep him up with something rhythmic, usually with an even stronger beat than in the morning. That's what we call programming. . . . We always have to be careful that arrangements aren't too intrusive. After all, this is basically music to hear, not to listen to."

The desirable effects on selling or production seem pretty well demonstrated. The proprietor of a Long Island supermarket who had installed Muzak reported that most of his customers "said it made the time go faster. Funny thing, though, we now find they spend more time here since we put in the music than before." During World War II, Muzak developed a music-for-industry program which was approved by the War Production Board. After the war, despite growing competition, Muzak steadily expanded. In some places, say in offices, Muzak alternated fifteen-minute periods of music with similar periods of silence, to prevent possible irritation from a steady stream of sound. Such periods were, of course, dictated by functional considerations or by the clock, not by the length of any individual composition.

Muzak has always looked for new ways of dissolving old musical units. "The point is," Mr. O'Neill once explained, "we just can't let ourselves get into a rut. A short while back we were looking for a type of music that would sound classical to people who like popular music and popular to people who prefer the classics. So we decided to record themes from movies—*Lydia, Blythe Spirit*—music like that. We received a lot of favorable response."

With the growing use of Muzak and other piped-in systems of musical programming, with juke-boxes and the universal installation of hi-fi systems in bars, restaurants, railroad stations, railroad trains, airports, airplanes, and shops, it becomes ever harder to avoid the flood of musical pseudo-events, the sounds which do not say what they seem to, but are only vehicles for personal moods and commercial images. In 1949 the management of Grand Central Terminal in New York installed a small broadcasting studio and eighty-two loudspeakers to flood with canned music and commercials the half-million commuters who daily passed through the station. Exasperated commuters appealed to the New York Public Service Commission. A psychiatrist, testifying for the Terminal management, declared that no normal person would be permanently harmed by the noise. Harold Ross, editor of *The New Yorker,* testifying for the commuters, confessed that he was thinking of having an eardrum punctured; a woman commuter vowed to protect herself by growing "earlids." After these protests, broadcasting in the Terminal stopped for a time. Perhaps some mid-twentieth-century Edison will develop for installation in public places a device by which a person who inserts a dime can purchase (or have piped in) a few minutes of silence. Then we could be comforted that, in this branch of technology at least, no further improvement would be possible.

XI

THE GRAPHIC REVOLUTION has produced a new fluidity in all experience. We are not quite clear where the air conditioning ends and where the Muzak begins. They flow into each other. The forms of books and magazines and dramatic offerings merge. "Through the pages of *McCall's,*" reads a full-page advertisement in *The New York Times* (August 18, 1960), "pass the most exciting books of our time." "Read any good books lately?" it asks. And answers by naming twenty-one books that had gone from pre-publication in *McCall's* to best-sellerdom. Three quarters of these were the ghostwritten lives of celebrities—what should more accurately have been called "non-books."

The more different forms it becomes possible to cast any work into, the more vague and wraithlike become all the forms. Is a hardcover book simply an unhatched paperback? Or rather is a paperback a hardcover book that has not yet grown a shell? "Do you know *War and Peace?*" "Yes." "Did you like it?" "Yes, pretty much." "Which, the movie or the book?" Was it the *un*abridged original (the negative is significant)?—or the "definitive modern abridgment"? Nobody is quite clear. Was it the 1931 or the 1961 version of *Cimmaron?* The "original" may mean the motion picture, the novel, the comic book (*Prince Valiant* and many other movies have derived from comics), the magazine article, the musical score, the phonograph record, the radio program, or the television show.

Not long ago I approached one of the best publishers in the country with a proposal for a book. The book I outlined, it seemed to me, was much needed. The climax of the publisher's consideration of my proposal was a conference in the firm's board room with several vice presidents and the heads of numerous departments. As we went around the table, the chiefs of different divisions debated whether the book could be taken apart and marketed in different pieces. Could it be made into an "Executive Gift"? Could it be made into pamphlets and sold separately, chapter by chapter? Could it be printed piecemeal on the back of maps? Could it be marketed as a premium for a mail order house? No one asked whether it could be shredded into a marketable breakfast food. We hardly discussed the need for the book itself, and that came to seem beside the point.

Multiplication of forms and improvements of technology inevitably make all experience a commodity. When the entertainment comes packaged in film, the movie-house owner need not know anything about drama. All he needs to know is what will sell. The rise of the paperback has made it unnecessary for the retailer to know about books. Most are marketed with newspapers, magazines, hair tonic, and canned foods. Advances in the merchandising of records now make it impossible for the customer to try before he buys. He had better buy a best seller or a nationally advertised brand. Yet the marketer of recorded music himself usually knows very little about music. Like the tour agent, who seldom knows where he is sending you (and need not know, when he can sell you a tour package), the record merchant need not know his music. To stay in business he need know only which music packages sell. All he sees is the package. The record package becomes more like that of the paperback, with lurid, full-color photographs on coated paper.

When the same theme can be put in so many different ways, and each way is a path to millions of viewers or readers or hearers, the pressures to repeat what has already proved successful become almost overwhelming. Much of modern publishing—whether of books, movies, television shows, or music—can be described as a reviewer once characterized the pat formula used by a successful imitator of Sir Walter Scott, whose novels were for a while outselling those of Scott himself. "For the last ten years, he has been repeating his own repetitions, and echoing his own echoes. His first novel was a shot that went through the target, and he has ever since been assiduously firing through the hole." The successful dealer in literary, dramatic, and musical commodities is one who discovers a formula for the public wants, and then varies the formula just enough to sell each new product but not enough to risk loss of the market. The artistic standards of the new multiform world of pseudo-events are best summarized, "A best seller is a best seller is a best seller." And which of us does not want to write (or at least to read) a best seller?

Wherever we turn we see the mirror, and in it (though we like to pretend we are seeing somebody else) we see ourselves. The most successful magazine is the digest which gives us not what is really in the other magazines, but what we already see (or think we see, or would like to think we see). The sure-fire successful movie or book—*Ben Hur, Spartacus,* a novel by Frank Yerby, Thomas B. Costain, Mary Roberts Rinehart or Micky Spillane—is apt to be the best mixture to the proved formula, a formula we have made for ourselves. Movies and books mirror each other. Both give us the fantastic, unreal image that we wish to believe of ourselves. Music becomes a mirror of moods. Experience becomes little more than interior decoration.

5

From Ideal to Image:

The Search for Self-Fulfilling

Prophecies

"You buy belief when you buy The Bulletin!'
ADVERTISEMENT FOR
THE PHILADELPHIA BULLETIN

TEMPTED, like no generation before us, to believe we can fabricate our experience—our news, our celebrities, our adventures, and our art forms—we finally believe we can make the very yardstick by which all these are to be measured. That we can make our very ideals. This is the climax of our extravagant expectations. It is expressed in a universal shift in our American way of speaking: from talk about "ideals" to talk about "images."

The Bible tells us that "God created man in his own image." Until recently skeptics titillated us by reversing the metaphor. "If God made us in his own image," observed Voltaire, "we have certainly returned the compliment." Dostoyevsky said, more profoundly, that it was the devil that man had created in his own likeness. But the God of the American Founding Fathers, whatever other qualities he might have had, was a constitutional monarch. He ruled by laws which he was not free to change at his whim. He had not yet become a chairman of the board, ruling under a policy-directive approved by and in the interest of the citizen-stockholders.

"The Laws of Nature and of Nature's God" governed an orderly universe. For neither God nor man was the world wholly plastic. But more recently, just as "adventure" has become a name for the unexpectedness we plan for ourselves (or pay others to plan for us), so we have emptied the word "value." We have moved away from a traditional meaning, found in older dictionaries: "Value. . . . *Ethics*. That which is worthy of esteem for its own sake; that which has intrinsic worth." Toward a newer and modern American meaning: "Value. . . . *pl*. in *sociology*, acts, customs, institutions, etc. regarded in a particular, especially favorable, way by a people, ethnic group, etc." Our new social scientists speak of "values" all the time. By it they mean the peculiar standards which a society has made for itself. By it they reassure us that we need not worry over the dissolution of ideals, since all ideals are obsolete. The most "civilized" peoples, in fact, are those who know they are guided by values of their own making.

Yet for most of our history we have believed ourselves a nation guided by ideals. Ideals given us by tradition, by reason, or by God. "Ideals are like stars," observed Carl Schurz on April 18, 1859, the anniversary eve of Lexington and Concord; "you will not succeed in touching them with your hands. But like the seafaring man on the desert of waters, you choose them as your guides, and following them will reach your destiny."

In nineteenth-century America the most extreme modernism held that man was made by his environment. In twentieth-century America, without abandoning belief that we are made by our environment, we also believe our environment can be made almost wholly by us. This is the appealing contradiction at the heart of our passion for pseudo-events: for made news, synthetic heroes, prefabricated tourist attrac-

tions, homogenized interchangeable forms of art and literature (where there are no "originals," but only the shadows
we make of other shadows). We believe we can fill our experience with new-fangled content. Almost everything we see
and hear and do persuades us that this power is ours. The life
in America which I have described is a spectator sport in
which we ourselves make the props and are the sole performers.

But to what end? How surprising if men who make their
environment and fill experience with whatever they please
could not also make their God! God himself becomes a
pseudo-event with all the familiar characteristics. He is not
spontaneous or self-created. He has been planned or planted
—primarily for the desirable effects of having him reported
and believed in. He is to be viewed like a television show
only at our convenience. His power can be measured by how
widely he is reported, how often he is spoken about. His relation to underlying reality is ambiguous. As with other pseudo-
events, about God, too, the most interesting question for us is
not what he does but whether he exists. We worry over his
prestige. By creating him we intend him to be a self-fulfilling
prophecy. He is the Celebrity-Author of the World's Best
Seller. We have made God into the biggest celebrity of all, to
contain our own emptiness. He is The Greatest of "the
greatest." What preoccupies us, then, is not God as a fact of
nature, but as a fabrication useful for a God-fearing society.
God himself becomes not a power but an image.

I

Now the language of images is everywhere. Everywhere it
has displaced the language of ideals. If the right "image"
will elect a President or sell an automobile, a religion, a cigarette, or a suit of clothes, why can it not make America herself—or the American Way of Life—a salable commodity
all over the earth? In discussing ourselves, our communities,

our corporations, our nation, our leaders, ourselves, we talk the language of images. In the minister's study and the professor's seminar room as well as in advertising offices and on street corners.

When the distinguished scientists and educators on the Science Advisory Committee reported to President Eisenhower on November 19, 1960, they criticized universities for making an artificial division between research and teaching. What was essential, they urged, was "that the environment as a whole should be an environment of learning, investigation, and teaching—all together. Only too often the universities fail to understand and support this image of their nature."

This devious, circumlocutory way of talking has become common. We do not even notice it. In an earlier age critics would have objected simply that universities failed to pursue this ideal or that ideal. But today universities, like other institutions—in fact like everybody—are judged by whether they fit into a well-tailored "image" of themselves.

Some characteristics of the image can be suggested by our use of the "corporate image." This is, of course, the most elaborately and expensively contrived of the images of our age. In a series of lectures on effective advertising at a recent meeting of the American Management Association (New York City, October 27, 1960), Mr. Mack Hanan, managing partner in Hanan & Son, discussed the problem of building a corporate image. He warned of the dangers of building a "positive corporate image." This might do a firm more harm than good. By its very nature, he explained, no positive image can be all things to all of a corporation's publics. The sharper and more precise the image, the more likely it will accommodate only certain subsections of the corporate publics while isolating others. He mentioned a corporation that had the image of being totally efficient but completely dehumanized. "A dehumanized image discourages present employees, warns off prospective employees and executive recruiters and may even dissuade certain discerning groups of investors." He then offered an escape from these "perils of positivism."

What he urged was a "neutral corporate image." This, he said, was not to be equated with a wishy-washy, vague, or unplanned image. "It is, instead, open-ended. It allows the various corporate publics to be drawn into the corporate picture. . . . A neutral corporate image is an invitation to management's public for a suspension of their critical judgment. Middle-of-the-road as it is, the neutral image attracts all but the marginal fringe groups at either attitudinal extreme. But because it is impartial, it repels none."

This interesting advice presupposes certain familiar characteristics in a corporate image. They are clues to all the image-thinking of our time. What the pseudo-event is in the world of fact, the image is in the world of value. The image is a pseudo-ideal. As we shall see, it is synthetic, believable, passive, vivid, simplified, and ambiguous.

(1) *An image is synthetic.* It is planned: created especially to serve a purpose, to make a certain kind of impression.

Older and more obvious illustrations are the trademark and the brand name, both of which have become increasingly important in this century. A trademark (intended to become a standard for judging all products of a certain kind) is a legally protected set of letters, a picture, or a design, identifying a particular product. Because trademarks and many of the other images flooding our experiences are, like most other pseudo-events, expensive to produce, someone always has an interest in disseminating, re-enforcing, and exploiting them. Unlike other standards, they can be owned. To keep them legally valid as trademarks, the owner must constantly reassert his ownership.

It was by elaborate design that the cumbersome name "International Business Machines Corporation" was made in the public mind into "IBM." This is probably the most expensive and most valuable abbreviation in history. Under the creative direction of Eliot Noyes and a design group consisting of Paul Rand, Charles Eames, and George Nelson, the firm developed its streamlined trademark, to project a "clean, impressive" image. Nowadays a trademark is seldom a simple by-product of other activities. It is not merely the name, initials, or signature of the maker or owner, or a hallmark assigned by a guild. Usually it is produced by specialists.

But the images which fill our experience are not only the few letters, the simplified picture, or the catchy slogan. They are not merely "IBM," "USS" staggered in a circle (for United States Steel Corporation), the graceful cursive "Coca-Cola." They are not merely "His Master's Voice" (the dog listening quizzically at the horn of a primitive phonograph), "Time to Re-tire," (a yawning infant wearing Dr. Denton pajamas and holding a candle), "Rock of Gibraltar" (Prudential Insurance Company), a Benjamin Franklin medallion (*Saturday Evening Post*), a sleek, speeding greyhound (Greyhound Buses). Nor are they merely memorable slogans: "All the News That's Fit to Print," "I'd Walk a Mile for a Camel," "The Beer That Made Milwaukee Famous," "When It Rains It Pours," "Breakfast of Champions," "Man of Distinction," "57 Varieties," "Milk From Contented Cows," "Hasn't Scratched Yet," "Don't Write—Telegraph," "Keep That Schoolgirl Complexion," "Say It With Flowers," "Next to Myself I Like B.V.D.'s Best," "Winston Tastes Good Like a Cigarette Should," etc. etc.

While all these uses of the image have become more important with each decade of the twentieth century, a more abstract kind of image is the peculiar product of our age. Its tyranny is pervasive. An image in this sense is not simply a trademark, a design, a slogan, or an easily remembered picture. It is a studiously crafted personality profile of an individual, institution, corporation, product, or service. It is a value-caricature, shaped in three dimensions, of synthetic materials. Such images in ever increasing numbers have been fabricated and re-enforced by the new techniques of the Graphic Revolution.

When we use the word "image" in this new sense, we plainly confess a distinction between what we see and what is really there, and we express our preferred interest in what is to be seen. Thus an image is a visible public "personality" as distinguished from an inward private "character." "Public" goes with "image" as naturally as with "interest" or "opinion." The overshadowing image, we readily admit, covers up whatever may really be there. By our very use of the term we imply that something can be done to it: the image can always be more or less successfully synthesized, doctored, repaired, refurbished, and improved, quite apart from (though not entirely independent of) the spontaneous original of which the image is a public portrait.

Examples could be multiplied. Systematically collected, they would be nothing less than an encyclopedia of the most vivid figments among which we live. A few examples will suggest the pervasiveness of image-thinking. Such a headline as "President Striving to Develop Public Image" (Kalamazoo *Gazette,* February 20, 1961) is common in our daily papers. "Goldwater Attempting to Shape a Popular Conservative Image," topped a front page story of *The New York Times* (January 16, 1961) showing a photograph of the Senator. There Senator Goldwater amplified his intention "to make sure the image of conservatism is not an obstructive image." "Do you read between the lines?" asked an advertisement for the S. D. Warren Paper Company. "Your customers certainly do. When a hi-fi enthusiast studies your catalog, he sees more than just text and pictures. Unconsciously he is reading between the lines for evidence of your company's character. He looks for the quality image that only a good printer can help you achieve." The pamphlet *Admission to Harvard College* (1960), a printed report by a special committee on college admission policy of the Harvard Faculty of Arts and Sciences, talks the same language. It devotes a special section to the "public image" of Harvard, recommending that Harvard undertake "a careful investigation of its public image or images." The committee urges "a much more systematic study of the public image question than the time and resources available to this committee would permit. The committee believes that such a study should be launched by the University, with all the thoroughness and sophistication of research technique it obviously deserves." Everywhere we meet the implication that if an image is damaging or unacceptable, it can and should be repaired.

(2) *An image is believable*. It serves no purpose if people do not believe it. In their own minds they must make it stand for the institution or the person imaged. Yet if an image is to be vivid and to succeed popularly in overshadowing its original, it must not outrage the ordinary rules of common sense. It would be a mistake, then, for Harvard College to claim that it selected its whole student body without any regard to family antecedents, alumni associations, or financial connections; no one would believe it. The most effective images are usually those which have been especially doctored for believability. One of the best paths to believability is understatement. "Ask the man who owns one." In the words of the great public relations genius of American higher education in this century, The University of Chicago was "not a very good university . . . simply the best there is." Ivory Soap is "99.44% pure." A prudent advertiser or master of public relations takes advantage of the increasingly reckless use of superlatives to make his own hyperbole seem a conservative truth.

(3) *An image is passive*. Since the image is already supposed to be congruent with reality, the producer of the image (namely, the corporation) is expected to fit into the image —rather than to strive toward it. The consumer of the image (namely, the viewer of the corporate image: a potential client or customer) is also supposed somehow to fit into it. All these relations are essentially passive. The real effort in relation to an image is not by the corporation as a whole, but by the experts and executives who have made the image and who are its chief custodians. The "projection" of an image is itself a way of touting reputed virtues. Both subject and object then will want to fit into the picture. Both will assume that a portrait so persuasive and so popular must be made from life. Once the image is there, it commonly becomes the

more important reality, of which the corporation's conduct seems mere evidence; not vice versa. In the beginning the image is a likeness of the corporation; finally the corporation becomes a likeness of the image. The image (unlike actual conduct) can be perfect. It can be a precise pattern which will satisfy everybody.

When the Container Corporation of America decided (according to one reporter) "to make itself known as a company both tasteful, resourceful, and design-conscious," this decision might have been made simply enough in the minds and inner councils of its executives. Such an ideal had all along existed and could have been privately pursued. Traditionally, such inward-dwelling convictions were those considered most real and most effective. But now this is not enough.

An image is the kind of ideal which becomes real only when it has become public. A corporation which decides to rebuild its image has decided less on a change of heart than on a change of face. The face-lifting operation can usually be done for hire, by the new professions of plastic surgeons and cosmetic experts. The Container Corporation redesigned everything from its checks to its delivery trucks. It sponsored a major advertising campaign featuring "Great Ideas of Western Man," embellished by reproductions of works by modern painters. In the jargon, Container Corporation was not "pursuing an ideal." It was "constructing an image." Once the image was constructed, the object was to make the corporation, its products, and, hopefully, its customers, all fit neatly into the picture.

Because an image is essentially passive, it need have very little to do with the activities of the corporation itself. In old-fashioned language, image building is the building of reputations, not of characters. When, for example, Daniel J. Edelman & Associates of Chicago undertook a "corporate image job" for Brunswick Corporation, the object, as a business journalist put it, was "to build an image of Brunswick as a company on the go—no longer merely a 115-year-old bowling equipment outfit, but an increasingly diversified company." Edelman's spectacular success, widely admired in public relations circles, was accomplished by offering a shrewdly selected range of stories—items of pseudo-events —each well suited to the interests of a particular newspaper or magazine. *Fortune* was given a personality piece on the president of the corporation, who was depicted as a sports- man turned business genius, and another piece on the sudden emergence of a smaller corporation as a giant; the Asso- ciated Press columnist was handed an item on how bowling had become a billion-dollar business; *The New York Times* received a more sober biographical feature; in the *Wall Street Journal* was placed a story on the boom in the school equipment industry (tied to a convention of the American Association of School Administrators); for *Life* Edelman planned the photogenic stunt of completely modernizing a classroom, with Brunswick school furniture, in a single week- end. Each of these was another brush-stroke in the painting of the image. Meanwhile, the company itself, of course, had to do nothing more than go about its business, avoiding scan- dals or any public information that might discredit the image.

Sometimes the image build-up is concentrated on the chief executive rather than on the corporation itself. Ben- jamin Sonnenberg built up an image of Charles Luckman (then president of Lever Brothers) as a supersalesman genius; the effort here was by Sonnenberg, not by Luckman, much less by the corporation as a whole. It was necessary for Luckman to do very little except not break the image. A build-up of Benjamin Fairless (then president of United States Steel Corporation) was accomplished in similar fash- ion. Perhaps most important were the speeches he gave. The decisive one of these, an attack in 1950 on "jugglers in Con- gress attempting to alter U.S. business economics," was writ- ten by Phelps H. Adams, who had come from the New York *Sun*'s Washington Bureau. This success in building up Fair- less helped make Adams a vice president for public rela- tions. The build-up of Charles Percy, the imaginative and energetic head of Bell & Howell (by features in *Life* and elsewhere) has shaped the image of his company.

When the Standard Oil Company of New Jersey took over the New York television program "Play of the Week" ($600,-000 for a thirteen-week sponsorship; later to be considered a bargain in image building), it was building its image as a public-serving corporation. The production of plays, of course, had nothing to do with the production of oil. In an age when the average consumer has only the vaguest notion of the actual activities of a vast, complex corporation, the public image of the corporation substitutes for more specific or more circumstantial notions of what is actually going on. Most corporations today, like most scientists, operate on unintelligible frontiers. Institutional advertising—which, for example, makes us think of the Du Pont Corporation no longer as "Merchants of Death," but as making "Better Things for Better Living through Chemistry"—is a form of corporate celebrity building. Far from being resentful, we are usually grateful for the image. It is a concrete, graspable picture, taking the place of our amorphous notions.

As consumers, too, we can similarly be persuaded to buy. When Edward Gottlieb & Associates undertook to promote cognac (and actually succeeded in tripling its sales), they did it by creating images. They distributed cognac free at gourmet dinners, to food editors, to TV cooking programs, and to the White House, where its use would be photographed and reported. When Communications Counselors Inc. took an assignment from the Millinery Institute of America, they gave elegant hats free to fashion models, fashion editors, movie stars, TV performers, and society celebrities. Marilyn Monroe and Mamie Eisenhower, wearing hats, were photographed for national magazines. Hat sales soon showed the profitable effect of people wanting to fit themselves into the picture.

Amidst lamentation of the rise of conformity in American life, it has seldom been noticed that to "conform" now commonly means to fit into an image. Since the Graphic Revolution the multiplying and vivifying of images has provided the new molds within which the new conformity becomes possible. In England, where the word "conform" had long been in use, it was primarily a transitive verb meaning "to form according to some model"; in the intransitive sense (to say simply, "he conforms") it meant primarily to comply with the usages of the Church of England. In twentieth-century America the word has acquired a new meaning. Commonly nowadays when we say "he conforms" or when we talk of "conformity," we usually mention no explicit object. This is because now there is always an object implied. We mean he is trying to fit into an image. "Conformity" is one of the most characteristic words of our age. Its widespread use is, I suspect, an unconscious, inevitable by-product of the rise (and the passivity) of images. Images themselves are invitations to conformity.

The passivity of conformity is the passivity of fitting into images. The prevalence of images makes possible the prevalence of conformity. Before the age of images, it was commoner to think of a conventional person as one who strove for an ideal of decency or respectability, or who simply wished to avoid being conspicuous. Since the Graphic Revolution we think of him as a "conformist"—one who tries to fit into the images found vividly all around him. In our world of pseudo-events, synthesized images take the place of external standards.

We have become thoroughly accustomed to the use of images as invitations to behavior. There was a time when if you wanted a lady to buy a hat you would ask her to do so, or if you wanted a man to buy cognac you would describe the virtues of your cognac. Now the persuasion is more indirect. The widely observed decline of salesmanship may be explained in part by the ways in which the Graphic Revolution has made the hypnotic appeal of the image take the place of the persuasive appeal of argument. Why be a salesman when a well-presented product is one which itself draws the consumer into the picture? Products have become props for images into which the seller confidently assumes we will try to fit ourselves.

(4) *An image is vivid and concrete.* It often serves its purpose best by appealing to the senses. "The Skin You Love to Touch." The Old Dutch Cleanser girl with upraised stick ("Chases Dirt"). The bearded cough-drop Smith Brothers. The Arrow Collar Man. "Man of Distinction." The image is limited. It must be more graspable than any specific list of objectives. It is not enough if the product, the man, or the institution has many good qualities appropriate to it. One or a few must be selected for vivid portrayal.

(5) *An image is simplified.* In order to exclude undesired and undesirable aspects, an image must be simpler than the object it represents. "This strong, vigorous symbol, with its four sections bordering a square center," The Chase Manhattan Bank explains, "is indicative of our Bank's character and diversity." "When people just see those initials, IBM, the mechanism is triggered. In a flash the entire corporate image is etched on the mind." An effective image has the capacity to become hackneyed. Yet it loses its imagic power as soon as it passes into the language. Then it has become a word in place of a pseudo-event. We have then forgotten that it was contrived on purpose by certain people for specific ends. The maker of an image wishes to hear it on every tongue. Yet when everybody uses it for his own purposes, it loses its pseudo-eventful quality and ceases to serve its original purpose. This happened to "aspirin," "mimeograph," "cellophane," and "linoleum," and has almost happened to Kodak, Technicolor, Band-aid, and Kleenex. The most effective image is one simple and distinctive enough to be remembered, yet not so handy as to seem the natural symbol for the whole class of objects it describes.

(6) *An image is ambiguous.* It floats somewhere between the imagination and the senses, between expectation and reality. In another way, too, it is ambiguous, for it must not offend. It must suit unpredictable future purposes, and unpredicted changes in taste. Many such changes may have

taken place before the image can be remade to contain them. It must be a receptacle for the wishes of different people. Seldom is this so plainly acknowledged as in the recent program by Pincus Brothers Maxwell, clothing manufacturers of Philadelphia. They advertise their new brand of men's suits, not by a sharply focused photograph, but by a blur standing on the street. "The agency, Zlowe Co., New York," *Printers' Ink* explained (January 20, 1961), "came up with a campaign that discards the fashion plate for personal image. Based on deliberately blurred reflection photography, the illustration is supposed to sell the man through a vague but attractive image he has of himself." Early in 1961 Volkswagen ran a series of advertisements entitled "The experimental X-93 Volkswagen" below a blurry full-page photograph of an automobile. The fuzzy outlines were designed to make it easier for the viewer to see whatever he wished to see. In advertising, as in painting, the non-representational technique is apt to become more popular, to give the viewer ample scope for his unpredictable but always exaggerating expectations.

*   *   *   *   *

Strictly speaking, there is no way to unmask an image. An image, like any other pseudo-event, becomes all the more interesting with our every effort to debunk it. For this reason, some of the most effective advertising nowadays consists of circumstantial descriptions of how the advertising images were contrived: how tests were devised, how trademarks were designed, and how the corporate cosmetics were applied. The stage machinery, the processes of fabricating and projecting the image, fascinate us. We are all interested in watching a skillful feat of magic; we are still more interested in looking behind the scenes and seeing precisely how it was made to seem that the lady was sawed in half. The everyday images which flood our experience have this advantage over the tricks of magic: even after we have been taken behind the scenes, we can still enjoy the pleasures of deception.

Paradoxically, too, the more we know about the tricks of image building, about the calculation, ingenuity, and effort that have gone into a particular image, the more satisfaction we have from the image itself. The elaborate contrivance proves to us that we are really justified (and not stupid either) in being taken in.

On a trip to Washington, I found in the usual travel kit at my airplane seat a copy of *Voyager: Capital's Magazine for Air Travelers* (May-June, 1960). A leading article, "Memory Triggers," recounted the effort that Capital Airlines (which issues the magazine) had spent in devising a new corporate image. "The planning for Capital's new corporate image began almost two years ago," an Editor's Note explained, "when the company undertook a thorough evaluation of its public identity." Numerous firms were considered for the project, and finally, in July, 1959, Lippincott and Margulies, Inc., was assigned the task. I was taken behind the scenes. I was expected to think well of Capital Airlines, not only because the service was good, but equally because so much effort had gone into making an image skillfully designed to impress me favorably:

> The trade-mark is a kind of shorthand symbol for a corporation. It is a memory trigger. If it is a good one, it can in an instant, utilizing conscious and unconscious forces, reflect a corporate image effectively and accurately. That corporate image can be worth tens of millions, perhaps hundreds of millions in sales. . . . trade-marks should be adaptable to all media. . . . visually effective when reduced to the size of a dime. . . . effective when blown up for use on a billboard . . . effective in black and white or in color, on television, on letterheads, on the sides of trucks, on packages or in displays.
>
> A good case in point of the kind of problem faced in this connection is the new Capital Airlines symbol introduced recently. This symbol had to be effective in

the highly competitive environment of the busy airport. . . .

The symbol must have eye-appeal. But at the same time it is important that it reflect the image that the company is trying to create. The IBM symbol, for example, would be totally wrong for Coca-Cola; Olivetti would be equally wrong for Esso. Yet each of these trade-marks is considered an excellent one in its own right.

In the battle for consumer recognition—1,581 messages a family every day—the shorthand message these trade-marks send is still being received.

By being told how the corporation has worked to entice him scientifically, the consumer is reassured that the corporation is really up to date. It cares enough for him to improve its means for attracting him. Thus, in some sense or other, he is not really being deceived at all. This is the first great seduction in history where the seducer's appeal is increased by disclosing his arts.

At a meeting of the American Statistical Association in Chicago on March 15, 1961, Mr. David Karr, President of Fairbanks Whitney Corporation, speaking on "A Case Study in Planning a Corporate Image," described with pride how in 1958 Fairbanks Whitney had taken over the Penn-Texas Corporation, which was then heavily in debt and had a low reputation. The subsidiary corporation was quickly put on a strong financial basis. Then, Mr. Karr explained, "the company's image building program moved forward rapidly." The company's name was changed, and an expensive newspaper advertising campaign was launched. The new company's establishment of a desalting plant at Elath, Israel, was a climax of these efforts, "typical of the importance played by research and development activities in establishing a proper corporate image. . . . Israel, with its injunction to 'make the deserts bloom' dating from biblical times, and Fairbanks Morse, with roots reaching back more than 100 years in the production of pumps and other water handling equipment, were natural partners in the desalting venture." "American industry," Mr. Karr concluded, "is increasingly recognizing the corporate image as a management responsibility equal in importance to finance, operations, and engineering." But, he warned, "an image program must be built on fact, not fantasy, if it is to gain public acceptance."

Fact or fantasy, the image becomes the thing. Its very purpose is to overshadow reality. American life becomes a showcase for images. For frozen pseudo-events.

II

THE PECULIARITIES of the modern image and the consequences of image-thinking appear even clearer by contrast to what has been displaced: thinking in ideals. The English word "image," which comes from the Latin *imago,* is related to the Latin word *imitari,* which means "to imitate." According to common American dictionary definitions, an image is an artificial imitation or representation of the external form of any object, especially of a person.

Images now displace ideals. But an ideal is much more difficult to define. It is, I suppose we would say now, an old-fashioned word and an old-fashioned notion. "Ideal" is related somehow to "idea." Our dictionaries define it as a conception of something in its most excellent or perfect form —something that exists only in the mind.

Differences between "ideal-thinking" and "image-thinking" are the differences between our thinking before and after the Graphic Revolution. An ideal, contrasted to an image, is not synthetic. When we think of an ideal we think of something already there. It was created by tradition, by history, or by God. It is perfect, but it is not simplified. It is not ambiguous (or ambiguous only in a very different sense). Its implications are not passive. An ideal is what we actively strive toward, not what we fit into. Credibility is irrelevant.

Charity, justice, equality, mercy, are no less ideals because no man or society ever lived up to them. Ideals are needed *because* in their perfect form they are somehow hard to believe.

An image is something *we* have a claim on. It must serve our purposes. Images are means. If a corporation's image of itself or a man's image of himself is not useful, it is discarded. Another may fit better. The image is made to order, tailored to us. An ideal, on the other hand, has a claim on us. It does not serve us; we serve it. If we have trouble striving toward it, we assume the matter is with us, and not with the ideal.

During the last century great historical forces have promoted both the rise of images and the decline of ideals. The Graphic Revolution has multiplied and vivified images. By new machines to make accurate, attractive replicas of face, figure, and voice, of landscape and events, and by new machines to disseminate these images. By newspapers, magazines, cheap books, telephone, telegraph, phonograph, movies, radio, television. The American system of manufacturing, mass production, which originated about a century and a half ago, was based on the revolutionary idea of interchangeable parts. For the first time, every musket or clock or lock would be an image of every other of the same design. Dies and jigs, calipers and machine tools, and thousands of refinements made each item indistinguishable from others of its kind. All this was supported and stimulated by the growth of advertising, by enlarging markets, by competition for markets—in a society where unprecedented numbers could afford to buy.

Advertising flourished, then, from the effort to produce *apparent* distinctions. Competing products were now more precisely similar and more unnoticeably different. This was one explanation of why modern advertising first flowered in the marketing of beers, soaps, and cigarettes. Different brands of these commodities could not readily be distinguished from one another by actual shape or function. Each had to be distinguished, therefore, by being attached to, or rather, "fitted into," a distinctive image. The masters of advertising, men like Albert Lasker, were adept at this. At the same time came the build-up of brand names. The Brand Names Foundation (established in 1943), by 1959 had almost a thousand members—firms manufacturing or promoting nationally advertised products. The Foundation conducted "educational programs" on the benefits and services of brand names and brand advertising. Brand names became household words. They were monuments to American wealth, American democracy, and technological progress in the Age of the Graphic Revolution.

The obvious next step, so recent it has only begun to enter our dictionaries, was from the "Brand Name" to the "Name Brand." The use of "brand" as a synonym for trademark had entered the English language as early as 1827. In American usage the expression "brand name" called attention to the private ownership of a certain trademark, to the fact that one firm alone was authorized so to designate its product. But the much newer expression "name brand" makes the name and not the product the center of attention. This is quite a natural way to distinguish commodities in the age of the celebrity and the best seller.

The fast pace of life and the increasing speed of movement across vast American spaces, well before the beginning of the twentieth century, had begun to put a premium on quickly impressive, attractive images. They were creating a new Iconography of Speed. Competition for attention put a premium on attention-getting. The word "billboard," which was invented in America, had first come in use about 1851, in the early days of the Graphic Revolution. The rise of the automobile, the improvement of highways in the 1920's and '30's, and the consequent vast spread of billboards were new incentives to produce images that could catch the eye in a flash and remain indelibly imprinted on the memory. The very multiplication and the increasing size of newspapers and magazines were incentives. How to produce images that could not be forgotten even if seen only fleetingly as one leafed the pages? Everything pointed to the invention and perfection of inescapable, unforgettable images, drawing the viewer willy-nilly to a salable product.

To broadcast and receive these images, devices multiplied: high-speed presses, photography, vast-circulation magazines, movies, radio, television. In everybody's consciousness, images became important as never before. Man's power to produce graven images exceeded the most diabolical imagination of Biblical times. And while images multiplied and became more vivid, ideals dissolved.

Ideals became "corny." The word "corny," now commonly used to describe the explicit statement of ideals, came into use about 1935. Derived from "corn-fed," it applied to music which was hill-billy or out of date. At first it signified the style of pre-1925, but it became slang (gradually being displaced in the '50's by "square") for any trite, banal, or sentimental expression, and was frequently applied to the most familiar formulations of the naive, homely aspirations of the era before the Graphic Revolution. Strong new currents of thought have carried us farther in this direction. Not only particular ideals, but the very notion of ideals, has become corny.

A whole new vocabulary began to dominate thinking about men's aims and motives. An example is the new use of the word "rationalization" which appeared in the present century. It came to mean the making of superficially plausible or "rational" explanations, which were only excuses for actions or beliefs. Soon it was a catchall label for everybody's habit of justifying his behavior by not talking about his real motives. To attack something as a "rationalization" became a kind of philosophic penicillin—a layman's cure-all for arguments he could not understand or would not take seriously. Under the influence of Karl Marx, in the United States as elsewhere, people came to think philosophies were nothing but smoke screens for economic interests. Our ideals, we were told, were no more than the shibboleths of a retreating bourgeoisie. Sigmund Freud then provided an even subtler apparatus to explain why people did not really believe the reasons they professed. All this spelled the distrust, then the decline of ideals. Intellectuals, even more than others, became apologetic for talking or thinking in ideals. It seemed naive to judge by abstract standards of perfection, rather than by congruence with images.

We reversed traditional ways of thinking about the relation between images and ideals. Instead of thinking that an image was only a representation of an ideal, we came to see the ideal as a projection or generalization of an image. Our ideal father, we were told, was nothing but our projection of our image of our own father—of what he was or what he was not. We came then to distrust the very concept of an ideal, as an abstraction. We distrusted any standard of perfection toward which all people could strive.

Ideals had once given form to the study and the writing of history and to the study of society. American historians had once been preoccupied with ideals. Francis Parkman vividly described the conflict between the ideals of Protestantism and the ideals of Catholicism in the Franco-British struggle for colonial empire in the American forests. George Bancroft saw the struggle for independence and for the Constitution as a struggle for the ideals of liberty, of democracy, and of a new nation. Other students of society focused on other ideals: equality, peace, and justice. But in this century, in America perhaps more than elsewhere, the new social sciences collected statistics and interpreted them in norms, modes, medians, and averages. Vast new accumulations of fact and ingenious applications of mathematics to social data brought new patterns of generalization. These bred a deeper, "fact"-founded, distrust of ideals.

Social scientists no longer focused on the unique event which had fascinated the old humanist-historians. Instead they themselves built up images. These soon dominated the ways in which literate Americans thought about themselves. Americans tried to fit themselves into social science images of the frontier, economic classes, and status. Social scientists built up these images from modal forms. In statistics the "mode" was the most frequently recurring type or form of a phenomenon. The historian conjured up "the frontiersman" (Turner), the "personalty-property owner" (Beard), the status-deprived Progressive reformer (Hofstadter). Sociologists then were able to describe the villager, the suburban housewife (a heroic figure featured on a *Time* cover), the scientist, the small businessman (who lived in Middletown), or the junior executive. Humanist-historians had aimed at individualized portrait. The new social science historians produced group caricature. Through various means of popularization, such caricature became the image into which an individual was expected (and often tried) to fit.

Oversimplified sociological concepts—"status," "otherdirection," etc.—appealed because they were so helpful in building images. These wide-appealing "modes," expressed in our dominating notions of norms and averages, led us unwittingly to try to imitate ourselves. We have tried to discover what it is really like to be a junior executive or a junior executive's wife, so we can really be the way we are supposed to be, that is, the way we already are. Naive emphasis on ideals had at worst tempted men to unrealistic pursuit of an abstract standard of perfection; emphasis on modes and images now tempts us to pursue the phantoms of ourselves.

Every age has its own peculiar circumlocutions that unwittingly show deference to its dominant beliefs. The language of aristocratic ages overflows with terms of rank: milord, milady, goodman, sir, sirrah, etc. Religious ages embroider language with "God be praised!" "God willing!" etc.

Our age similarly betrays its deference to images. Each of us hopes for a pleasing "personality"—and our personality is the attention-getting image of ourselves, our image of our behavior. Each of the Presidential candidates aims, we say, not to improve what the electorate thinks of him, but rather to improve his public image. Stewart L. Udall, Secretary of the Interior in the Kennedy Administration, puzzled people when he came into office in early 1961 by his complex and partly-contradictory objectives—(a) his fierce Democratic partisanship and (b) his determination that the Government encourage writers and artists. The Washington correspondent does not put it that way. Instead, he reports that the Secretary is "creating two contradictory reputations," and the headline reads: "Udall building a Double Image." At their annual meeting in the summer of 1961, doctors of the American Medical Association are reported to be discussing their concern over the A.M.A.'s public image; they urge "the streamlining of organizational machinery to bolster the image." The London correspondent of *The New York Times* explains to us, when Dr. Geoffrey Francis Fisher retires as Archbishop of Canterbury, that he "has served as the chief 'image' of the Anglican Church for sixteen years." Protestantism in America, a minister tells us, is being "badly presented": the image of protestantism is not what it should be.

During the Presidential campaign of 1960 the editors of the Philadelphia *Inquirer* decided to drop the column by Dr. Norman Vincent Peale because of "his approach to the 'so-called religious issue' in this political campaign." They announced on their front page that until then they had regarded Dr. Peale's weekly article "as a non-sectarian feature, strongly inspirational to men and women of all faiths. To our regret Dr. Peale has impaired this public image" (September 13, 1960). When scholars of the American Studies Association prepare a collection of essays asking what Americans think of themselves, they characterize themselves as "students of the American image, in all its variety." A distinguished historian, reviewing their volume, observes that "Americans have attempted to hold on to some cohesive image of their land." Universities, we say, have the wrong "image" of themselves; or the public has an unfortunate "image" of them. The advertising industry itself, we read, is undertaking a program of ads (initiated by Gordon Chelf, publisher of the Philadelphia *Daily News*) directed to the general public "to improve the image of advertising."

The fantastic growth of advertising and public relations together with everybody's increasing reliance on dealers in pseudo-events and images cannot—contrary to highbrow clichés—accurately be described as a growing superficiality. Rather these things express a world where the image, more interesting than its original, has itself become the original. The shadow has become the substance. Advertising men, industrial designers, and packaging engineers are not deceivers of the public. They are simply acolytes of the image. And so are we all. They elaborate the image, not only because the image sells, but also because the image is what people want to buy.

To men unfamiliar with our way of life, our language would seem strangely circumlocutory. A world where people talk constantly not of things themselves, but of their images! Yet it is by these circumlocutions that we unwittingly express our deepest unspoken beliefs. Belief in the malleability of the world. Belief in the superior vividness of a technicolor representation to a drab original. Our language has the look of being indirect. In our age everybody uses the monstrous cliché, "in terms of" this or that. But not without reason. For in our time the old direct statement has become inaccurate, untrue to our experience. When images have become more vivid than originals, it is only natural that we should commonly prefer to speak of the more vivid copy. More important than what we think of the Presidential candidate is what we think of his "public image." We vote for him because his is the kind of public image we want to see in the White House. More important than what a Buick really is, is our image of it. We are sold it and we buy it and enjoy it for its image and how we fit into the image. The language of images, then, is not circumlocution at all. It is the only simple way of describing what dominates our experience.

III

THE MOMENTOUS sign of the rise of image-thinking, and its displacement of ideals is, of course, the rise of advertising. Nothing has been more widely misunderstood. Daring not to admit we may be our own deceivers, we anxiously seek someone to accuse of deceiving us. "Madison Avenue," "Public Relations," "Organization Men," and similar epithets have given us our whipping boys. We refuse to believe that advertising men are at most our collaborators, helping us make illusions for ourselves. In our moral indignation, our eagerness to find the villains who have created and frustrated our exaggerated expectations, we have underestimated the effect of the rise of advertising. We think it has meant an increase of untruthfulness. In fact it has meant a reshaping of our very concept of truth.

Advertising, from its modern American beginnings, was a classic example of the pseudo-event. It was a prototype of "made news." The modern era in American advertising dates from the epoch when advertisements ceased to be repetitive announcements naively describing services or products for sale and, by being contrived and being given the artificial aroma of news, took on the aspect of other pseudo-events. Modern advertising began when the advertisement was no longer a spontaneous announcement and had become "made news." James Gordon Bennett (1795–1872), who founded the New York *Herald* on May 7, 1835, as a one-cent daily paper, and who was one of the pioneers of modern American journalism, inaugurated the new era when he abolished the old "standing ad." Formerly a commercial announcement would be left standing in type; sometimes it ran unaltered for as long as a year at a time. Such standing ads were in fact the rule in the advertising columns of newspapers. Advertising matter of this kind obviously could offer readers little or nothing of newsworthy interest. Wishing to make the advertisements as newsworthy as everything else in his *Herald,* Bennett announced in 1847 that he would take no advertisement for more than two weeks' insertion; then, in 1848, he began the policy of accepting no advertisment for more than one day's insertion. This required advertisers to change their notices daily. Bennett's son, who succeeded him as editor of the *Herald,* showed a similar vigor and ingenuity in devising stunts to advertise the newspaper itself; for example, he sent Stanley to Africa to look for Livingstone (1871).

The news interest in advertisements has increased with the rising American standard of living, the rising level of expectations, and the growing ingenuity of copy writers. Readers enjoy the sense of being courted, they luxuriate in the knowledge that so much money, time, effort, and art have gone into making all these pseudo-events especially for them. The newspaper *PM,* launched on its brief life as a self-righteously "adless" daily in 1940, failed in part because readers missed the advertising news to which they had become accustomed. Statistical studies of reader interest made by the Market Research Foundation, 1940–1950, indicated an increased interest in advertising. Readers seemed to find about as much interest in advertising as in regular news and editorial features. It has become a commonplace of American journalism that the most successful (that is, the most appealing) newspapers and magazines are those with the most advertising. *The Reader's Digest* had long been an exception. But when in November 1954 inflation and mounting costs made Wallace decide to include advertising in order to avoid raising the price of the magazine, *The Digest* promised to print only advertising "of unusually high reader interest." Three years' experience justified *The Digest's* official historian in concluding that "most Americans like advertising. They expect to find it in their magazines. They read it as news. They are conscious of advertising and look to it for excitement and novelty . . . When *The Reader's Digest* began to take advertising in 1955 it added to its value as a complete magazine." This is not merely a way of saying that nothing succeeds like success. It is also a way of saying what has not always and everywhere been true: that the public enjoys an ever greater abundance of advertising "news."

The successful American advertiser knows how to make news. A notorious pioneer was P. T. Barnum (1810–1891), whom advertising textbooks still treat as the first large-scale practitioner of many modern publicity techniques. He was a genius at making pseudo-events, although they were often so crude that they could not titillate us today. He made news even by his attitude toward advertising. "I thoroughly understood the art of advertising," boasted Barnum in his autobiography, "not merely by means of printer's ink, which I have always used freely, and to which I confess myself much indebted for my success, but by turning every possible circumstance to my account." In 1835 he exhibited Joice Heth, an aged Negress whom he advertised as the 161-year-old former nurse of George Washington. For a while he made fifteen hundred dollars a week from her. Showing his mastery of the art of compounding pseudo-events, he then increased his publicity by attacking the whole exhibition as a hoax. "The fact is, Joice Heth is not a human being," he wrote the newspapers, ". . . simply a curiously constructed automaton, made up of whalebone, india-rubber, and numerous springs ingeniously put together and made to move at the slightest touch, according to the will of the operator. The operator is a ventriloquist." An autopsy done at the time of her death indicated that Joice Heth was about eighty years old. Barnum then multiplied publicity by having her buried in his family plot; he wrote a series of articles exposing the fraud and reasserting his own good faith.

In 1841, Barnum managed to buy Scudder's American Museum, a private collection of curiosities exhibited for profit. The museum, once well known and profitable, was then losing money. When Barnum told a friend that he intended to buy the museum (the asking price was $15,000), the friend replied in astonishment, "What do you intend buy-

ing it with?" "Brass," retorted Barnum, "for silver and gold
have I none." He increased and diversified the transient
attractions, exhibiting, according to his own list, "educated
dogs, industrious fleas, automatons, jugglers, ventriloquists,
living statuary, tableaux, gipsies, Albinoes, fat boys, giants,
dwarfs, rope-dancers, live Yankees, pantomime, instrumen-
tal music, singing and dancing in great variety, dioramas,
panoramas, models of Niagara, Dublin, Paris, and Jeru-
salem; Hannington's dioramas of the Creation, the Deluge,
Fairy Grotto, Storm at Sea; the first English Punch and Judy
in this country, Italian Fantoccini, mechanical figures, fancy
glass-blowing, knitting machines, and other triumphs in the
mechanical arts; dissolving views, American Indians who
enacted their warlike and religious ceremonies on the stage—
these, among others, were all exceedingly successful." Barnum's American Museum soon became one of New York's
major tourist attractions.

It was to advertise this museum that he invented his famous "brick man"—a perfect, if somewhat primitive, example of the connection between "pseudo-events" and advertising. Barnum hired a stout, hearty-looking man for $1.50 a
day and handed him five bricks. He instructed the man to lay
one brick at each of four points which Barnum indicated
near the American Museum. The man kept the fifth brick in
his hand and marched rapidly from one brick to another, at
each point exchanging the one in his hand for the one on
the street; he kept this up in a constant circuit. At the end of
every hour, however, the brick man entered the American
Museum, spent fifteen minutes solemnly surveying all the
halls, then left, and resumed his work. Each time, a dozen or
more persons would buy tickets and follow him into the museum hoping to learn the purpose of his movements. Their
entrance fees more than paid the brick man's wages. Additional interest was created when a policeman (who had been
let in on the trick) objected that the crowds were obstructing
traffic, and ordered Barnum to call in his brick man. "This
trivial incident," Barnum recounted, "excited considerable

talk and amusement; it advertised me; and it materially advanced my purpose of making a lively corner near the Museum."

One of Barnum's great successes was his mermaid. A painting outside the museum depicted an attractive half woman, half fish about eight feet long. Illustrated handbills portrayed her capture on a Pacific island. The specimen was said to have been purchased by a Dr. Griffith as agent for the Lyceum of Natural History in London. Barnum had this "Dr. Griffith" (who was in fact a Barnum assistant named Lyman) exhibit it before a large meeting of New York scientists in the Concert Hall. Actually what was being exhibited was only the preserved head of a monkey attached to the dried body of a fish. "The public appeared to be satisfied," Barnum recalled, "but as some persons always *will* take things literally, and make no allowance for poetic license even in mermaids, an occasional visitor, after having seen the large transparency in front of the hall, representing a beautiful creature, half woman and half fish . . . would be slightly surprised to find that the reality was a black-looking specimen of dried monkey and fish that a boy a few years old could easily run away with under his arm." Other Barnum triumphs were General Tom Thumb, a five-year-old dwarf who was less than two feet high and weighed sixteen pounds when he was first displayed on Thanksgiving Day, 1842, and who attracted over a hundred thousand people in the first year; and Jenny Lind, the "Swedish Nightingale" whose real name was Mme. Otto Goldschmidt. She was advertised as being paid a thousand dollars a concert, all of which she supposedly gave to charity. Barnum first opened "The Greatest Show on Earth" in Brooklyn in 1871. There, and on tour, he displayed countless freaks and monstrosities, among them "Jumbo," a large, gentle African Elephant advertised as "The Only Mastodon on Earth."

Contrary to popular belief, Barnum's great discovery was not how easy it was to deceive the public, but rather, how much the public enjoyed being deceived. Especially if they could see how it was being done. They were flattered that anyone would use such ingenuity to entertain them. Barnum argued that his "clap-trap" was perfectly justifiable so long as it was occasionally "mixed up with the great realities which I provide. The titles of 'humbug,' and 'prince of humbugs,' were first applied to me by myself. I made these titles a part of my 'stock in trade.' " Barnum's autobiography, *Struggles and Triumphs* (published in 1854, the year of Thoreau's *Walden*), recounted his exploits with disarming candor and precise detail. It soon became a best seller.

Barnum was perhaps the first modern master of pseudo-events, of contrived occurrences which lent themselves to being widely and vividly reported. When his winter circus quarters burned, he managed to pyramid the news by announcing that insurance had covered only a fraction of the losses. When newspapers disputed him, he remained unconcerned, finding that the insurance controversy itself was a fruitful source of additional publicity. When Jumbo, the African elephant, was killed in a railroad accident, Barnum put out the story that Jumbo died sacrificing himself to save a baby elephant; he then imported "Alice," whom he billed as Jumbo's widow, posing her next to the stuffed body of her deceased "husband." Barnum was a doubly appropriate symbol of the opening of the era of the Graphic Revolution: by making colossal pseudo-events, he himself became a celebrity.

A talent for advertising and a talent for making news have ever since been connected. Albert D. Lasker, an advertising master of the twentieth century, once characterized all good advertising as news.

Advertising, however, contained an ingredient not generally found in the other pseudo-events which were mere "made news." For while any pseudo-event—an interview, for example—was a happening incited into existence for the purpose of being reported, an advertisement was designed to suggest not merely that something had happened, but also that something was good. An advertisement usually conjured up an image in order to persuade people that something was worth buying. It combined a pseudo-event with a pseudo-ideal. The pseudo-event must be vividly newsworthy, the pseudo-ideal must be vividly desirable.

Much of the appeal of advertising has actually consisted in its effort, which we all appreciate, to satisfy our extravagant expectations. The deeper problems connected with advertising come less from the unscrupulousness of our "deceivers" than from our pleasure in being deceived, less from the desire to seduce than from the desire to be seduced. The Graphic Revolution has produced new categories of experience. They are no longer simply classifiable by the old common sense tests of true or false.

I V

OUR FRENETIC earnestness to attack advertising, our fear of advertising, and our inability to fit advertising into old-time familiar cubbyholes of our experience—all these prevent us from seeing its all-encompassing significance as a touchstone of our changing concept of knowledge and of reality. Our attitude toward advertising is comparable to the eighteenth-century English and American attitude toward insanity and mental disorders. Unable to understand the insane, the sane, respectable people of London saw in them something wicked and diabolical, put them in chains, confined them in Bedlam, punished them with whips. Madmen ceased to be treated as half witch, half criminal only in the later nineteenth and early twentieth century when physicians, psychiatrists, and psychoanalysts helped us see that "madmen" suffered from mental diseases. The great forward steps in public understanding came only when people began to realize that the disorders of the "insane" and the perverted—hysteria, paranoia, schizophrenia, homosexuality, etc.—were only extreme examples of tendencies in each of us "normal" people. The understanding of "insanity" in this way has gradually led each of us to a better understanding of himself.

Similarly with advertising. Baffled and suspicious, we deride the "witch doctors" of Madison Avenue. It is they, we say, who want to involve us in the figments of their disordered imaginations. They lie to us; they persuade us against our will. Accusing them, we fail to see what their activities can teach us about ourselves. Since the Graphic Revolution, the multiplication of images has had a revolutionary effect on all our imaginations, on our concept of verisimilitude, on what passes for truth in common experience.

This can be summed up as the shift in common experience from an emphasis on "truth" to an emphasis on "credibility." All of us—not merely the supposed witch doctors of Madison Avenue, but all American citizen-consumers—are daily less interested in whether something is a fact than in whether it is convenient that it should be believed. Today the master of truth is not the master of facts but the practitioner of the arts of self-fulfilling prophecy. What seems important is not truth but verisimilitude. In this new world, where almost anything can be true, the socially rewarded art is that of making things seem true. It is the art not of discovery, but of invention. Finding a fact is easy; making a fact "believed" is slightly more difficult. The greatest effort goes into the realization not of dreams, but of illusions. God makes our dreams come true. Skillful advertising men bring us our illusions, then make them seem true.

The whole American tradition of pragmatism—from Benjamin Franklin, who insisted that it was less important whether any religious belief was true than whether the consequences of the belief were wholesome, down to William James, who explored the consequences of the "Will to Believe" and focused interest on how whatever people believed or wanted to believe overshadowed whatever might be out there in the "real" world—this tradition has expressed a consuming interest in the appearances of things.

One explanation of increasing American interest in credibility is a simple paradox of the Graphic Revolution. While that Revolution has multiplied and vivified our images of the world, it has by no means generally sharpened or clarified the visible outlines of the world which fill our experience. Quite the contrary. By a diabolical irony the very facsimiles of the world which we make on purpose to bring it within our grasp, to make it less elusive, have transported us into a new world of blurs. By sharpening our images we have blurred all our experience. The new images have blurred traditional distinctions.

The broadest of the old distinctions which no longer serve us as they did is the distinction between "true" and "false." Well-meaning critics (including many in the advertising profession) who say the essential problem is false advertising are firing volleys at an obsolete target. Few advertisers are liars. A strong advertising profession has its own earnest ethic. Lies are not so readily diffused through newspapers and magazines, over radio and television. They are not so eagerly believed. The "evils" of advertising could be easily enough reduced if they came only from lies. The deeper problem is quite different. In some ways it is quite opposite. Advertising befuddles our experience, not because advertisers are liars, but precisely because they are not. Advertising fogs our daily lives less from its peculiar lies than from its peculiar truths. The whole apparatus of the Graphic Revolution has put a new elusiveness, iridescence, and ambiguity into everyday truth in twentieth-century America.

The so-called "Baltimore Truth Declaration," which was adopted at an early convention of advertising men in 1913, committed them to "Truth in Advertising." This later became the slogan of the Advertising Federation of America and its local affiliates. Advertisers were welcomed to that historic convention by the word TRUTH displayed in the largest electric sign yet erected in Baltimore. On the whole, the advertising profession has since then followed its credo with a dangerously literal persistence. The advertising profession was founded on "Truth," but it has survived by its power to give Truth a new meaning.

Several novel appeals have come to characterize the most successful advertising statements. All are both effects and causes of our exaggerated expectations: products and by-products of image-thinking. These first developed in advertising, but have spread out to all our experience. As nature now imitates art, as the geysers in Yellowstone now provide us tourist attractions, more and more of our experience now-adays imitates advertising. The pseudo-event, or that which looks like a pseudo-event, seldom fails to dominate.

(1) *The appeal of the neither-true-nor-false.* The larger proportion of advertising statements subsist in this new limbo. They cannot be parsed in the old grammar of epistemology because modern experience is newly ambiguous. The complexity of new manufacturing processes, the new vagueness that can be designed into vivid images, the new uncertainty of relation between the image and the thing imaged (Is it an actual photograph?)—all these make the simple question, "Is it true?" as obsolete as the horse and buggy. Here, too, the once-simple notion of an "original" has acquired a tantalizing ambiguity bordering on meaninglessness.

The advertiser's art then consists largely of the art of making persuasive statements which are neither true nor false. He does not violate the old truth-morality. Rather, like the news maker, he evades it. It is not only advertising which has become a tissue of contrivance and illusion. Rather, it is the whole world. The ambiguities and illusions of advertising are only symptoms. Advertising events are no less or more unreal than all other pseudo-events. A few commonplace examples will suffice.

One of the most familiar is the use of the open comparative adjective—"the better beer"—without specifying that with which it is being compared. This can hardly fail to be true of every beer which is not the worst in the world.

When Claude C. Hopkins, one of the pioneers of American advertising, took on the Schlitz Beer account some years ago, he prepared himself by learning all he could about brewing. On his tour through the Schlitz brewery Hopkins noticed that bottles were purified by live steam before being filled. This caught his fancy. He developed an advertising program around the notion that Schlitz beer was pure because the bottles were steam-sterilized. Schlitz quickly rose from fifth place in national sales to near first place. What he said was, of course, gospel truth. Consumers simply did not know enough about beer making to realize that the beer of every respectable brand was bottled in this way. The use of live steam by Schlitz became a more vivid fact than its use by any of the competitors. Hopkins had concocted the pseudo-event he was looking for. He had made news. This pseudo-event was then given a nationally advertised dignity making it predominate over the same prosaic fact which was equally "true" about all reputable beers. Competitors dared not match the boast for fear they might seem to be imitating Schlitz. Schlitz continued to sell as *the* beer in sterilized bottles. This was a "fact" if there ever was one. Yet by being touted as a pseudo-event it became only a quasi-truth. This itself made it overshadow the simple facts.

Lucky Strike cigarettes sold well by pre-empting the slogan "It's Toasted." They *were* toasted! So was every other American cigarette. Soon the sales of Lucky Strike reached nearly six billion cigarettes a year.

The growing field of packaged foods, drugs, and cosmetics is a world of just such quasi-information. Toothpastes are "ammoniated." Hair tonics contain "lanolin"—one even contains "cholesterol, the heart of lanolin." Of course they really do contain what they say. Advertisers are so honest they will even concoct a chemical in order to be able truthfully to advertise it.

Statements are given a peculiar, specious kind of truth— and an overshadowing vividness—in the process of being made into pseudo-events. What is called for in these advertising situations is less a verifiable fact than a credible statement. The credibility cannot exist without the "truth"; the seduction cannot exist without the "falsehood." As pseudo-events, of course, they are all quite reputable.

(2) *The appeal of the self-fulfilling prophecy.* The Graphic Revolution has given advertisers—like news makers, celebrity makers, tour agents, movie directors, do-it-yourself photographers, and each of us in a thousand new ways—an unprecedented power to make things "true." Much of our befuddlement, I have suggested, comes from the fact that advertisers insist on offering only statements that are "true." They go to the most devious lengths, employing the most ingenious devices, to procure a persuasive credibility which passes for truth in our everyday life. The successful advertiser is the master of a new art: the art of making things true by saying they are so. He is a devotee of the technique of the self-fulfilling prophecy.

An elementary example is testimonial-endorsement advertising, which has been elaborated in this century. Even at common law, statements employed to promote sale were called "puffs" and were allowed wide latitude. A puff, even if not literally true, was not necessarily legally actionable. Much of the ingenuity of modern advertising derives from the refusal to accept this traditional latitude; and the effort, instead, to force other facts into being in order to make an improbable fact seem true.

So straightforward a statement as one that someone approves or uses a product has become one of the most interesting of pseudo-events. From a most simple declaration of fact, it has become a formula of compounding ambiguity. What could have been a more unambiguous statement, once upon a time, than to say about any product that a particular person, say Mr. J. Edgar Hoover, Director of the Federal Bureau of Investigation, used it? Nowadays the commercial value of such statements, plus the insistence of reputable advertising agencies on being truthful, has loaded just such simple declaratory sentences with all kinds of innuendo. We can read about this in William M. Freeman's *Big Name* (1957), a practical handbook on how to secure credible testimonials and how to use them in advertising. Endorsements have become a specialized and profitable enterprise. Dealers in big names have made them big business.

According to Jules Alberti, president of Endorsements, Inc., a firm specializing in bringing together advertiser and endorser, the endorsement business has prospered. Between 1945 and 1957, he observed:

> Approximately 8,000 celebrities have been used in all combined media, including television, for approximately 4,500 separate products. They have covered apparel, household appliances, cosmetics, beverages, food, tobacco, jewelry, autos, etc. This was through approximately 1,400 agencies. The combined cost of media space and time in twelve years runs well over $700,000,000. The combined fees paid to celebrities were probably about 1 per cent of this amount.

Rarely does anyone become a celebrity solely by selling his name or his picture for endorsements. But even this phenomenon (no paradox in the world of celebrities, where a celebrity is a person known for his well-knownness) occasionally does occur: for example, the Hathaway Shirt man with the patch on his eye; the bearded Commander Whitehead, Schweppes tonic endorser; the attractive "Fire and Ice" model for Revlon nail polish and lipstick; and Miss Rheingold. The endorsement business usually deals in personalities who have already become celebrities in some way (namely, movie stars, sports figures, and beauty queens).

Planning an endorsement requires as much finesse as planning a newsworthy interview, or any other successful pseudo-event. It is partly, as Freeman says, a matter of "good casting"—of matching the right product to the right name. "The celebrity, of course, need not be always the actual user of a product," Freeman explains. "On a household item such as an air refresher, the testimonials are wanted from the domestic staffs of well-known persons. The resulting advertising then would say, 'This is the product used in the home of Mr. and Mrs. Hollywood Star.' Presumably the celebrities would not know what products are used in their establishments, and the endorsement is all the more believable when it comes from an employee."

The dangers of "miscasting" are considerable, observed Edward Carroll, sales promotion manager of Hess Brothers Department Store in Allentown, Pennsylvania, a store noted for its progressive merchandising methods. He notes the mistake of using pretty girls indiscriminately to sell all kinds of products. "Sleepy, seductive models shouldn't be shown in advertising holding pots and pans. The Marjorie Main phototype of model belongs with the pots and pan ads, while the mannequin who looks like Marilyn Monroe is just fine in bathing suits. No sincere advertiser would think of advertising a roasting pan for $1.95 and then marking it up to $2.95 when the customer came into the store. . . . That would be outright misrepresentation. And so is a beautiful, enticing Marilyn Monroe type pictured in an ad holding a mop in a typical family kitchen scene. The same goes for a Marlene Dietrich shown struggling over the kitchen range or the Ava Gardner counterpart wielding a vacuum cleaner. The latter role should cast the Spring Byington type." The sense of appropriateness must often be delicate. Mr. Carroll advised that Marilyn Monroe herself, although an eminently appropriate endorser for bathing suits, strapless and backless evening gowns, negligees, diamonds, and furs, should not be "cast" in underwear advertising. Here credibility would be sacrificed, since as he says, Miss Monroe has actually stated publicly that she does not wear such garments.

Experience and know-how are useful in securing endorsements. Certain celebrities are unobtainable, or will endorse only certain kinds of products. For example, Clyde Beatty, the lion trainer, will not endorse anything linked to alcohol; Buster Crabbe, starred on television as Captain Gallant of the Foreign Legion, will not endorse any product he does not think good and healthy; Gene Autry, Roy Rogers, and some other celebrities who appeal primarily to a juvenile audience, are reluctant to endorse a cigarette or any other product not for young people.

Endorsement agencies maintain lists of the most-wanted names, arranged both by the fields in which each name is a celebrity and by the kind of product for which each would be appropriate. Almost any celebrity has a well-knownness which can be attached to some product, service, or institution. In the decline of American "Society," as Cleveland Amory notes, an epoch was marked when the first member of authentic Society signed her first commercial testimonial. Mrs. James Brown Potter, under a Tuxedo Park address, endorsed Harriet Hubbard Ayer's cold cream. Soon thereafter, in 1923, two agencies, William Esty and J. Walter Thompson, made heavy use of Society names: Mrs. Oliver Harriman and the Duchess de Richelieu of Baltimore for Hardman pianos; Mrs. Oliver Harriman, Mrs. August Belmont, and the formidable Mrs. Longworth of Washington for Pond's cold cream. Amory remarks that by 1960, whether because some persons of Society (for example the Duke and Duchess of Windsor) had worn out their names by commercialism or simply because fewer celebrities were real Society, not a single authentic Society name was on the "most-wanted" list.

A more attenuated form of endorsement does not even make any statement about a person's use or approval of the advertised product. This is the so-called "implied" endorsement. In this technique, the big name does not say in so many words that he uses the product. Instead his name is associated with the product in such a way as to give it the aura of his name. A series of advertisements was run by the Cyma Watch Company, announcing, under a large portrait of J. Edgar Hoover, that he had been given the "Cyma Honor Award Watch."

In the fabricating of endorsements, the planning and casting are all-important. The least troublesome problem of all is how to make the statement true. In many cases (the implied endorsement, for example) the project is accomplished, the pseudo-event is created, merely by public association of the celebrity's name or photograph with the product. A sign of a celebrity is often that his name is worth more than his services. For an endorsement the use of a name is frequently all that is wanted. A legend, true as fable if not as fact, tells that at the end of the Civil War an insurance company offered its presidency to General Robert E. Lee with the salary of $50,000 a year. General Lee was puzzled by the large salary, saying he did not think his services worth so much. "We don't want your services," he was told, "but only your name." "My name," Lee is reported to have said, "is not for sale." There are, of course, a few literal-minded celebrities who are hard to get. Some will actually refuse to say they use a product which they are not already in the habit of using. General Douglas MacArthur, for example, before 1957, had endorsed only the Cyma watch; Mrs. Eleanor Roosevelt had endorsed only the Cyma watch and the Zenith hearing aid.

Sometimes the endorsement itself makes the endorser into a user; he is given a large supply of the product as payment for the endorsement.

By the law of pseudo-events, the staging of the event inevitably becomes more interesting than the event itself. Everybody knows that big names are usually paid for their endorsements. A clever advertiser can actually increase interest by describing the process by which the endorsement was secured—even if it was paid for. The advertising agency working for Thom McAn's low-priced men's shoes published an ingenious series which attracted more than the usual attention simply by having the endorsers purport to explain how their endorsements were paid for. In each case, a photograph of the endorser, wearing Thom McAn shoes, appeared with a facsimile of his signature alongside the statement. Admiral J. J. ("Jocko") Clark, U.S.N. (Ret.), for example, included the following in his endorsement:

MY PREJUDICE AGAINST THOM MCANS

In general I have made it a personal rule to buy expensive shoes—at $25 and $30 a pair. When asked to join the Thom McAn Shoe Jury, I was frankly skeptical. It's not always easy to teach an old sea dog new tricks.

But Thom McAn's offer to send a check to my favorite charity, Navy Relief, was a strong inducement. Also, my Navy experience has shown me that it's never too late to learn. So I approached the test with an open mind.

In America today—where popularity and well-knownness are themselves such valuable qualities of a product—the consumer himself is given an enticing opportunity to make advertising prophecies come true. The nationally advertised product is a celebrity of the consumption world. It is well known for its well-knownness, which is one of its most attractive ingredients. Just as each of us likes a movie star or television celebrity more when we think we have had a hand in making him a celebrity, the same is true with commercial products. We know that by buying a product we increase its popularity; we thus make it more valuable. Each of us has a power to help transform it into the leader in its field. This itself makes it more attractive to us and nearly everyone else. Each of us has the power to help make true the assertion that Chevrolet is the most popular car in the low-price field.

One of the most effective efforts to increase beer consumption among women (and incidentally among men, too) was the ingenious campaign by Liebmann Breweries, aided by Foote, Cone & Belding, Chicago advertising agency, and by Paul Hesse, the well-known photographer, to promote Rheingold beer. Their simple device was to let the consumers themselves vote for Miss Rheingold. This attractive model would then declare that Rheingold was her favorite beer and help entice those who had chosen her to entice them. The first national election for Miss Rheingold took place in 1941, when Ruth Ownby won. (Jinx Falkenburg, who was the first Miss Rheingold, was undemocratically appointed, not elected.) By 1957 the 20,000,000 ballots cast in the election of Miss Rheingold made it the largest election in the United

States outside of that for President. The fact that customers were allowed to vote more than once simply added to the tantalizing verisimilitude.

Customers themselves seemed more effectively persuaded, more personally interested in being sold by a pseudo-event which in this fashion they themselves had helped create. No one worried much over how to fabricate the essential fact— how to persuade the most popular model of the year to prefer Rheingold over all other beers. The contract which candidates were required to sign contained no mention of beer. A cynical advertising man observed that since beer was fattening, it was always unlikely that a model slim enough to win the election would actually be a heavy beer drinker. Reputedly only one of the early winners drank much beer. But was it untrue for Miss Rheingold to say, "My beer is Rheingold, the dry beer"? Any model who won the election, with its $50,000 in fees and prizes, would have been preternaturally callous not to like Rheingold best of all. What better way of securing truthful testimonials?

In a world where brand names dominate, the consumer's power to bring the brand name into common use can make the brand name synonymous with the product itself. This, despite the legal perils of dissolving the right to the name, is much desired by the manufacturer. This is a verbal symbol of the consumer's power to make the product the success it claims to be. By daily use of the product and the word, the consumer actually makes "Kodak" his synonym for camera, "Kleenex" his synonym for paper tissue. In an expanding economy, where the very function of a commodity is often an aspect of the claimed qualities of a particular brand (for example of a mouthwash like Listerine, or of a deodorant like Dial soap or Ban), the consumer, by believing in the function and by developing his "need," actually gives the product a new reality.

(3) *The appeal of the half-intelligible.* In fast-moving, progress-conscious America, the consumer expects to be dizzied by progress. If he could completely understand ad-

vertising jargon he would be badly disappointed. The half-intelligibility which we expect, or even hope, to find in the latest product language personally reassures each of us that progress *is* being made: that the pace exceeds our ability to follow.

Who would want to live in an economy so stagnant, in a technology so backward, that the consumer could actually understand how products were made and what their real virtues were? The very obscurity of advertising language proves that manufacturers are really at work for our benefit —developing new processes, discovering, perfecting, and adding mysterious new ingredients, elaborating subtle and complicated new features. The consumer cannot be wholly satisfied, then, unless he is partly bewildered.

Advertising is, of course, our most popular reading, listening, and watching matter. Precisely because it transports us to where the rigidities of the real world have dissolved. As we stroll through the world of advertising, the half-intelligibility of what we see and read and hear encourages us to hope that our extravagant expectations may be coming true.

To people who want the latest model, but who do not understand automobiles, a "V-type" engine, "hydro-matic drive," "wide-track wheels," and "uniweld body" are especially appealing. These are scrupulously true statements of fact. Their appeal consists in our half-understanding.

When the function of newly contrived objects becomes more attenuated, when an automobile is no longer merely a transportation machine, but something we wear and luxuriate in or something that gives us "that carefree feeling" and "that sense of indescribable luxury"; when a ball-point pen is no longer something to keep accounts with or to write checks with, but something vaguely useful for writing on butter or under water; when a soap is not merely for washing, but to give us "round-the-clock protection"—then we can no longer be "deceived" about the "function" of anything.

On a full-page, full-color portrait of an enticing woman who might be oneself, the lady reader is told:

'ULTIMA' GOSSAMER TINTS

THE ASTONISHING NEW COLOR COSMETOLOGY

Dedicated by Revlon to the exciting woman who spends a lifetime living up to her potential. For the first time, you can be porcelain pale or spun gold . . . or any exquisite anything . . . without the vaguest feel of make-up on your skin. The key to this paradox? The limitless tints and the almost bodiless textures of these gossamer powders, nutrient foundations and lipsticks. Do let a Revlon consultant help you to a gossamer complexion. At only the most distinguished stores.

THE 'ULTIMA' MAKE-UP COLLECTION BY REVLON
New York   *   London   *   Paris

In a world of functions so vague, so derivative, so attenuated, we read advertisements and listen to commercials to discover functions, ogres, needs, and perils of which we never dreamed and never would have known. Advertising attenuates, making everything more interesting, more fanciful, more problematic.

(4) *The appeal of the contrived.* And we enjoy being courted. Like the little girl pleased to see her best beau stand on his head for her sake, we delight in the headstands and handsprings of advertisers. Not necessarily because we especially enjoy acrobatics, or even because the acrobatics are done so well, but because we are flattered that anyone would go to such trouble for us. When we see an elegant living room ensemble by Dunbar Furniture spread on a lawn; when we see "The Pepperell family on Cotton Cay—Imaginary Island in the Sun" poised improbably in an array of three hammocks, one above another; when we see a man hunting, fishing, or playing poker while chained to a large egg ("For a better way to take care of your nest egg talk to the people at Chase Manhattan") we are pleased. Not so much because we know what is happening or what it all

means, or because the spectacle is anything but ludicrous; but because we cannot help being pleased that so elaborate a pseudo-event should be made especially for us.

The shrewd planner of advertising pseudo-events plays on our puzzlement. Even our own suspicions and doubts themselves become themes for new pseudo-events. An advertising campaign in 1960 by Clairol, Inc., makers of a hair dye for women, featured a photograph of an attractive model with beautiful hair. Over the photograph appeared the question: "Does she . . . or doesn't she?" And underneath: "Hair color so natural only her hairdresser knows for sure!" The advertising copy which followed did not answer the tantalizing question. Someone wrote to the company for the facts. The enterprising publicity director then made news by releasing the story of the correspondence, and the company's reply as follows:

> In response to your letter, the answer to your question "Does She or Doesn't She?" is "Yes, Always."
>
> I guess we at Clairol always knew that somewhere, someone would be bright enough to ask the very intelligent questions which you have put forth. Consequently, for as long as we have been doing national advertising, we have had an iron-clad rule that all models used in our advertisements must use Miss Clairol on their hair . . . girls who do not use our products on their hair just don't look good enough to reflect the true qualities of our hair-coloring.

The unanswered question, of course, was what relation if any there really was between using Clairol and having beautiful hair. The fact offered was that a girl with hair naturally beautiful enough to make her a cosmetic model had not spoiled her appearance by one application of Clairol. Here obviously the real interest centered not on the qualities of the product but on the advertisement itself—the mechanics and mystery of the pseudo-event.

*   *   *   *   *

When "truth" has been displaced by "believability" as the test of the statements which dominate our lives, advertisers' ingenuity is devoted less to discovering facts than to inventing statements which can be made to seem true. Making them seem true is relatively easy. With the apparatus of the Graphic Revolution, almost anything can be made to seem true—especially if we wish to believe it. The advertising man resembles the newspaperman for whom he was in some ways the prototype. He artfully develops his pitch as the journalist cleverly develops his story. The happening which the reporter sends over the wire has often been incited into being in the same way in which the advertising man has produced the "facts" for his copy. Both aim at newsworthiness and believability. The advertising man who, according to Endorsements, Inc., may approach as many as five big names for a particular endorsement before he secures a single acceptance is like the conscientious Washington reporter who approaches seven senators before he finds the one to make the statement needed for his story. Both work hard to incite the pseudo-event into being. Both are inhibited by prudence and ethics: believability is produced only if quasi-facts are invented within certain limits. But the problem is both complicated and simplified by the fact that in many fields of marketing (for example, drugs, cosmetics, automobiles, or home appliances) a statement cannot be most attractively believable unless it is only partly intelligible.

The readers of advertisements are always playing a game with themselves. Momentarily they enjoy the pleasurable illusion that an extravagant expectation has been satisfied. Then they enjoy the revelation that they have seen through the illusion: the fairy princess is not really a fairy princess at all, but only Jinx Falkenburg dressed up like one. Ample room is left for the advertiser's "creativity." His imagination, like a poet's, enlarges our world for us. In the contest between the creative imagination of ad men and the disillusioning information and sophistication of ad readers, the successful advertiser stays one step ahead. He can keep us in "that willing suspension of disbelief for the moment, which [according to Coleridge] constitutes poetic faith." He is always conceiving new legends for a world governed by its own legendary rules to take the place of those legends which have been disenchanted. The citizen-consumer enjoys the satisfactions of being at the same time the bewitched, the bewitcher, and the detached student of witchcraft.

The difficulty of curing us of our ever exaggerating expectations comes from the very fact that not truth, but credibility, is the modern test. We share this standard with the advertising men themselves. For everybody, then, it is more important that a statement be believable than that it be true. This is illustrated by the spectacular success of a series of Rheingold beer testimonials. These were, of course, written by copywriters, to suit the personalities of the celebrities who gave the endorsements. "Although the agency helps out," Freeman explains in his *Big Name,* "the endorsement is none the less sincere or believable. The foundation for the endorsement is the fact that these are well-known persons, believable as beer drinkers, who are well liked and trusted by their publics. [Some examples are Van Heflin, Victor Borge, Louis Armstrong, Ernest Borgnine, Nat (King) Cole, Sir Cedric Hardwick, Raymond Loewy, Joanne Dru, Beatrice Lillie, Charles Coburn, Dorothy Kilgallen, and Groucho Marx.] They would not put their names to a statement unless it were true, the readers believe, so that it is of little consequence that the actual choice of the words used to convey their approval of Rheingold is the work of another hand."

The advertising world can never collapse so long as believability remains the test. Even as each old advertising formula becomes ritualized and its mechanics become widely known, the mechanics themselves become the pseudo-eventful center of interest. When a manufacturer of shaving cream was cited by the Federal Trade Commission for using tooth paste instead of shaving cream on a television commercial to show the supposedly remarkable under-water staying qualities of the shaving cream, the manufacturer inevitably benefited from the repetition of the brand name in this widely reported pseudo-event. We have already seen that in the news world, when the press conference became ritualized as a form of pseudo-event, it lost some of its charm and much of its function; when a looser, more ambiguous form of communication was required, the institutionalized leak was developed. Similarly, in the world of advertising, when the straight endorsement becomes ritualized and loses its appeal, new interest can be created by such devices as letting the public elect their own endorser (Miss Rheingold) or by showing them how the endorsements are bought and paid for (Thom McAn). There still remains enough of an always novel kind of believability.

P. T. Barnum's flamboyant explanation of his success as a showman can serve now as prosaic description of our everyday experience. The world's way, Barnum observed, was "to excite the community with flaming posters, promising almost everything for next to nothing."

> I confess that I took no pains to set my enterprising fellow-citizens a better example. I fell in with the world's way; and if my "puffing" was more persistent, my advertising more audacious, my posters more glaring, my pictures more exaggerated, my flags more patriotic and my transparencies more brilliant than they would have been under the management of my neighbors, it was not because I had less scruple than they, but more energy, far more ingenuity, and a better foundation for such promises.

This might be the appropriately immodest motto for an expanding American economy, which thrives on our ever more extravagant expectations.

V

THE CENTRAL PARADOX—that the rise of images and of our power over the world blurs rather than sharpens the outlines of reality—permeates one after another area of our life. There is hardly a corner of our daily behavior where the multiplication of images, the products and by-products of the Graphic Revolution, have not befogged the simplest old everyday distinctions.

Life in medieval times, remarked the Dutch historian Johann Huizinga in his classic *Waning of the Middle Ages* (1924), offered sharp edges and bright contrasts. Each season, each time of day, each station in society, was clearly distinguished from others. Perhaps we can never recapture the poignancy which a medieval man felt in a warm fire on a winter day, in the sound of the leper's bell, in the dark of night, in the splendor of a nobleman's brocade. Equality and economic progress have leveled sensations. In rich, adept America, distinctions of social classes, of times and seasons, have been blurred as never before. With steam heat we are too hot in winter; with air conditioning, too cool in summer. Fluorescent lights make indoors brighter than out, night lighter than day. The distinctions between here and there dissolve. With movies and television, today can become yesterday; and we can be everywhere while we are still here. In fact, it is easier to be there (say on the floor of the national political convention) when we are here (at home or in our hotel room before our television screen) than when we are there.

In twentieth-century America we have gone one step beyond the homogenizing of experience. Not only do we begin to erase the distinctions of nature. Our own distinctions become more impressive than nature's. Even as we try to sharpen our artificial distinctions they become ever more blurry. A couple of examples will suffice.

Take, for instance, our notion of time and the seasons. Measured by our economy, they become pseudo-events. As the machinery of production becomes more complex, as "progress" becomes ever more certain and more predictable, we must cautiously measure it out. Next year's model of an automobile (always out *this* year) is not the farthest step to which our technology can reach. But it is the farthest stage to which the pseudo-events of publicity and advertising can profitably be accommodated. It often represents not where progress has reached, but where it has been conveniently arrested.

Advance publicity becomes more important for everything produced. To change next year's model of automobile we must have begun retooling eighteen months before; planning must have begun over two years in advance. The vast machinery of progress then makes every product express an obsolete imagination. Women's dresses for next summer must go on sale this winter, which means that they must have been designed, and the new styles decided on, at least last summer. Next year's designs are made before this year's have been sold. In publishing, for example, Books for Fall are announced before summer has come. In *Publishers' Weekly,* Santa Claus arrives with his Christmas picture book gift items on the Fourth of July. We anticipate ourselves so that manufacturers and merchandisers always live in several seasons at once. Not only news, but more and more other items of daily consumption are made for future release.

The increasing importance of public relations in the world of politics and pressure groups has blurred the meaning of so simple a notion as "membership." People cannot remember the names of the organizations they belong to. Money-raising counselors and professional managers of pressure groups must be adept not only at handling people, but especially at using names. Every year, more thousands of reams of stationery are printed with lists of "advisory committees," "sponsoring committees," and other fictitious bodies. Organizations are set up and dissolved to serve any purpose.

The United States has historically been par excellence the country of "voluntary" organizations. Here even churches have a voluntary character which they have had almost nowhere else in the world. But in the twentieth century ours has become the country of "front" organizations. In the United States, more and more organizations are pseudo-events, set up not because their members wish to collaborate for a common purpose, but because it serves someone's purpose that the founding and the activities of such organizations be widely reported. They are appendages of the media. They are front organizations, but not in the sense that they front for subversive causes. Rather in the sense that their membership and sponsorship and leadership are carefully constructed not to do a job but to produce an image. The "fellow-traveler" (also a characteristic product of our age) is a person—of whatever political complexion—who allows himself to be associated with that image.

Pressure to participate leads to more and more nominal membership: in churches, service clubs, professional societies, pressure groups, charitable organizations, and political associations. Our joining is itself one of the most perfunctory of pseudo-events. We wish our membership to be reported. We do not care to participate. Multiplication of these personal pseudo-events confuses and dilutes our personal loyalties. The very idea of membership becomes hopelessly blurred. *The Reader's Digest* offered itself not as a magazine to be subscribed to, but as an "association" to be joined. We have book clubs and travel clubs and Christmas clubs, and clubs and associations ad infinitum. Nowadays it would be pedantic to say these are not clubs. But if they *are* properly clubs it is simply because so few associations (except rural, obsolete, or snobbish groups—country clubs and downtown dining clubs and small sewing and reading circles) remain clubs at all in the traditional sociable sense. "Are you a member or aren't you?" "I can't remember."

The mark of an educated man, Irving Babbitt once shrewdly observed, is the clarity of the line in his mind between what he knows and what he does not know. Of course this is only an ideal. But today it is more difficult than ever to reach for it. When in our schools the study of "current events" (that is, of what is reported in the newspapers) displaces the facts of history, it is inevitable that the standard of knowledge propagated by newspapers and magazines and television networks themselves (that is, whether one is "up on" what is reported in the newspapers, magazines, and television) overshadows all others. When to be informed is to be knowledgeable about pseudo-events, the line between knowledge and ignorance is blurred as never before. No wonder we use the quiz formula to test knowledge. No wonder our estimates of books and movies and television programs are shaped by whether they have won prizes (Pulitzers, Oscars, and Emmies) or have attained best-sellerdom. We *should* know them simply because they are well known. Having made celebrities, we have a duty to worship them. We worship them by keeping them alive, by keeping them well known. Distinction between "knowledge" and "ignorance" itself has become old-fashioned. It is displaced by the minute and barely discernible degrees of well-knownness.

VI

ALONG WITH the blurring of knowledge, the multiplication and sharpening of images brings the blurring of our intentions and desires. Do not improved marketing techniques enable manufacturers to know what we want better than we do ourselves? New ambiguities enter into "desire" and "function." Does the public really want fins on its new-model automobiles? If the fins do satisfy a public want, are they not then somehow functional? We become more and more confused about our desires in an ever expanding economy where products are always remoter from primitive needs.

We read advertisements, then, to discover and enlarge our desires. We are always ready—even eager—to discover, from the announcement of a new product, what we have all along wanted without really knowing it. The ambiguity of "desire" and of "function" come along together. "Function" was once a word for describing a simple standard of utility. By contrast, an ornament was supposed to be only subsidiary to the object's function. But we become more uncertain what is the precise usefulness of any particular product. That usefulness itself becomes a kind of pseudo-event—a utility made up for the purpose of being reported. We then find ourselves occupied less with finding products to perform certain obvious functions than with discovering what is the real function of objects that we think we want. The search for function—as anyone who has lived in a modern "functional" house knows —is just as uncertain as the search for beauty.

A symptom of the blurring of our intentions and desires by the increase of images is the rising interest in public opinion, and especially in public opinion polls. Although the expression "public opinion" dates from at least as early as the end of the eighteenth century (Jefferson used it), it came into common use only in the era of the Graphic Revolution. The multiplication of news reports multiplied the supposed evidence of the opinion of the people generally. Of course what was printed as "opinion," and what was therefore most widely available, was not everybody's opinion, but only a few symptoms. Still, with rising literacy and extending circulation, there came an increasing tendency to take the symptom for the fact. The digests—*The Literary Digest* and *The Reader's Digest,* for example—and the many new forms of opinion reporting in other magazines and newspapers gave public opinion a specious new reality.

In his brilliant pioneering book, *Public Opinion* (1922), Walter Lippmann made a valuable distinction. "The pictures inside the heads of these human beings, the pictures of themselves, of others, of their needs, purposes, and relationship, are their public opinions. Those pictures which are acted upon by groups of people, or by individuals acting in the name of groups, are Public Opinion with capital letters." After the Graphic Revolution it was possible to make "images" of Public Opinion—with many of the general characteristics I have observed for all images. Public Opinion now became synthetic, believable, passive, vivid, concrete, simplified, and ambiguous as never before. If you wanted to know what the public thought, you could simply pick up a newspaper. Changes were recorded daily, or twice daily, opinions were vivified by journalese and by photographs, they were forced into being by earnest newspapermen trying to make news, they were played against one another.

Inevitably, then, "Public Opinion" became itself a kind of pseudo-event, forced into existence for the primary purpose of being reported. Expressions of public opinion became among the most powerful, the most interesting, and the most mysterious of pseudo-events. The more fabricated and factitious public opinion became—true to the law of pseudo-events—the more interesting and titillating the news about it became. "Democracies," Lippmann shrewdly observed, "have made a mystery out of public opinion. There have been skilled organizers of opinion who understood the mystery well enough to create majorities on election day. But these organizers have been regarded by political science as low fellows or as 'problems,' not as possessors of the most effective knowledge there was on how to create and operate public opinion. The tendency of the people who have voiced the ideas of democracy, even when they have not managed its action, the tendency of students, orators, editors, has been to look upon Public Opinion as men in other societies looked upon the uncanny forces to which they ascribed the last word in the direction of events." Lippmann made a plea for a better, more effective, more widely understood news apparatus. He observed that the quality of the news about modern society was an index of its social organization: the better the institutions, then the more objective the news, the more effectively issues could be disentangled, and "the more perfectly an affair can be presented as news." Lippmann's interpretation did not take sufficient account of how the mere existence and proliferation of media would produce pressures to fabricate, complicate, and dramatize; and hence to misrepresent. And how the interestingly contrived account would tend to overshadow the naively accurate facts.

Again, true to the laws of pseudo-events, public opinion bred its own interest-awakening novelties. Even if there was no opinion spontaneously expressed, elaborate new devices would incubate opinions into expression so they could be reported, discussed, and set against one another. These devices, one critic warned, "seek to turn the people into a great beast which is asked to roar when it is not ready to do so."

Public opinion polls are an example. There had been "straw" polls in the United States as early as July 24, 1824, when the Harrisburg *Pennsylvanian* sent to Wilmington, Delaware, to gather samples of opinion on the Presidential campaign and reported: Andrew Jackson, 335 votes; John Quincy Adams, 169; Henry Clay, 19; William H. Crawford, 9. Since then there have been many straw polls. They have often helped increase the circulation of magazines and newspapers. The best known in this century were the *Literary Digest* polls between 1916 and 1936.

The modern scientific sampling technique for surveying public opinion did not, however, develop out of these crude earlier polls. Instead it grew, appropriately enough, out of research in marketing and advertising. Market surveys were devised about 1912 by Roy O. Eastman to find out who was reading the magazines in which his breakfast food ads were appearing. By 1919 a survey department appeared within an advertising agency; then independent surveying organizations were established. More recently opinion surveying has become a sizable industry, training and employing thousands of interviewers, mailing out hundreds of thousands of questionnaires, sparing neither time nor expense in lengthy depth-interviews. A host of novel techniques have been elaborated for securing expressions of opinion and for finding the motives behind the opinions. These have been directed mostly to consumers.

In 1935 market research techniques were applied to politics and public issues. *Fortune* was the first to publish widely the results of such surveys (conducted under the direction of Elmo Roper and others), and then George Gallup offered his features on a regular syndicated basis to numerous newspapers. Beginning in 1936 "what the polls say" during national campaigns became one of the most interesting and widely featured pieces of news.

The spectacular failure in 1936 of the *Literary Digest* poll —which until then had been remarkably accurate, but which forecast a sweeping victory for Landon over Roosevelt and mispredicted the popular vote by a full 20 per cent—actually stimulated a wider interest in opinion polls. The *Digest* fiasco was itself one of the biggest pieces of news about the election. When the *Digest* collapsed, other polls—for example, those by *Fortune,* by Archibald M. Crossley, by George Gallup, by the National Opinion Research Center—took over. In 1944 a poll by a national polling agency showed that over half of its informants had heard of public opinion polls. In 1948, once again, the best known national opinion polls predicted the wrong result, choosing Dewey over Truman. Elmo Roper's *Fortune* poll missed the actual popular vote by 12 per cent; both Crossley and Gallup had given Dewey a 5 per cent popular lead. Yet, again, within six months of this fiasco, market research agencies and public opinion polls were functioning at their 1948 levels. In the succeeding Presidential elections, as more elaborate polling techniques were perfected and as voters became accustomed to following the polls, the polls became the political equivalent of the *Racing Form.* They became more and more interesting for their own sakes. Now politicians and pundits were constantly being asked not merely about the issues and the candidates and the state of public sentiment, but about the meaning of specific polls. People speculated about the effect on voters of revealing this or that set of figures. After each election, one of the most widely interesting news items was the degree of accuracy of each of the different polls. Prominent pollsters were interviewed, encouraged to speculate, explore, defend, and wonder over their results.

The experts have, of course, been preoccupied with explaining and defending the basis of their mispredictions. In their post-mortems they have focused their interest not on the actual opinions gathered (never, of course, gathered at the moment and in the places where legally valid votes are actually cast), but rather on comparison of the "artificial" election (by opinion pollers) with the real election (at the ballot box). Some scientific polling experts, like George Gallup, have been anxious to prove that opinion polling is an aid, rather than a menace, to representative democracy. In his *Pulse of Democracy* (1940), Gallup concludes with an unintended ominousness that "the limitations and short-comings of the polls are the limitations and shortcomings of public opinion itself." The deepest peril of polls comes, however, not from their inaccuracy, but from their accuracy. If and when polls become so scientific that they can precisely predict our opinions at the ballot box, at that moment they may cease to be very interesting; at the same time, of course, the process of voting will have become superfluous. The defenders of the polls, like Gallup, declare that polls are valuable—even essential—for what they now define as our representative government: "government responsive to the average opinion of mankind."

The larger problem which the rising interest in public opinion and public opinion polls illustrates is the rise of images and their domination over our thinking about ourselves. We hopefully exaggerate our expectations of the power of these polls to predict how we will decide. The more confidence pollsters can inspire in their power to offer us an image of what we will really believe or will choose at some future time, the more blurred becomes our notion of what is our own real preference as voters.

Here again arise some of our most bewildering blurs—produced by some of the most sharply contrived images. Just as in the world of news the roles of the actor and the reporter have been more and more intermixed (through press conferences, news releases, institutionalized leaks, and other devices), so the same is true of manufacturer and consumer, political leader and political follower, statesman and citizen. Now the consumer can look at advertisements to see what he "really" wants (the best manufacturers make only products which they are convinced the consumer really wants). Now the citizen can see himself in the mirror of the opinion polls. Having been polled as a representative of the public, he can then read reports and see how he looks. As polls become more scientific and detailed—broken down into occupations, counties, income groups, religious denominations, etc.—the citizen can discover himself (and the opinions which he "ought" to have or is likely to have) in the views reported as predominant among people like him. Public opinion—once the public's expression—becomes more and more an image into which the public fits its expression. Public opinion becomes filled with what is already there. It is the people looking in the mirror.

6

From the American Dream to American Illusions? The Self-Deceiving Magic of Prestige

"WHEN the gods wish to punish us," Oscar Wilde might have said, "they make us believe our own advertising." The God of American destiny has answered our prayers beyond Jules Verne's imaginings. He has given us domination over the fish of the sea, and over the fowl of the air, and over every living thing that moveth upon the earth. But no power is without price.

Have we been doomed to make our dreams into illusions?

A dream is a vision or an aspiration to which we can compare reality. It may be very vivid, but its vividness reminds us how different is the real world. An illusion, on the other hand, is an image we have mistaken for reality. We cannot reach for it, aspire to it, or be exhilarated by it; for we live in it. It is prosaic because we cannot see it is not fact.

America has been a land of dreams. A land where the aspirations of people from countries cluttered with rich, cumbersome, aristocratic, ideological pasts can reach for what once seemed unattainable. Here they have tried to make dreams come true. The American Dream was the most accurate way of describing the hopes of men in America. It was an exhilaration and an inspiration precisely because it symbolized the disparity between the possibilities of New America and the old hard facts of life. Only the stagnators of America—the prophets of rigid Puritan theocracy, of Southern slaveocracy—ever mistook the dream for reality. Only profitless visionaries—the utopians in narrow ideal communities like New Harmony and Brook Farm—ever thought they could make the dream a mold in which to live. If America was also a land of dreams-come-true, that was so because generations suffered to discover that the dream was here to be reached for and not to be lived in.

We have been notorious as a country where the impossible was thought only slightly less attainable than the difficult. The unprecedented American opportunities have always tempted us to confuse the visionary with the real. America has not been plagued by utopianism, for the very reason that here, finally, dreams could be striven for and made real.

Yet now, in the height of our power in this age of the Graphic Revolution, we are threatened by a new and a peculiarly American menace. It is not the menace of class war, of ideology, of poverty, of disease, of illiteracy, of demagoguery, or of tyranny, though these now plague most of the world. It is the menace of unreality. The threat of nothingness is the danger of replacing American dreams by American illusions. Of replacing the ideals by the images, the aspiration by the mold. We risk being the first people in history to have been able to make their illusions so vivid, so persuasive, so "realistic" that they can live in them. We are the most illusioned people on earth. Yet we dare not become disillusioned, because our illusions are the very house in which we live; they are our news, our heroes, our adventure, our forms of art, our very experience.

Formerly we were saved from the menace of ideology by the elusiveness and the promise of the American dream. Now we replace the dogmas by which men live elsewhere, by the images among which we live. We have come to think that our main problem is abroad. How to "project" our images to the world? Yet the problem abroad is only a symptom of our deeper problem at home. We have come to believe in our own images, till we have projected ourselves out of this world.

The "problem" abroad is valuable, however, as a symptom. It can remind us that men need not live in a world of images, that our life of images is a strangely modern, New World life. And it can remind us also of some of the dangers of having so successfully persuaded ourselves.

I

ALL AROUND the world we have revealed a shift in our thinking from ideals to images. Everywhere we have been the victim of this shift. Without reflecting on consequences, we have become preoccupied with creating "favorable images" of America. Yet by doing so, we may be defeating ourselves.

Almost everywhere today American images overshadow American ideals. The image of America overshadows the ideals of America. How has this happened? Some of the explanations are obvious. Many I have already recounted in describing the Graphic Revolution, the rise of pseudo-events, the multiplication of images, the improvement of instruments for making and receiving images, and the rise of image-thinking here at home. Abroad, some special accidental factors have been at work: our wealth, our technological precocity, and especially our ability to make attractive motion pictures. All these have enabled us to flood with American images the people who have never heard of American ideals, and who do not know whether we have any ideals.

The most important single influence in parts of the world which *have* heard of the United States has been the prevalence of American movies. I encountered this myself in a trip to South Asia in 1960. For example, in Bangalore in southern India, we had an admirable United States Information Agency library with a wide selection of books. It was being visited by perhaps 250 people a day. Of these, a considerable number were coming in to escape the dust, or because they had no other place to do their schoolwork. Some came to learn about the United States or other Western cultures. At the same time a half-dozen motion picture houses in the city customarily showed American movies. Here the language barrier almost disappeared. The people reading in the USIA library were a handful. Any one of the movie houses offered images of America to many more people and at a far greater rate than that at which the library was offering them ideas about America.

The motion picture is to real life in America what any image is to the commodity or corporation it stands for. The motion picture, seen abroad, is of course synthetic. It is believable. It is passive. It is concrete. It is simplified, and it is ambiguous. Thus the world has been flooded with images of America. The selling of American images abroad is a remunerative business.

Our government operations also have had a large part in spreading these images. Much of our propaganda has been trying to create an image (we always say, of course, a "true," by which we mean a favorable, image) of the United States. Through our libraries, our mobile movie and exhibit units, and our displays at world fairs, we offer photographs and models of skyscrapers, farmhouses, factories, clubs, suburbs, and churches. We offer samples of farm implements, automobiles, farm machinery, and home conveniences. Our documentary films depict town meetings, drugstores, schools, churches, and countless other American activities and artifacts. Even where people cannot read, or read very little, they can have a more concrete (and I believe a more accurate) picture of life in America than of life in any other country equally remote from them.

Most of the efforts we make to educate people (especially "underdeveloped" people) about our country are the offering of vivid concrete images. During the winter of 1960, I attended the International Agricultural Fair in Delhi. There we were making one of our most strenuous and expensive (and by conventional standards one of our most successful) efforts. The American pavilion, a light and graceful structure, danced in the sun. Inside, it was neat and uncluttered. One of the sights most impressive to all comers was an American farm kitchen—a dazzling porcelain-and-chrome spectacle, complete with refrigerator, disposal, deep-freeze, automatic washer and dryer, and electric stove. Before it walked a procession of Indian peasant women. Long pendant earrings, bangles on arms and ankles, objects piercing their noses— these pieces of gold were their savings which they dared not put in the hands of banks. In their arms they carried bare-bottomed infants. They stopped and stood in bewilderment. What was this? It was the image of America.

That was an almost perfect example of how an image can emphasize irrelevance. A vivid image, well-tailored to a spectator, can entice him to lose himself and fit perfectly into it. But an irrelevant image reminds another that he has no community with its makers. A large banana would have been easily enough understood. The ideal of abundance or of health or nourishment or well-being was not irrelevant to these people. They were eager for it and would embrace it. But the image of an American kitchen was meaningless: a barrier between them and America.

In our cliché-ridden "Battle for Men's Minds," perhaps our problem is not so much that peoples abroad have an "unfavorable image" of America while they have a more favorable image of life among our enemies. Some of our difficulty may be much simpler, and too obvious for us to notice. I suspect we suffer abroad simply because people know America through images. While our enemies profit from the fact that they are known only, or primarily, through their ideals. That is, through their professed goals of perfection.

Images are the pseudo-events of the ethical world. They

are at best only pseudo-ideals. They are created and disseminated in order to be reported, to make a "favorable impression." Not because they are good, but because they are interesting.

We suffer unwittingly from our own idolatry. The more images we present to people, the more irrelevant and perverse and unattractive they find us. Why? The image, because it invites comparison, is irrelevant. Few people are not sensible enough to see that the image does not relate to them. Our images suggest arrogance: in them we set ourselves up as a mold for the world. Even the most belligerent and unrealistic Communist ideals do not seem to do that. Instead, they present people with standards of perfection which they are supposed to apply to themselves.

The image—limited, concrete, and oversimplified—inevitably seems narrow and unadaptable. Because it is a projection of ourselves, it declares our conceit. Images always seem more static and rigid than ideals. Utopianism has a happy fluidity and vagueness. What people in self-conscious, turbulent Asia and Africa want is fluidity: something dynamic, something iridescent, something that changes. Least of all do they want somebody else's image to fit into.

Much of what we have been doing to improve the world's opinion of us has had the contrary effect. Audio-visual aids which we have sent over the world are primarily aids to belief in the irrelevance, the arrogance, the rigidity, and the conceit of America. Not because they are poorly made. On the contrary, *because* they are well made and vividly projected. Not because they are favorable images or unfavorable images, but because they are images.

This helps us explain, too, why we seem "materialist" to all the world. To future historians it may seem bizarre that in our age Communism, a historical movement which most explicitly based itself on materialism, should have been called "idealistic." And that the United States, a nation explicitly built on ideals, should have had a reputation for being materialist. Any prosperous country will, of course, be blamed (and envied) for its materialism by its less prosperous neighbors. Discovering we cannot have another people's virtues, we call them vices. They similarly reproach us. But in addition we especially suffer in the eyes of the world because our prosperity and our technological success have doomed us to present ourselves to the world in images.

Although we may suffer from idolatry, we do not, I think, suffer from materialism—from the overvaluing of material objects for their own sake. Of this the world accuses us. Yet our very wealth itself has somehow made us immune to materialism—the characteristic vice of impoverished peoples. Instead, our peculiar idolatry is one with which the world till now has been unfamiliar. Others have not been rich enough nor had the technology to flood their consciousness with shadows. Nor to flood the world with images of themselves. It is to these images and not to material objects that we are devoted. No wonder that the puzzled world finds this unattractive and calls it by the name of its own old-fashioned vices.

The multiplication of images, by stimulating our economy and arousing extravagant expectations, has, of course, helped make us the richest country in the world. Despite some flagrant injustices and inequalities, we have diffused opportunity more equally and more widely than ever before. Yet by no image-magic can we extend the American continent, nor can we include others in American history. If we must speak to other peoples, we might do better to speak more simply. Not with the devices by which we sell ourselves on images of things we are not sure we want, nor in the new rhetoric of the neither-true-nor-false.

Of all nations in the world, the United States was built in nobody's image. It was the land of the unexpected, of unbounded hope, of ideals, of quest for an unknown perfection. It is all the more unfitting that we should offer ourselves in images. And all the more fitting that the images which we make wittingly or unwittingly to sell America to the world should come back to haunt and curse us. Perhaps, instead of announcing ourselves by our shadows and our idols, we would do better to try to share with others the quest which has been America.

II

To DO THIS has never been easy. It is doubly difficult since the Graphic Revolution and the rise of images have transformed our thinking. A great obstacle, itself a product of the Graphic Revolution, is our belief in "prestige."

It is on this very quest for prestige that we now spend our efforts. Formerly our statesmen—Washington or Adams or Jefferson or Jackson or Lincoln—would have said they wished others to admire, love, or fear the United States. They sought respect for America and for American ideals. Today we no longer speak so directly. Instead we hope America will have a "favorable image" abroad. We hope our nation will have "prestige." What does this mean?

It means we hope the world will be attracted to, or dazzled by, our image! Formerly, when we worried about our reputation, we worried about what the world would think of us or our way of striving. Now we worry about what the world will think of our image.

Although the word "prestige" in its dominant twentieth-century American usage is novel, it has not strayed too far from its etymological origins. It is probably not unrelated to the word "prestidigitate"—to perform a juggler's trick or magic. "Prestige," which came into English through the French language, came ultimately from the Latin *praestigium,* which meant an illusion or a delusion, and was usually employed in the plural, *praestigiae,* to signify jugglers' tricks. This in turn had come from *praestringere,* which meant to bind fast, or to blindfold—hence to dazzle. In English, too, the word "prestige" originally meant deceit or illusion; "prestigious" (an adjective especially closely related to the noun "prestidigitation") until recently meant deceitful, cheating, or illusory. For a long time "prestige" had only an unfavorable sense. The new favorable sense is probably an American invention. In our common American parlance, the merest hint of the old unfavorable sense still remains. A person who has prestige has a kind of glamor: he momentarily blinds or dazzles by his image.

While the word "prestige" is, of course, common enough in our talk about people and things here at home, its significance for all our thought is clearest when we look abroad. There the indirectness of our thinking becomes most obvious. When we talk of prestige abroad we are talking not of ourselves, but of the shadows of ourselves which we can somehow project. To compare prestige, then, is to compare the appeal of images. To insist on our prestige is to insist on the appeal of our image.

In addressing the Republican National Convention in Chicago on July 26, 1960, President Eisenhower remarked:

> The Soviet dictator has said that he has, in his recent journeys and speeches, succeeded in damaging the prestige of America. . . .
>
> Concerning this matter of comparative national prestige, I challenge him to this test: Will he agree to the holding of free elections under the sponsorship of the United Nations to permit people everywhere in every nation and on every continent, to vote on one single, simple issue?
>
> That issue is: Do you want to live under a Communist regime or under a free system such as found in the United States? . . .
>
> Are the Soviets willing to measure their world prestige by the results of such elections?
>
> But the United States would gladly do so.

This proposal called for a world-wide market research project by the United Nations to see whether the United States or the Soviet Union offered the world a more attractive package. One did not need to be oversubtle to suspect that the proposal itself was meant to be a piece of skillful packaging. A "bold proposal" like this (of course there was not the slightest chance it would be adopted) would supposedly improve the image of America abroad. In our world of pseudo-events the dramatic gesture of American openness and honesty was as contrived, as devious, and as disingenuous as could be imagined.

The very notion of "high" or "low" prestige, of people "accepting" or "rejecting" the "Russian Way" or the "American Way," itself betrays unconcern for the complex, inwardly conflicting reactions of real people to other real people. It reveals a naive take-it-or-leave-it mentality that is at one with the oversubtlety and indirectness of all our thinking about our relations to other peoples. In our popularity game we ask the world not, "Do you like me?" but, "Do you like my shadow?"

During the Presidential campaign of 1960 there was much discussion over whether the Eisenhower Administration would or should publish the results of a "prestige" poll conducted by the United States Information Agency under the auspices of the Department of State. Candidate Kennedy bitterly attacked the Administration for failing to publish the figures (the data, it was assumed, must have been simple and statistical, with an obvious, damaging moral). Supposedly in the national interest, the figures were not revealed. If people did not like our image, it was not good public relations to announce it, or to reveal why. Better deftly repair the image for better results.

Our thinking has become so blurred, we have so mixed our image and our reality, that we assume our place in the world is determined by our prestige—that is, by others' respect for our image. "Not least of all," Walter Lippmann warned in December, 1960, "our prestige in the world has diminished. We have ceased to look like a vigorous and confident nation."

In competition for prestige it seems only sensible to try to perfect our image rather than ourselves. That seems the most economical, direct way to produce the desired result. Accustomed to live in a world of pseudo-events, celebrities, dissolving forms, and shadowy but overshadowing images, we mistake our shadows for ourselves. To us they seem more real than the reality. Why should they not seem so to others? Our technique seems direct only because in our own daily lives the pseudo-event seems always destined to dominate the natural facts. We no longer even recognize that our technique is indirect, that we have committed ourselves to managing shadows. *We* can live in our world of illusions. Although we find it hard to imagine, other peoples still live in the world of dreams. We live in a world of our making. Can we conjure others to live there too? We love the image, and believe it. But will they?

III

ABROAD the making of credible images seems a problem. It is hard to persuade others to fit themselves into our molds, to be at home among our illusions, and to mistake these for their own reality. At home our problem is the opposite. What to do when everybody accepts the images, when these images have pushed reality out of sight?

Here, in the United States, the making of images is every-day business. The image has reached out from commerce to the worlds of education and politics, and into every corner of our daily lives. Our churches, our charities, our schools, our universities, all now seek favorable images. Their way of saying they want people to think well of them is to say they want people to have favorable images of them. Our national politics has become a competition for images or between images, rather than between ideals. The domination of campaigning by television simply dramatizes this fact. An effective President must be every year more concerned with projecting images of himself. We suffer more every day from the blurriness and the rigidity of our image-thinking.

Examples are everywhere. Life becomes more and more

illusory. We have become so accustomed to our illusions, they have become so routine, that they seem no longer produced by any special magic. The forces I have described in this book converge on our everyday experience. They are revealed in almost everything we do, in almost everything we see, in the very words we use.

One example is especially significant to me. I came upon it casually, but it focuses many of the problems I have discussed in this book.

Early in the fall of 1960, I received an elaborate color brochure advertising the Chevrolet for 1961. Inside, the only full-page illustration is a brilliant portrait of a man in the front seat of a de luxe new model. His hard-top convertible (advertised for its unobstructed view) is parked near the edge of what seems to be the Grand Canyon, a background of indescribable natural beauty. The man is not, however, peering out of the car window at the scenery. Instead he is preoccupied with a contraption in his hand; he is preparing to look into his "Viewmaster," a portable slide viewer using cardboard disks holding tiny color transparencies of scenic beauty. On the seat beside him are several extra disks. Standing outside the car are his wife and three small children. The eldest of them, a little girl about ten years old, at whom his wife is looking, is herself preoccupied with a small box camera with which she is preparing to take a picture of her father seated in the car.

Here, if ever, is a parable of twentieth-century America. All the ingenuity of General Motors, Eastman Kodak, generations of Fords, Firestones, and Edisons, the accumulated skills of fifty years of automotive engineering, of production know-how and industrial design, all the imagination and techniques of full-color printing, of junior and senior executives, and the whole gargantuan paraphernalia of the American economy have brought us to this. An opportunity for me to be impressed by the image of a man (with the Grand Canyon at his elbow) looking at an image, and being photographed as he does it!

While this example is beautifully symbolic, others are all around us. Almost any evening on television I can watch in my own home a celebrity performing in a skit which is the television version of a movie (made from a novel), to the accompaniment of dubbed-in laughter and applause—the whole performance sponsored by a steel manufacturer or an oil company, by a manufacturer of cosmetics to cure imaginary ailments, or by a brewer or cigarette manufacturer of products indistinguishable from those of his competitor—all put on in order to create a more favorable corporate image.

I well remember my disappointment when the Democratic National Convention was being held in Chicago in the summer of 1956 and I finally secured some tickets to the visitors' galleries at the International Livestock Amphitheatre. It was the first time I had ever attended a National Party Convention, and I took my young sons along. Finally admitted to our seats, we found ourselves confused by the floor events. Along with the other "actual spectators," we spent our time watching the television screens which the arrangements committee had considerately placed there. These sets showed us precisely the same programs we would have seen from our living room. The unlucky delegates on the floor below (those were the days before portable television) without the aid of a television screen must have been more confused than we were about what was going on.

Not long ago I met a public relations counsel who held a responsible position in a large and influential firm. His specialty was writing—speeches, articles, letters—for public figures. I asked him how much he consulted with his clients. He explained that of course he had to meet and know the men for whom he wrote in order to be able to write like them. But, he said, a difficulty in working for the same clients over an extended period was that, if you were successful in writing for them, it became harder and harder to know what they were really like. His clients, he said, had an incurable tendency to forget that they had not written their own speeches. When he asked them in briefing sessions what they thought of this or that, they were increasingly inclined to quote to the public relations counsel the very speech which the counsel had supplied them a few weeks before. It was disturbing, he said, to hear yourself quoted to yourself by somebody else who thought it was himself speaking: you began to wonder whether it was your language after all.

This suggested to my public relations counsel friend another example of the same problem. A client had decided to move his plant away, and therefore to change his public relations counsel to a firm in the city where his new plant would be located. This client telephoned my friend, explained the situation, and asked that he ghostwrite a letter to be sent to the head of the public relations firm, explaining the situation, enumerating his regrets, and generally keeping up the image which the firm had helped him build up over the years. My friend wrote the letter. A few days later the head of the public relations firm called in my ghostwriting friend, told him he had a piece of bad news, namely, that Mr. X was moving his firm away and would have to drop their services. But, the boss said, there were only the warmest feelings (as he had just learned from the letter he had received); now he wanted my friend to draft a nice letter which he as head of the firm could send, explaining *his* regrets that the business connection was being terminated. My friend remarked that he was probably the highest-paid man ever employed to write letters to himself.

We have heard ours called an age without direction—a "directionless" age. It would be better to call us the age of indirection. Everything I have described helps us produce secondhandness. We make, we seek, and finally we enjoy, the contrivance of all experience. We fill our lives not with experience, but with the images of experience. The most popular—most "functional"—styles of modern architecture are not necessarily those most comfortable to live in, but always those which photograph well. "Money," we are told on the radio by a "friendly" personal loan company promising to give us cash without security so we can rid ourselves of worrisome debts—"Money is the magic ingredient that gives you financial status."

The awkward monstrosities of our everyday speech betray the secondhandness of our way of looking at everything. We no longer talk about something; we talk "in terms of" it. In an organization a man is no longer important; he is "at the policy level." What we seek, we are told, is no longer wealth or glory or happiness, but a sociological concoction called "status." We do not simply "believe"; instead we talk of "the values we hold." We cannot do something in our spare time, we must cultivate it as a "hobby." We do not study music or art or literature; we study the "appreciation" of music or art or literature. We do not rest; we "seek relaxation." We are not asked to go see our Ford Dealer, but rather to "visit our local dealership." We no longer do a job; we play a role. We do not learn parental virtues; instead we are prompted on how to "play the role of" parents. We less often say we like a man or find him sympathetic; instead we prefer to observe that he has "made a good impression on us." We do not simply plan to meet again; we must arrange to "set up" another meeting. We do not find a person; we "contact" him. We do not discuss a problem; we look at it "policy-wise."

The technology of our daily lives has, of course, prepared us for all this. When we have a letter from a person, it is no longer in his own hand (as it would have been if Franklin or Washington or Jefferson had written us); it is a typewritten, mimeographed, or Thermofaxed image of what he has written. Often it is a transcription not of his writing at all, but of the words he spoke into his dictaphone, copied by a secretary he has not seen. The voice we hear, more and more often, is not in the physical presence of the speaker, but a sound in a telephone receiver, or from a phonograph record, or over radio, or on television.

This is the age of contrivance. The artificial has become so commonplace that the natural begins to seem contrived. The natural is the "un-" and the "non-." It is the age of the "*un*filtered" cigarette (the filter comes to seem more natural than the tobacco), of the "*un*abridged" novel (abridgment is the norm), of the "*un*cut" version of a movie. We begin to look on wood as a "*non*-synthetic" cellulose. All nature then is the world of the "*non*-artificial." Fact itself has become "*non*fiction."

But people—even twentieth-century Americans—will not so supinely allow themselves to be deprived of the last vestiges of spontaneous reality. By a new residual effect, then, we become doubly interested in any happenings which somehow seem to offer us an oasis of the uncontrived. One example is the American passion for news about crime and sports. This is not simply an effect of the degradation of public tastes to the trivial and the unserious. More significantly, it is one expression of our desperate hunger for the spontaneous, for the non-pseudo-event.

Of course, many sports events become pseudo-events; and some (professional wrestling, for example) have actually flourished by exploiting their reputation for being synthetic. But there still remain many areas (for example, amateur sports and professional baseball) where we have succeeded to a certain extent in guarding the uncorrupted authenticity of the event. Our outrage when we find that a boxing match was rigged or that an amateur basketball team was bribed comes not merely from our feeling that our morality has been violated. It also expresses our angered frustration at being deprived of one of our few remaining contacts with an uncontrived reality: with people really struggling to win, and not merely to have their victory reported in the papers.

The world of crime, even more than that of sports, is a last refuge of the authentic, uncorrupted spontaneous event. Of course there are rare exceptions (the planned "violators" of law for political purposes, like the suffragettes, or more recently the Freedom Riders in the South). But, generally speaking, crimes are not pseudo-events, however industriously they may be exploited by the press. Only seldom are they committed for the purpose of being reported. Quite the contrary, a man who commits a murder or a rape, who robs a bank, or embezzles from his employer, hopes to get away with it. Our hunger for crime news and sports news, then, far from showing we have lost our sense of reality, actually suggests that even in a world so flooded by pseudo-events and images of all kinds, we still know (and are intrigued by) a spontaneous event when we see one.

The same quest for spontaneity helps explain, too, our morbid interest in private lives, in personal gossip, and in the sexual indiscretions of public figures. In a world where the public acts of politicians and celebrities become more and more contrived, we look ever more eagerly for happenings not brought into being especially for our benefit. We search for those areas of life which may have remained immune to the cancer of pseudo-eventfulness.

I V

ONE OF the deepest and least remarked features of the Age of Contrivance is what I would call the mirror effect. Nearly everything we do to enlarge our world, to make life more interesting, more varied, more exciting, more vivid, more "fabulous," more promising, in the long run has an opposite effect. In the extravagance of our expectations and in our ever increasing power, we transform elusive dreams into graspable images within which each of us can fit. By doing so we mark the boundaries of our world with a wall of mirrors. Our strenuous and elaborate efforts to enlarge experience have the unintended result of narrowing it. In frenetic quest for the unexpected, we end by finding only the unexpectedness we have planned for ourselves. We meet ourselves coming back. A Hollywood love triangle, according to Leo Rosten, consists of an actor, his wife, and himself. All of us are now entangled with ourselves. Everywhere we see ourselves in the mirror.

Some schools of philosophers have long told us that all experience consists only of the images we have in our mind.

This has been expressed in various forms of Neoplatonism. In the eighteenth century it was given classic modern expression by George Berkeley (1685–1753). In his *New Theory of Vision* (1709) he argued that what we see is not simply the imprinting on the mind of the characteristics of external objects, but the mind's reconstruction of the fragmentary visual signs received, into the images which alone make sense to the mind. He went on to argue that only these mental images were "real"—and anything in the whole world was therefore real only insofar as it was held together in the mental experience of some being. According to him, the all-imaging, all-perceiving being was God. But, though we are not philosophers, we can see a difference between what bothered Berkeley and what bothers us. Even if we agree with Berkeley that all experience everywhere in some special sense consists of nothing but images, there remains a great difference between the older philosopher's world of omnipresent images and our own. The difference is not that never in the past has it been possible persuasively to describe experience as consisting only of mental images. Rather that such an overwhelming proportion of the images *we* live among have been contrived by man himself.

More and more of our experience thus becomes invention rather than discovery. The more planned and prefabricated our experience becomes, the more we include in it only what "interests" us. Then we can more effectively exclude the exotic world beyond our ken: the very world which would jar our experience, and which we most need to make us more largely human. The criterion of well-knownness overshadows others, because the well-known is by definition what most people already know. We seek celebrities, not only among men and women, but even among books, plays, ideas, movies, and commodities. We make our whole experience a *"reader's* digest" where we read only what we want to read, and not what anyone else wants to write. We listen for what we want to hear and not for what someone wants to say. We talk to ourselves, without even noticing that it is not somebody else talking to us. We talk to ourselves about what we are supposed to be talking about. We find this out by seeing what other people are talking to themselves about. "All I know," Will Rogers remarked in the earlier days of the Graphic Revolution, "is what I read in the papers." Today he might modernize his complaint: "All I see in the papers is what I already know."

We have all heard the story of how, once upon a time in ancient Greece, a handsome youth named Narcissus was beloved by Echo, a mountain nymph. She died of a broken heart when he spurned her love. The gods decided, then, to punish Narcissus; they doomed him to fall in love with his own image. A soothsayer predicted that Narcissus would live only until the moment when he saw himself. This was, of course, in the days before photography or television. And the only way they could make him see himself was to have him see his own reflection in the limpid waters of a spring one day as he was leaning over it. When he saw his reflection his passion for this phantom so obsessed him then and there that he could not leave the waterside. On that very spot he died of languor. His name was later given to the flower which grows at the edge of springs, whose bulbs were supposed to be a sedative. Through the Greek word which means numbness or stupor (*narke:* whence "narcotic"), love of a self-image is closely connected with languor, sleepiness, and inactivity.

As individuals and as a nation, we now suffer from social narcissism. The beloved Echo of our ancestors, the virgin America, has been abandoned. We have fallen in love with our own image, with images of our making, which turn out to be images of ourselves.

How can we flee from this image of ourselves? How can we immunize ourselves to its bewitching conceitful power?

This becomes ever more difficult. The world of our making becomes ever more mirror-like. Our celebrities reflect each of us; faraway "adventures" are the projections of what we have prepared ourselves to expect, and which we now can pay others to prepare for us. The images themselves become shadowy mirror reflections of one another: one interview comments on another; one television show spoofs another; novel, television show, radio program, movie, comic book, and the way we think of ourselves, all become merged into mutual reflections. At home we begin to try to live according to the script of television programs of happy families, which are themselves nothing but amusing quintessences of us.

Our new New World, made to be an escape from drab reality, itself acquires a predictable monotony from which there seems no escape. This is the monotony within us, the monotony of self-repetition. Our tired palates will not let us find our way back. When we look for a "natural" flavor all we can find is one that is "non-artificial." We become more and more like the character (described by the English wit, Sydney Smith) who had spent his youth "in letting down empty buckets into empty wells; and he is frittering away his age in trying to draw them up again." A juvenile critic recently said that television was "chewing gum for the eyes." In the late nineteenth century a bitter critic called cheap novels "the chewing gum of literature, offering neither savor nor nutriment, only subserving the mechanical process of mastication." But chewing gum (an American invention and an American expression) itself may have a symbolic significance. We might say now that chewing gum is the television of the mouth. There is no danger so long as we do not think that by chewing gum we are getting nourishment. But the Graphic Revolution has offered us the means of making all experience a form of mental chewing gum, which can be continually sweetened to give us the illusion that we are being nourished.

More and more accustomed to testing reality by the image, we will find it hard to retrain ourselves so we may once again test the image by reality. It becomes ever harder to moderate our expectations, to shape expectations after experience, and not vice versa. For too long already we have had the specious power to shape "reality." How can we re-discover the world of the uncontrived?

V

WE ARE DECEIVED and obstructed by the very machines we make to enlarge our vision. In an earlier age, an architectural symbol of small-town, growing America was the friendly front porch. In our day, the architectural symbol of our domestic life is the picture window. The picture window is as much to look into as to look out of. It is where we display ourselves to ourselves. When from the outside you look in, what you usually see is not people going about their business, but a large, ornate, tasteless electric lamp, which during the day prevents the natural sunlight from coming in. When we look out our own picture window, if we do not see our neighbor's garbage pail, we are apt to see our neighbor himself. But he too is apt to be doing nothing more than looking at us through *his* picture window.

In the simpler years of the depression of the 1930's, Will Rogers said the United States might be the only country in history to go to the poorhouse in an automobile. We had not then yet discovered the deeper, scientifically distilled poverty of our abundance. If Will Rogers were alive today, he might add to his portrait the paradox of a people taking pictures of themselves—even on their way to that same poorhouse.

How escape? How avoid a life of looking in and out of picture windows?

Here enters a providential peculiarity of our ailment. In the last stages of Albert Camus' *Plague,* Dr. Rieux remarks that a man "can't cure and know at the same time." Dr. Rieux says that his job, the more urgent job, is not to know but to cure. Our plague, our disease of extravagant expectations, is different. To know our disease, to discover what we suffer from, may itself be the only possible cure.

"Discontent," Oscar Wilde once observed, "is the first step in the progress of a man or a nation." This is surely true today. Our problem is complicated by the fact that the prescriptions which nations offer for themselves are also symptoms of their diseases. But illusory solutions will not cure our illusions. Our discontent begins by finding false villains whom we can accuse of deceiving us. Next we find false heroes whom we expect to liberate us. The hardest, most discomfiting discovery is that each of us must emancipate himself. Though we may suffer from mass illusions, there is no formula for mass disenchantment. By the law of pseudo-events, all efforts at mass disenchantment themselves only embroider our illusions.

While we have given others great power to deceive us, to create pseudo-events, celebrities, and images, they could not have done so without our collaboration. If there is a crime of deception being committed in America today, each of us is the principal, and all others are only accessories. It is dangerously tempting to treat our illusions by compounding them. To try to cure the ills of advertising by creating a more favorable image of advertising. To salve mediocrity by mediocre appeals for "excellence." To drown our illiteracy in illiterate appeals for literacy. To hide our individual purposelessness in the purposelessness of a committee fabricating an attractive image of the national purpose.

Each of us must disenchant himself, must moderate his expectations, must prepare himself to receive messages coming in from the outside. The first step is to begin to suspect that there may be a world out there, beyond our present or future power to image or to imagine. We should not worry over how to export more of the American images among which we live. We should not try to persuade others to share our illusions. We should try to reach outside our images. We should seek new ways of letting messages reach us; from our own past, from God, from the world which we may hate or think we hate. To give visas to strange and alien and outside notions. Notions of which neither we nor the Communists have ever dreamed and which we can never see in our mirror. One of our grand illusions is the belief in a "cure." There is no cure. There is only the opportunity for discovery. For this the New World gave us a grand, unique beginning.

We must first awake before we can walk in the right direction. We must discover our illusions before we can even realize that we have been sleepwalking. The least and the most we can hope for is that each of us may penetrate the unknown jungle of images in which we live our daily lives. That we may discover anew where dreams end and where illusions begin. This is enough. Then we may know where we are, and each of us may decide for himself where he wants to go.

Suggestions for Further Reading

(and Writing)

(Note: The following discussion of books has three purposes: (1) to tell the reader where he may learn more about topics I have mentioned, (2) to acknowledge my debt to the books, articles, and other materials which I have found most useful, and (3) to point out some unexplored territories.)

The deeper, more revolutionary changes in human experience of the kind I have tried to describe in this volume enter our history books only slowly. This is usually after the new ways have come to seem normal, and therefore have ceased to threaten the respectable thinking patterns of scholars. "The Renaissance," a European movement of awakening which began at least as early as the fourteenth century and had run its course by the end of the seventeenth century, did not enter common use among historians until the mid-nineteenth century. Not until the later nineteenth and early twentieth century did historians energetically explore the Industrial Revolution, which had begun at least as early as the seventeenth century. The more professionalized and more respectable the historian's profession becomes, the more he is tempted to classify fluid experience into rigid categories: political history, economic history, intellectual history, etc., etc. Each of these becomes a recognized specialty with its own professional associations, its own learned journals, and with "No Trespassing" signs erected against outsiders. Inevitably, then, there is no respectable place to put the great revolutionary changes which occur in between or entirely outside of the old categories. Facts which fit neatly under traditional chapter headings are not apt to be radical novelties; facts which do not fit are apt to be left out.

In the last several decades we have made great progress in providing accurate texts of the writings of the political leaders of the early age of our republic—of Franklin, Jefferson, Adams, Madison, Hamilton, and many others. We continue to gather in the national archives and the Library of Congress, in state archives, in local historical societies, and elsewhere, the correspondence files of public figures, data on the drafting of government documents, and many other traditionally important historical remains. We should continue to do so, and should still further improve our means for preserving, cataloguing, calendaring, and editing these monuments of our national tradition. But except for a few books (mostly on the history of newspapers and magazines), except for some sporadic progress in business history and on scattered other topics, and for a few ingenious projects like those of Columbia University's Oral History Department, almost all the great changes of the Graphic Revolution have remained outside the stream of our best historical scholarship.

Numerous subjects like the history of photography, of techniques of art reproduction, of group travel, of the hotel or the motel, of radio or of television, are still generally considered beneath the dignity (or at best on the periphery) of the historian's profession. Despite some loosening of categories encouraged by new American Studies programs and the American Studies Association, many of the most important topics in the history of our civilization remain academic outcasts. They fit into no familiar academic category, they are not examinable for the Ph.D.; or they require a combination of scientific and humanistic knowledge which is too rare. If professors themselves do not know a subject, why should the students? Who will say, then, whether a thesis is "competent"? Our historical scholarship, including much that calls itself "interdisciplinary," continues to pour almost exclusively into old molds, into the background of this or that tariff bill, into the proto-history of minor political parties, into chronicling the literary treatment of political or economic subjects; or, at most, into finding novel ways of relating the statistics of the new social sciences to the same conventional categories—the history of labor in the Jacksonian era, "status" and the Progressive movement, etc.

If this book serves no other purpose, it might offer a rough map of some too-little-known territories in the new American wilderness. It might suggest how little we still know, and how slowly we are learning about the inward cataclysms of our age.

The main impetus to this book has been my personal experience: the billboards I have seen, the newspapers and magazines I have read, the radio programs I have heard, the television programs I have watched, the movies I have attended, the advertisements I receive daily through the mail, the commodities I have noticed in stores, the salesmen's pitches which have been aimed at me, the conversation I hear, the desires I sense all around me.

The tendencies and weaknesses I remark in twentieth-century America are my own. Whether or not I can persuade my contemporaries, I suspect that some future historian, with undue reverence for the printed word, may treat me as a "primary source." I would like to persuade my fellow-Americans today that they, too, are primary sources. The trivia of our daily experience are evidence of the most important question in our lives: namely, what we believe to be real.

The following is not intended to be a complete, or even a basic, bibliography. Instead it is a list of items I have happened to find most suggestive and which the reader may also find helpful in opening up these subjects.

For this purpose some of the most useful books (and some of those most neglected by the historian, professional or amateur) deal with the history of our spoken and printed language. No subject is more exacting of its scholars; but the fruits of linguistic scholarship are handy to us all. We must certainly beware of dogmatic statements concerning the first use of a word, yet this is no more than the good historian's caution of all statements resting on absence of evidence. Those who record the history of our language give us a mine of suggestions of when certain ways of talking and thinking became widespread.

The language record has an intimacy, a color, and a nuance hard to find elsewhere. The basic, epoch-making work here is, of course, James A. H. Murray and others, *A New English Dictionary on Historical Principles* (10 vols. and a supplement, 1888–1933 and another in preparation), commonly known as the Oxford English Dictionary (or OED). Its American counterpart is Sir William A. Craigie and James R. Hulbert (eds.), *A Dictionary of American English* (4 vols., 1938–1944), carrying the history of the American language down to about 1900. For the twentieth century, we are fortunate to have Mitford M. Mathews (ed.), *A Dictionary of Americanisms* (2 vols., 1951), which picks up where Craigie and Hulbert left off. Mathews' work is confined to "Americanisms," that is, words, expressions, or usages that originated in the United States; it revises some items in the earlier work. In addition to these we have the classic volumes by H. L. Mencken, *The American Language* (1937), *The American Language: Supplement One* (1945; Chs. 1–6) and *Supplement Two* (1948; Chs. 7–11), all presently being revised by Raven I. McDavid, Jr., whose valuable updated and abridged version of these works will appear shortly. The history of twentieth-century spoken usage is recorded in the sensible but incomplete Bergen Evans and Cornelia Evans, *Dictionary of Con-*

temporary American Usage (1957) and the brilliant and meticulous Harold Wentworth and Stuart Berg Flexner, *Dictionary of American Slang* (1960). A few hours spent with Wentworth and Flexner will teach the student more about the history of American feeling, customs, and social attitudes than twice that time spent with any other book I know on American social history. Of current dictionaries of the American language, I have found most useful *Webster's New World Dictionary of the American Language* (1957). Another excellent dictionary is the *American College Dictionary* (1959). We may refuse explicitly to describe our innermost sentiments, but the quality of our reticence is willy-nilly recorded in the words we use to conceal our feelings. The master of the history of our language can confront us with ourselves.

Other specially valuable sources for the history of the changes I describe in this volume are the practical handbooks (e.g., *Trademark Management: A Guide for Businessmen,* published by the United States Trademark Association, N.Y., 1955; William M. Freeman, *The Big Name* (1957), on securing and policing endorsements) and the trade journals (e.g., *Printers' Ink, Advertising Age, Variety, Publishers' Weekly, Public Opinion Quarterly, Editor and Publisher*). These are reliable and undeniable sources of what people in the profession want to know, what they discuss and worry about.

Chapter 1. *From News Gathering to News Making: A Flood of Pseudo-Events*

The main source for these observations is, of course, the magazines, newspapers, radio and television programs. So far we have no adequate general history of what Americans have thought of as "news," nor on the general history of communications or of image making, although we do have valuable scholarly works on a few traditionally classifiable items like newspapers and magazines. What I call the Graphic Revolution has remained virtually unchronicled, except in popular works, practical professional handbooks and textbooks, and scattered trade and technical journals.

The background of the Graphic Revolution in the history of the American economy is not easy to trace because, despite our widespread (and largely unwitting) adoption of an economic interpretation of history, much of American economic history remains virgin territory. Colleges all over the country vainly seek qualified economic historians. They remain extremely rare, both because the more fluid, unconventional topics have been pre-empted by the newer social sciences (political science, sociology, psychology, and social anthropology) and because, as economic theory has become more and more mathematical, fewer and fewer historians can qualify as literate in a world of graphs and equations. On all sorts of topics much valuable information for the layman is handily available in the United States Department of Commerce, Bureau of the Census, *Historical Statistics of the United States, Colonial Times to 1957* (Government Printing Office, Washington, D.C., 1960). Among the most suggestive books are those of the Swiss historian, Siegfried Giedion: *Space, Time and Architecture* (1941) and *Mechanization Takes Command* (1948).

On the beginnings of an American system of manufacturing and the system of interchangeable parts, which was a forerunner and prototype of the Graphic Revolution, see Jeannette Mirsky and Allan Nevins, *The World of Eli Whitney* (1952), especially Chs. 13–16, and Constance McL. Green's cogent *Eli Whitney and the Birth of American Technology* (1956). A book on an extremely technical subject which is nevertheless quite intelligible to the layman is Joseph W. Roe, *English and American Tool Builders* (1916). This volume introduces us to the master mechanics, die makers, and inventors of measuring machines who had a large role in devising our present system of manufacturing and producing our American standard of living. John A. Kouwenhoven, *Made in America* (1948) is a sprightly and original exploration of (among other topics) the artistic consequences of American technology. Suggestive short introductions to this subject are: John E. Sawyer, "The Social Basis of the American System of Manufacturing," *Journal of Economic History*, XIV (No. 4, 1954), 361–379, and "Social Structure and Economic Progress," *American Economic Review*, XLI (May, 1951), 321–329; and D. L. Burn, "The Genesis of American Engineering Competition," *Economic History*, II (1930–1933), 292–311.

A detailed history of modern machine printing techniques and especially of new techniques of speed-printing and paper manufacture would give us much of the background we still need for the history of the newspaper. We are fortunate to have the epoch-making books by Frank Luther Mott: *A History of American Magazines*, (4 vols., which carries the story to 1905; 1938–1957), *American Journalism* (Revised ed., 1950), and *The News in America* (1952). I have leaned heavily on Mott's work, which is admirable from almost any point of view; it is readable, factually scrupulous, and imaginative, although somewhat lacking in large organizing ideas. A valuable earlier work which emphasizes the social background is Alfred M. Lee, *The Daily Newspaper in America* (1937). A briefer, more recent book, with emphasis on general trends and the newspaper profession itself is Bernard A. Weisberger, *The American Newspaperman* (Chicago History of American Civilization Series, 1961). An excellent survey of the literature is found in the bibliography at the back of Weisberger's short volume; or in Allan Nevins, "American Journalism and Its Historical Treatment," *Journalism Quarterly,* XXXVI (Fall, 1959), 411–422, 519. A helpful but incomplete introduction to an important related topic is Lyman H. Weeks, *A History of Paper-Manufacturing in the United States, 1640–1916* (1916).

We can learn much about the development of modern journalistic techniques in the autobiographies of particular newspapermen (like Lincoln Steffens, *Autobiography* (1931)), in their biographies (for example, Don C. Seitz, *The James Gordon Bennetts Father and Son: Proprietors of the New York Herald* (1928); Oliver Carlson, *The Man Who Made News: A Biography of James Gordon Bennett, 1795–1872* (1942); Francis Brown, *Raymond of The Times* (1952)), or in their credos (Charles A. Dana, *The Art of Newspaper Making* (1900)). Newspapermen now alive—both the pioneers and the developers of news-gathering and news-making crafts and professions—could perform a lasting public service by writing their intimate professional autobiographies.

The history of press agentry and public relations is still to be written. The best sources are fragmentary, like Edward L. Bernays' pioneer handbook *Crystallizing Public Opinion* (1923) and his later writings, *Public Relations* (1952), and the collection of essays which he edited, *The Engineering of Consent* (1955); or topical, like the helpful article, "Public Relations Today," *Business Week* (July 2, 1960), pp. 41–62, and occasional articles in *Fortune.* Bernays' writings are among the most sophisticated, philosophically self-conscious, and literate works on public relations—the institution and the profession. See his valuable bibliography: *Public Relations, Edward L. Bernays and the American Scene: Annotated Bibliography . . . from 1917 to 1951* (1951; supplement, 1957). His autobiography, now in preparation, could be a major document in American social history. See Eric F. Goldman's useful brief introduction to the history of this subject, *Two-Way Street* (1948); and David Finn's effective brief article, "The Price of Corporate Vanity," *Harvard Business Review,* XXXIX (July–August, 1961), 135–143, which came to my attention just as this book was going to press. From his extensive experience in public relations Finn comes to conclusions very close to mine.

The relation of the rise of newspapers to American politics, perhaps because it is more obviously a matter of public interest, has been more adequately, though still fragmentarily, treated. Walter Lippmann early in this century produced succinct and prophetic books, *Public Opinion* (1922) and *The Phantom Public* (1925), which envisaged the out-reaching implications of changing news-gathering techniques for political theory and democratic institutions. Douglass Cater, *The Fourth Branch of Government* (1959) is a profound and fundamental book on which I have drawn freely; it deserves a large audience. The rise of the Washington press corps and the development of its techniques and protocol are traced in James E. Pollard, *The Presidents and the Press* (1947), a treasure house of neatly arranged information on the press-personalities of our Presidents; and Leo C. Rosten, *The Washington Correspondents* (1937), which gathers valuable statistical and sociological data on 127 correspondents who were in the capital between September, 1935, and December, 1936. The critical views expressed by magazine and newspapermen themselves can be sampled in T. S. Matthews, *The Sugar Pill: An Essay on Newspapers* (1959), which attacks the effort to make news into entertainment, from the point of view of an ex-*Time* editor, and Carl E. Lindstrom, *The Fading American Newspaper* (1960), which describes the technological, financial, and social forces which help explain the declining influence of the newspaper. Some interesting suggestions are found in Oswald Garrison Villard's collection of essays, *The Disappearing Daily* (1944), especially in the title essay. On the first interview see George Turnbull, "Some Notes on the History of the Interview," *Journalism Quarterly*, XIII (Sept., 1936), 272–279.

For the implications of changes in news-gathering techniques for American politics see my "Direct Democracy of Public Relations: Selling the President to the People," in *America and the Image of Europe* (1960), pp. 97–117, and more generally, Walter Johnson, *1600 Pennsylvania Avenue: Presidents and the People, 1929–1959* (1960). Richard H. Rovere, *Senator Joe McCarthy* (1959) is an acute and knowledgeable interpretation supported by the personal insights and on-the-spot knowledge of one of the most literate reporters of our age. We can glimpse the techniques of the first master of modern Presidential press relations in the reminiscences of those close to F.D.R.: for example, Robert Sherwood, *Roosevelt and Hopkins* (1948), Samuel I. Rosenman, *Working With Roosevelt* (1952), and in the several brilliant volumes of Arthur M. Schlesinger, Jr., *The Age of Roosevelt* (1957–   ).

A bright light on the uses of news-gathering, news-making, and news-disseminating techniques in Presidential politics is Theodore H. White, *The Making of the President: 1960* (1961). On the interrelation of the media, and on the television debates, see especially Chapter 11.

There is not, to my knowledge, an adequate history of the *Congressional Record*. To do it properly would require a Rabelaisian sense of humor and a Sophoclean sense of tragedy. A hint of the problems I mention can be found in Clarence Cannon, *Cannon's Procedure in the House of Representatives* (4th ed., Washington, D.C., 1944). The speech of the reformer I refer to is that of Senator George Graham Vest of Missouri, delivered in the Senate, December 23, 1884 (found in *Congressional Record:* Senate, Vol. 16, Pt. 1, 48th Congress, 2d Session, p. 422); it is worth reading in full. A citizen with the curiosity, the time, and the stamina may secure a subscription to the *Record* through his Senator or Congressman. Before doing so, however, he should prepare himself to take the consequences. He should be thoroughly confident of his own devotion to democratic institutions; and there are other risks. It is harder to turn off the flood than to turn it on.

A few sociological studies have been made of the effect of the different media and their relation to one another. One of the best is the study of the MacArthur Parades in Chicago: Kurt Lang and Gladys Engel Lang, "The Unique Perspective of Television and Its Effect: A Pilot Study," *American Sociological Review*, XVIII (1953), 3–12. In more extensive form this study is available as an unpublished doctoral dissertation (1953) in the Sociology Department of the University of Chicago. It won the 1952 prize of the Edward L. Bernays Foundation, and is a study of great subtlety and originality. See also, Reuben Mehling, "Attitude Changing Effect of News and Photo Combinations," *Journalism Quarterly*, XXXVI (Spring, 1959), 189–198; and Elmer E. Cornwell, Jr., "Presidential News: The Expanding Public Image," at pp. 275–283.

The great background changes in the Graphic Revolution still await their historians. Despite some valuable biographies like Carleton Mabee, *The American Leonardo: The Life of Samuel F. B. Morse* (1943), Matthew Josephson, *Edison* (1959), and company histories, like Robert L. Thompson, *Wiring a*

Continent: The History of the Telegraph Industry in the United States, 1832–1886 (1947), the social history of the telegraph, the telephone, the phonograph, radio, and television remains mostly untold. We may hope that the Annenberg School of Communications at the University of Pennsylvania, under the able direction of Gilbert Seldes, and with the assistance among others of Patrick D. Hazard, will fill some of these gaps. We can learn about the development of the typewriter and its pervasive significance for American life in Richard N. Current's concise *The Typewriter and The Men Who Made It* (1954) and in Bruce Bliven, Jr., *The Wonderful Writing Machine* (1954). The history of shorthand could reveal some neglected facets of our life; the history of penmanship and the decline of handwriting might also be suggestive. So far as I know, there is not yet an account of such influential techniques of duplication as the mimeograph, photoduplication (Thermofax, etc.), planograph, or photo-offset printing.

We have valuable and highly readable specialized books like James D. Horan, *Matthew Brady, Historian with a Camera* (1955) and Dorothy Norman, *Alfred Stieglitz* (1960); and "picture histories" galore—of the Civil War, the Spanish-American War, World Wars I and II, and everything else from plumbing to Presidents. But we still need more comprehensive and up-to-date histories of American photography worthy of this great subject. A book which sees in photography something of its full grandeur and philosophic importance is André Malraux's magnificent *The Voices of Silence: Man and His Art* (trans. by Stuart Gilbert, 1953). For the broad outlines and large tendencies in the history of the subject, the reader unfortunately cannot do better than refer to the article "Photography" in *Encyclopaedia Britannica* (14th ed.).

Chapter 2. *From Hero to Celebrity: The Human Pseudo-Event*

Much of our great literature—the Bible, the Iliad, the Odyssey, the Aeneid—is, of course, a chronicle of heroes and hero-worship. Biography as a genre is relatively recent; in England it does not date much back of the Renaissance—say the seventeenth century. Critical biography—which in English literature we may date from the happy coincidences which eventually produced James Boswell's *Life of Samuel Johnson* (1791)—appeared still later. The self-conscious study of the phenomenon of heroes and of the nature of biography is not much over a century old. The most influential work has been Thomas Carlyle's *Heroes, Hero-Worship, and the Heroic in History* (1841). Ralph Waldo Emerson's *Representative Men* (1850) was probably suggested by Carlyle's work; Emerson's book, a compilation of popular lectures on such diverse figures as Plato, Swedenborg, Montaigne, Shakespeare, Napoleon, and Goethe, is the best-known American statement of the "divine right" theory of the hero. Many old-time Fourth of July orations were variations on this theme of the heroism (that is, divine inspiration) of the founders of our nation. All these works usually asked the reader or listener to share the writer's or speaker's reverence for his hero's greatness. In the late nineteenth and early twentieth century—with the rise of a cult of critical and scientific history, the growth of sociology and anthropology, the ascendancy of various forms of economic ("rationalizing") interpretations of history, and the elaboration of Freudian and Jungian psychology—many writers in many new ways began inviting readers to look with a detached and suspicious eye on the "greatness" of all past heroes. The phenomenon of human greatness came to seem no expression of divinity (divinity itself had become a human figment), but some kind of collective social illusion. European works of world-wide influence (all delightfully readable and stimulating) which illustrated and re-enforced these tendencies were: Ernest Renan, *Life of Jesus* (1863), Sir James George Frazer, *The Golden Bough* (11 vols., 1890–1915), and Sigmund Freud, *Moses and Monotheism* (1939).

There is no quite satisfactory treatment of hero-worship as a phenomenon in American history. A brief general discussion is found in Sidney Hook, *The Hero in History* (1943). Dixon Wecter's *The Hero in America: A Chronicle of Hero-Worship* (1941), an elegantly written compilation of American Greats, with the story of their adulation, is very much in the old style. It aims "to look at a few of those great personalities in public life . . . from whom we have hewn our symbols of government, our ideas of what is most prizeworthy as 'American.' " An admirable book which lies halfway between the older, symbolic, and the newer, critical, view of American heroes is Richard Hofstadter, *The American Political Tradition and the Men Who Made it* (1948; Vintage paperback, 1954). A valuable specialized study is John W. Ward, *Andrew Jackson: Symbol for an Age* (1955). For a lively reinterpretation of the history of the making of our colonial heroes, see Wesley Frank Craven, *The Legend of the Founding Fathers* (1956). And for another view of the special place of the foresighted American hero in the

American political tradition, see my *Genius of American Politics* (1953; Phoenix paperback, 1958). Adolf Hitler's doctrine that "The Strong Man is Mightiest Alone," along with his dogma that "coalition successes" have never built anything great, is expounded in Chapter VIII of *Mein Kampf.*

Sophisticated applications of psychology, anthropology, and the techniques of critical history are found in Lord Raglan, *The Hero: A Study in Tradition, Myth, and Drama* (1936; Vintage paperback, 1956), and Joseph Campbell, *The Hero with a Thousand Faces* (1949; Meridian paperback, 1956).

More studies of the social history of American biography would be invaluable in helping us chronicle the history of American ideals. John A. Garraty, *The Nature of Biography* (1958), a useful book aiming at general definition, does not focus primarily on America. W. Burlie Brown, *The People's Choice: The Presidential Image in the Campaign Biography* (1960) surveys the virtues attributed to Presidential candidates by their campaign biographers. Catherine Drinker Bowen describes many of the problems of the biographer today in suggestive essays in *Adventures of a Biographer* (1959). Avenues into the literature of American biography can be found in Oscar Handlin and others, *The Harvard Guide to American History* (1954) and in relevant sections, well indexed in the admirable bibliographical Volume III, of Robert Spiller and others, *Literary History of the United States* (3 vols., 1948). Handy surveys are: Edward H. O'Neill, *A History of American Biography, 1800–1935* (1935), *Biography by Americans, 1658–1936* (a bibliography, 1939); and Marion Dargan, *Guide to American Biography, Part I: 1607–1815* (a classified bibliography, 1949). Raw materials for another approach to the American hero are listed in Louis Kaplan and others, *Bibliography of American Autobiographies* (1961). An introduction to the hero in American folklore is found in Richard Dorson, *American Folklore* (Chicago History of American Civilization Series, 1959).

The literature on the history of celebrities and of celebrity worship is meager. Few recent writers have had as delicate a sense of the transforming standards of social recognition as has Cleveland Amory. His *Celebrity Register* (1959), compiled with the collaboration of Earl Blackwell, is one of the most symbolic documents of our age: it is an index to the new categories of American society. The *Celebrity Register* is as expressive of our standards of social preference as was *Burke's Peerage* (1826) or *Burke's Landed Gentry* (1833–1838) for an earlier age in England. Cleveland Amory's *Who Killed Society* (1960), a treasure house of miscellaneous information on changing standards of admiration, describes itself with brilliant accuracy on its jacket: "The Warfare of Celebrity with Aristocracy in America—from the 'First Families' to the 'Four Hundred' to 'Publi-ciety.' " On the endorsement business, see William M. Freeman, *The Big Name* (1957). Leo Lowenthal's invaluable "Biographies in Popular Magazines," is found in *American Social Patterns* (selected and edited by William Peterson; Anchor paperback, 1956). See also Jerome Ellison and Franklin T. Gosser, "Non-Fiction Magazine Articles: A Content Analysis," *Journalism Quarterly*, XXXVI (Winter, 1959) 27–34.

An important book could be written on the press secretary and his role in politics and American public life. The most suggestive treatments I have come upon are Lela Stiles, *The Man Behind Roosevelt: The Story of Louis McHenry Howe* (1954); and miscellaneous items in current magazines, like the cover story on James C. Hagerty, President Eisenhower's secretary, in *Time*, LXXI (Jan. 27, 1958), 16–20; the article on Pierre Salinger, President Kennedy's press secretary in *Time*, LXXVI (Dec. 5, 1960), p. 57. Patrick D. Hazard of the Annenberg School of Communications has kindly let me see his unpublished paper, "The Entertainer as Hero: The Burden of an Anti-Intellectual Tradition," which I have found invaluable.

For the facts from which I reconstruct my account of the transformation of Lindbergh from hero into celebrity I have leaned heavily on Kenneth S. Davis, *The Hero: Charles A. Lindbergh and the American Dream* (1959). This meticulous book combines the vividness and warmth of a good novel with a relentless objectivity. It is brilliant evidence that the techniques of the sociologist do not require the abandonment of the humanist's literary elegance or dramatic flair. Davis gives us a parable for our time, which no serious student of American morals in the twentieth century should fail to read. Similar studies, with comparable insight, sympathy, and objectivity, of figures like Al Capone, Rudolph Valentino, Charlie Chaplin, Frank Sinatra, Marilyn Monroe, and Elvis Presley, would teach us more about ourselves than many of the more lengthy studies of less significant but more conventionally "important" minor figures in our political, literary, and academic life. Some suggestive notions and much valuable detail, especially on popular attitudes to figures like Capone, are found in Orrin E. Klapp, "Hero-Worship in America," *American Sociological Review*, XIV (Feb., 1949), 53–62, and in a longer version of the same study, "The Hero as a Social Type" (1948), unpublished doctoral dissertation in the Department of Sociology of the University of Chicago. A constantly useful tool for exploring the uncompiled social history of our time is *The New York Times Index*.

George Waller's copiously detailed *Kidnap: The Story of the Lindbergh Case* (1961) appeared as this volume was going to press.

Chapter 3. *From Traveler to Tourist: The Lost Art of Travel*

Just as a large proportion of our great literature has been the chronicle of heroes, so, much of it has been a chronicle of travel. Many great epics have been both at the same time. In fact, if one defined an epic as the adventures of a hero who travels, one would exclude few of enduring importance. This itself may be evidence to support the theses of my Chapters 2 and 3. The story of a hero on his travels—Ulysses against Polyphemus —can excite the minstrel talents of great poets; but a celebrity at his relaxation (that is, on vacation)—Bob Hope in Palm Springs—can inspire few but gossip columnists. The decline of the hero and the decline of travel have come together. Except for religion and war, travel was for centuries the most hero-producing, hero-inciting of man's activities. In religion many epic heroes (the Buddha, Moses, Mohammed) have been notable travelers.

The literature of travel is so abundant (even for the United States alone) that one hardly knows where to begin. It comprises some of the most readable, most exciting, and most neglected of Americana. We may divide the American travel literature into three large classes which overlap both logically and chronologically: (1) travel epics; (2) travel surveys; and, (3) travel reactions (or tourist diaries).

First is the travel epic, whose central figure is a hero doing great deeds, encountering risks, exploring and enjoying the exotic and the dangerous. It includes some of the basic sources of American history: for example, such works as those by Captain John Smith, *True Relation of Such Occurrences and Accidents of Note as hath hapned in Virginia since the first planting of that Colony* (1608), *True Travels, Adventures, and Observations of Captain John Smith in Europe, Asia, Africa, and America, from . . . 1593 to 1629* (1630). The Pocahontas story, a characteristic travel exploit, is recounted in detail by Smith himself in his *General Historie of Virginia . . .* (1624). William Bradford's *History of Plymouth Plantation* is in large part a travel epic. This first group also includes such later American classics as the *History of the Expedition under the Command of Captains Lewis and Clark* (ed. Nicholas Biddle and Paul Allen, 2 vols., 1814); John Lloyd Stephens, *Incidents of Travel in Central America* (1841) and *Incidents of Travel in Yucatan* (1843); Francis Parkman, *Oregon Trail* (1849); Josiah Gregg, *Commerce of the Prairies* (2 vols., 1844); Mark Twain, *Roughing It* (1872), *A Tramp Abroad* (1880), and *Life on the Mississippi* (1883); and Charles Warren Stoddard, *South-Sea Idyls* (1873), *The Lepers of Molokai* (1885), *Hawaiian Life* (1894), and *The Island of Tranquil Delights* (1904), which, like many of the pseudo-classics of day-before-yesterday, become the staple of secondhand furniture stores.

Books of the second class, the travel surveys, sometimes overlap with those of the first. They offer us fewer accounts of derring-do, of exciting action, and risky encounter, and are primarily compilations of outlandish or useful information. Much of the writing by Europeans about America in the colonial period had this character. Such works were in demand because of the helpful information (or interesting misinformation) they offered about the New World. The rise of natural history in the eighteenth and early nineteenth centuries produced such works as *Observations on the Inhabitants, Climate, Soil, etc. . . . made by John Bartram in his travels from Pensilvania to . . . Lake Ontario* (1751), and by his son William Bartram, *Travels through North and South Carolina, Georgia, East and West Florida, etc.* (1791); Thomas Jefferson, *Notes on the State of Virginia* (1784); John James Audubon, *Birds of America* (1827–1838), and his journals, selected as *Delineations of American Scenery and Character* (1926). For an excellent selection of writings by Americans about their experiences abroad (most of which take the form of social survey or encounters with famous men and women), see Philip Rahv (ed.), *Discovery of Europe* (Anchor paperback, 1960).

The rise of the social sciences further encouraged such collection and classification of information from faraway places. Examples of such works are: again, Thomas Jefferson, *Notes on the State of Virginia* (1784), which was prepared expressly for a European reader, the Marquis de Barbois, secretary of the French legation in Philadelphia, whose twenty-odd Baedeker-like questions formed the frame of the book; Alexis de Tocqueville, *Democracy in America* (2 vols., 1835; first American edition, 1838), which grew out of a stay of less than a year (May, 1831–Feb., 1832) in the United States; and George

Catlin, whose illustrated *Manners and Customs of the North American Indians* (2 vols., 1841) was the product of eight years of travels and observations from the Yellowstone to Florida. Some of the most delightful books to come out of eighteenth-century America are the too-little-read travel surveys by William Byrd, who retails facts and fictions of natural history, geography, and social customs with a rare wit. His works include *History of the Dividing Line* (1728), *Progress to the Mines* (1732), and *Journey to the Land of Eden* (1733), all of which were first published only in 1841.

In the early decades of the nineteenth century, the approaching conflict between North and South incited an additional large number of remarkable social-survey travel volumes. Important examples are the influential books by Frederick Law Olmsted: *A Journey in the Seaboard Slave States* (1856), *A Journey Through Texas* (1857), and *A Journey in the Back Country,* abridged and revised as *The Cotton Kingdom* (2 vols., 1861; ed. by Arthur M. Schlesinger, 1953). Admirable analytical bibliographies are Thomas D. Clark, *Travels in the Old South* (3 vols., 1956–1959) and E. Merton Coulter, *Travels in the Confederate States* (1948). Many of the best travel surveys of the American West are collected by Reuben G. Thwaites in his multivolumed *Early Western Travels, 1748–1846* (32 vols., 1904–1907).

Compared to either of these earlier classes, both of which continue to be exemplified in many excellent works, the third, and distinctively modern, class, the book of travel reactions (or tourist diary), is pretty flimsy stuff. Characteristically, instead of recording action, recounting mortal risks, or surveying the social scene and interesting customs, it records the confusion, amused bewilderment, and disorientation of the tourist himself, or his frustrated search for adventure. The focus is on a puzzled, self-conscious quest for the "interesting," rather than on inevitable encounters. An example is Tats Blain, *Mother-Sir!* (1951), "a navy wife's hilarious hap-hazardous adventures in Japan." A more substantial work is Herbert Kubly, *American in Italy* (1955), which, precisely because it is deftly written and expertly constructed, reveals the limits of this kind of travel literature.

We need some good histories of travel as an institution. Paul Hazard, *The European Mind, 1680–1715* (1953) is the book I know which best puts old-style travel in the large framework of thought, belief, and feelings. Seymour Dunbar's copious *History of Travel in America* (1915; 1937) is valuable mainly as a readable chronicle of the forms of transportation, on which it gathers a large stock of unassimilated information. For a special study of the varying motives which have taken Americans to one part of the world, see Van Wyck Brooks, *The Dream of Arcadia: American Writers and Artists in Italy, 1760–1915* (1958). For some of the philosophical and epistemological implications of the means of travel in different epochs, see Harold A. Innis' profound and remarkable brief books, *Empire and Communications* (1950) and *Changing Concepts of Time* (1952). I have raised some questions about the relations between travel styles and styles in sight-seeing in "An American Style in Historical Monuments," in my *America and the Image of Europe* (1960), pp. 79–96.

The literature on the history of tourism is, for the most part, even more rudimentary. F. W. Ogilvie, *The Tourist Movement: An Economic Study* (1933) is written mainly from the British point of view, and focuses on statistics and currency effects. A broader view is taken by A. J. Norval, *The Tourist Industry* (1936), a study originally undertaken under the auspices of the government of the Union of South Africa. Neither of these books, nor any other book I know, explores the many implications of the rise of the package tour, the tour agent, and middle-class touring, for standard of living and social attitudes in general. An essay on the history of travelers' checks and credit cards could be quite suggestive. The rise of conventions (commercial, professional, etc.) in the United States—a subject with wide implications—still needs treatment. An excellent regional study showing the many-sided possibilities of the history of tourism for social history in general is Earl Pomeroy, *In Search of the Golden West: The Tourist in Western America* (1957).

Government statistics, and reports of committees to promote tourism, are a valuable source. Here again I have found indispensable *Historical Statistics of the United States, Colonial Times to 1957* (Statistical Abstract Supplement; U.S. Department of Commerce, Bureau of the Census; Government Printing Office, 1960), especially the figures on consumer expenditure, transportation, and distribution and services (for example, on hotels and motels). Miscellaneous facts can be found in such reports as: League of Nations (Economic Committee), *Survey of Tourist Traffic considered as An International Economic Factor* (Geneva, 1936); U.S. Department of Commerce, Bureau of Foreign Commerce, *Survey of International Travel* (Washington, D.C., 1956) and *United States Participation in International Travel, 1959 Supplement* (Washington, D.C., 1959); Clarence B.

Randall, *International Travel: Report to the President of the United States* (Washington, D.C., April 17, 1958).

An oblique approach to the subject is found in the history of the formalities of foreign travel, and especially in the history of the passport. On this topic, however, much of the printed matter now concerns either the bare Government regulations and formalities, or questions of public administration and political theory, such as how to administer the issuance of passports, whether restrictions on issuance are an infringement of the right of movement or of expatriation, etc. Current passport regulations, and especially the impressive easing and speeding of procedures for securing passports (in 1961, citizens in Chicago were receiving their passports in three days), evidence the changed character of foreign travel. Some historical perspective can be secured by a glance at documents from the turn of the century, for example, United States Department of State, *Passport Regulations of Foreign Countries* (Washington, 1897) and *The American Passport* (Washington, 1898). See Theodore M. Norton, "The Right to Leave the United States," unpublished doctoral dissertation in the Department of Political Science, University of Chicago (1960).

The history of particular tour agencies can be approached through John Pudney, *The Thomas Cook Story* (1953), a vivid and literate essay, showing imagination, a sense of humor, and an even-handed impartiality; and its contrasting counterpart Alden Hatch, *American Express: A Century of Service* (1950), a much thinner book, naive in its social history, with all the provincialisms and synthetic enthusiasms of "authorized" company history. On American Express see also: Ralph T. Reed, "American Express: Its Origin and Growth," in *Publications of The Newcomen Society*, Vol. 15 (1952); and "Uncle to the Tourists," *Fortune*, LXIII (June, 1961), 140–149.

The rise of the modern American hotel is difficult to study, except by personal exploration. This rich and colorful subject deserves more attention from historians. The kind of thing which could be done is illustrated in Doris Elizabeth King, "T First-Class Hotel and the Age of the Common Man," *Jo*ole *of Southern History*, XXIII (May, 1957), 173–188. A rem 7); piece of Americana is Conrad N. Hilton, *Be My Gues*meri for naiveté, self-revelation, and unintended confession reli can mores—in business, publicity, celebrity, marri ure. The gion—it has few equals in the whole of recen lthough it book is made available to guests in Hilton H iting assist was obviously written with some technical ance, these ghost writers have done their job admirably; they allow their "author" to speak unmistakably in his own voice, to ramble, to "enthuse," to pat himself on the back, and to moralize in his own unghostable fashion.

The motel, still unchronicled except in movies, novels, and on the television screen, must be traced through the statistics of government agencies and the publications of professional associations. Valuable sources are architectural planbooks, like *Motels, Hotels, Restaurants and Bars: An Architectural Record Book* (F. W. Dodge Corp., N.Y., 1953).

On the history of museums, a useful starting point is George Brown Goode, "Museum History and Museums of History," in Smithsonian Institution, *Annual Report . . . 1897, Report of the U.S. National Museum*, Pt. II (Washington, D.C., 1901), pp. 65–81. See Walter Pach's *The Art Museum in America* (1948); and, on the relation of wealthy collectors to the museums, Aline B. Saarinen's amusing, anecdotal *The Proud Possessors* (1958). Some of the profounder aesthetic implications of the rise of museums and of photography are explored again in André Malraux's magnificent *Voices of Silence: Man and His Art* (1953), especially Part I, "Museum without Walls," and Part III, "The Creative Process." On the rise and significance of world fairs, see Merle Curti's suggestive article, "America at the World Fairs, 1851–1893," *American Historical Review,* LV (July, 1950), 833–856. For a general survey of museum history one must still turn to the article in *Encyclopaedia Britannica* (14th ed.).

While sailing ships, steam navigation, canals, turnpikes, wagon trails, and railroads have attracted the expert interest of many scholars, the automobile and the airplane have yet attracted too few serious historians. John H. Morrison, *History of American Steam Navigation* (1903) and John L. Stover, *American Railroads* (Chicago History of American Civilization Series, 1960) offer admirable introductions. For wider implications of these older innovations, see George R. Taylor, *The Transportation Revolution, 1815–1860* (1951; Vol. IV in the valuable Rinehart Economic History of the United States). All these subjects have, of course, attracted buffs and hobbyists; there have been a number of useful picture books.

The automobile is an epic subject; a panoramic history of the automobile could make a grand parable of modern America. The most useful works so far have been biographies or company histories, like Allan Nevins and Frank Ernest Hill, *Ford: The Times, the Man, the Company* (1954) and *Ford: Expansion and*

Challenge (1957), which incidentally touch the social effects of the automobile. Roger Burlingame, in *March of the Iron Men* (1938), *Engines of Democracy* (1940) and *Machines that Built America* (1948), covers a broader subject, but hints the possibilities of more narrowly focused works. Hints are also found in works of sociology like Robert S. and Helen M. Lynd, *Middletown* (1929) and *Middletown in Transition* (1937). Social epics of America in the twentieth century, like F. Scott Fitzgerald, *The Great Gatsby* (1925), John Dos Passos, *U.S.A.* (1938), and John Steinbeck, *Grapes of Wrath* (1939) inevitably give the automobile a leading role; they probably remain the best expositions of its importance for a future historian.

The history of motor highways and highway practice is important as a chronicle of the man-made motorist's landscape, a major episode in the homogenization of our continent. A brief introduction is United States Public Roads Administration, *Highway Practice in the United States of America* (Washington, 1949).

The airplane and air travel generally are much in need of historical treatment. We have admirable histories of the Air Force in World War II, but we could still learn much from a scholarly and detailed history of civilian air travel and air tourism, compiled while pioneer figures are still alive. On the airline stewardess, see Joseph Kastner, "Joan Waltermire: Air Stewardess," *Life,* X (April 28, 1941), 102–112; and "Glamor Girls of the Air," *Life,* XLV (August 25, 1958), 68–77. On the increasing speed of civilian air travel, see George A. W. Boehm, "The SST: Next Step to Instant Travel," *Fortune,* LXIII (June, 1961), 159–164, 238–244.

Tourist guides should be consulted as a source of what people have been told to look for, and what they like to think is important. I have toured France and Italy with the constant companionship of Baedeker. Most large libraries have a collection of old Baedekers, which can be consulted with much amusement and profit. I have found *Japan: The Official Guide* (Japan Travel Bureau, Revised and Enlarged, Tokyo, 1957) especially helpful for underlining the characteristics of modern guide books, although it is almost useless for any other purpose. It is a caricature of the tourist guidebook, showing how a mechanical following of the tourist-guide pattern can multiply trivia and omit matters of the greatest significance. The reader is told which items are considered "Important Cultural Property," and is given the dimensions of every garden, pagoda, palace, shrine, and temple, but he is almost never told the meaning of social customs or the uses of buildings. On Baedeker, see Francis Watson, "The Education of Baedeker," *The Fortnightly*, CXLVI (Dec., 1936), 698–702; Arnold Palmer, "The Baedeker Firmament," *The Fortnightly*, CLXXII (Sept., 1949), 200–205; W. G. Constable, "Three Stars for Baedeker," *Harper's*, CCVI (April, 1953), 76–83; Arthur J. Olsen, "A Tour of Baedeker," *The New York Times Magazine*, Nov. 29, 1959, pp. 92, 94; and "Peripatetics: Two-Star Civilization," *Time*, IV (Jan. 9, 1950), 15–16. To my knowledge there is no adequate biography in English either of the first Karl Baedeker or of the Baedeker enterprises, nor is there a satisfactory history of travel guidebooks. All these are most amusing and instructive subjects. Unfailing and omnipresent sources on attitudes toward travel are, of course, the articles and advertisements in current magazines and newspapers, travel posters, advertising brochures, and television commercials —to all of which we have much better access than will future historians.

Chapter 4. *From Shapes to Shadows: Dissolving Forms*

Academic critics, however little they may understand the processes of artistic creation, still determine which forms of art are to be considered "serious." This they do mainly on pedagogical or professional grounds. Subjects which have "always" been lectured on and examined about are of course those which continue to be easiest to lecture on and examine about. If you have nothing else to say, you can always comment on what others have said on the same subject. This situation is worst in the most respectable institutions. At Oxford University, England, for example, the study of the English common law and of English literature entered the curriculum only very late; there the study of American history has hardly yet come to be taken seriously. Such institutions set a tyrannic pattern: books on American history still have a surprisingly small audience in England.

In our age of fluid art forms and rapidly changing techniques of art and dramatic reproduction, the customs of the academic community have a more insulating effect than ever before. These customs inevitably lead us to ignore the profound implications of great current changes in our forms of art, literature, and drama. I do not know of a regular course on the art of the movies in a department of literature in a single major university, although there may be such. A result is that many of our scholars who are best equipped to judge contemporary dramatic forms against those of earlier ages ostracize the leading forms of our own age. Meanwhile, there are numerous courses on the far less significant dramatic works (written in conventional form for the stage) of minor playwrights.

One symptom of this freezing of categories is the long separation of the study of the history of printing and of publishing from the history of literature. An admirable introductory volume which helps bring all these together is Hellmut Lehmann-Haupt and others, *The Book in America: A History of the Making and Selling of Books in the United States* (2d ed., 1952).

A comprehensive history of the popularization of knowledge could help us understand the effect of the rise of liberalism and democratic institutions on our ways of thinking about everything, and on our very conceptions of "knowledge" and "art." An important chapter in this story is the history of translation. See, for example, F. O. Matthiessen, *Translation, An Elizabethan Art* (1931). There have, of course, been numerous histories of Biblical translation; but we could learn much from a broader study of how in recent times paths have been made from works in learned or foreign languages to the masses of the new literates who read only their own vernacular.

Donald Sheehan, *This was Publishing: A Chronicle of the Book Trade in the Gilded Age* (1952) draws on the records of Henry Holt and Company, Harper & Brothers, Dodd, Mead and Company, and Charles Scribner's Sons (and the files of *Publishers' Weekly*) to produce a valuably detailed and unromanticized account of publishing practices between the Civil War and World War I; this was a crucial period for the purposes of the present volume. The chapter by Malcolm Cowley, "How Writers Lived," in Robert E. Spiller and others (eds.), *Literary History of the United States* (3 vols., 1948), II, 1263–1272, is a knowledgeable and incisive account of the relation of new publishing techniques and opportunities to the writer's profession between World War I and the mid-1940's.

We are fortunate to have some excellent books—both meticulous in facts and readable in style—on the history of popular and best-selling books in the United States. Frank Luther Mott, *Golden Multitudes: The Story of Best Sellers in the United States* (1947) was a pioneer work and remains a lively and readable introduction to a miscellaneous subject. Defining a "best seller" as a book that had a sale equal to 1 per cent of the population of the continental United States (or the English Colonies in the years before the Revolution) for the decade in which it was published, Mott carries his story from Michael Wigglesworth, *The Day of Doom* (1662; required sale before 1690: 1,000) to Kathleen Winsor, *Forever Amber* (1945; required sale 1940–1949: 1,300,000).

James D. Hart, *The Popular Book: A History of America's Literary Taste* (1950) deals with a broader, subtler, and less statistically precise subject, namely the relation of popular reading tastes to social pressures. Besides providing a treasure house of information, Hart offers many penetrating observations on the relation between the popularity of books and their enduring literary value. He is especially shrewd in showing how a capacity to "re-create the sense of the present" tends to make a book popular. In other words, he gives evidence to show how the increasing prevalence of "popular" or "best-selling" books increases the mirror effect in literature. Hart (p. 290) objects to Mott's criterion of best-sellerdom: "Using population statistics of one period and sales statistics of another, Professor Mott finds that Mark Twain's *Life on the Mississippi* is one of the best sellers rising from the 1880–89 decade (when population was about 50,000,000) because in 1946 it reached a sale of half a million copies as the first of a series of 25-cent, pocket-size reprints. Thus Professor Mott includes as best sellers *Leaves of Grass,* Poe's *Poems, Moby Dick,* and other works that when related to the periods of their first publication are found to have interested only a very small public." Hart concludes that the most popular books of past eras tended always to include a larger proportion of ephemeral works than of classics. Alice Payne Hackett, *Sixty Years of Best Sellers: 1895–1955* (1956) is valuable for its year-by-year lists and its figures on actual sales, separated also by hard-cover and paperback.

Much valuable information about the problems of book publishing—as seen from inside the publishing trade—is found in O. H. Cheney, *Economic Survey of the Book Industry, 1930–1931* (1931), a study undertaken for the National Association of Book Publishers, which nevertheless is unsparing in its criticism of prevalent trade practices. A more recent survey especially instructive to the layman is Chandler B. Grannis, *What Happens in Publishing* (1957). *Publishers' Weekly* (established 1872) is an indispensable source with which the layman should become more familiar.

The book club phenomenon can be examined in Charles Lee, *The Hidden Public: The Story of the Book-of-the-Month Club* (1958), full of many valuable little-known details about the "BOMC." Yet it has the unmistakable character of an "authorized" company history; it is defensive, even when defense is not called for. On how the BOMC and other popular book clubs re-enforce the mirror effect, see Lee's conclusion in his final Appendix C: *"Publishers' Weekly's* regular best seller lists show that BOMC titles almost invariably score on its monthly popularity listings. In *PW's* annual summaries of the 10 best sellers in fiction and in non-fiction, the Club has registered between 1926 and 1953 the remarkable total of 129 best sellers (exclusive of dividends). Of the 560 titles reported, the Club accounted for 23%. With dividends, the Club score rises to 25½%." See also Dorothy Canfield Fisher, "Book Clubs" (R. R. Bowker Memorial Lecture, 1947), interpreting her twenty years' experience on the selection committee of the BOMC and offering a sensible defense of book clubs as one of many mechanisms "to keep up the book habit" in a democracy. For a sampling of the book clubs and their selections, see Leo M. Hauptman (compiler), "Current Monthly Book Clubs: A Descriptive Review" (mimeographed), compiled for the Research Division of the National Education Association (1944).

A lively and perceptive examination of the effect of the rise of paperback publishing and of the moviefying of novels on publishing ways and on the contents of books is Albert Van Nostrand, *The Denatured Novel* (1960), to which I am much indebted. Van Nostrand offers many facts and suggestions on the growing mirror effect in this area. Two classic discussions of the aesthetic and philosophic problems of the relations among art forms are Gotthold E. Lessing, *Laokoon* (1766) and Irving Babbitt, *The New Laokoon* (1910). The effect on book publishing of accelerating mergers and of putting publishing stock on the open market is explored in R. W. Apple, Jr., "The Gold Rush on Publishers' Row," *Saturday Review,* XLIII (Oct. 8, 1960), 13–15, 47–49, which ought to be required reading for all students of contemporary American literature. Other valuable articles on mid-twentieth-century developments include: Eleanor Blum, "Paperback Book Publishing: A Survey of Content," *Journalism Quarterly,* XXXVI (Fall, 1959), 447–454; William Dow Boutwell, "The Coming of the Compact Book," *Library Journal,* LXXXV (May 15, 1960), 1859–1862; Frank L. Schick, "The Future of Paperbacks," *Library Journal,* LXXXV (May 15, 1960), 1863–1865; Harvey Swados, "Must Writers be Characters?" *Saturday Review,* XLIII (Oct. 1, 1960), 12–14, 50. Budd Schulberg, "Why Write It When you Can't Sell It to the Pictures?" *Saturday Review,* XXXVIII (Sept. 3, 1955), 5–6, 27, explores the peculiar problems of the writer in an age of dissolving forms, through his eloquent account of his experiences with the movie script for (and later the novel) *Waterfront*. Malcolm Cowley reflects on these and related problems in his *The Literary Situation* (Compass paperback, 1954), especially, Ch. 6, "Cheap Books for the Millions," and Ch. 7, "Hardbacks or Paperbacks?"; see also his "The Paperback Title Fight," *The Reporter*, XXIII (July 7, 1960), 44–47. The rise of the "nonbook" is wittily reported in "The Era of Non-B," *Time*, LXXVI (Aug. 22, 1960), 70–71.

The history of abridgment is an important subject, much in need of treatment. On *The Reader's Digest* we do have two useful books, at opposite ends of the critical spectrum. James Playsted Wood, *Of Lasting Interest: The Story of The Reader's Digest* (1958) is an "authorized" company history, saccharine and adulatory. But the volume gives much additional information about *Digest* procedures and internal company history not available elsewhere and I have learned a great deal from it. John Bainbridge, *Little Wonder or, The Reader's Digest and How It Grew* (1946), originally a series in *The New Yorker*, is critical and often snide, but full of useful detail, statistics, and anecdote, including a valuable chapter, "Plant you now, dig you later" on the *Digest* practice of "planting" articles, and a delightful account of the exploration of the *Digest's* headquarters at Chappaqua, by "Nicolai Popkov," mythical Soviet editor of *"Minimag."*

Many books have been written and much reforming energy properly spent advocating the freedom to print and attacking book censorship. See, for example, the reports of the Commission on the Freedom of the Press (Robert M. Hutchins, Chairman): among them, *A Free and Responsible Press* (1947). But in the United States, as in many western European countries since the rise of popular literacy, censorship has had a much narrower influence than the universal practices of abridging, bowdlerizing, and anthologizing. While censorship is attacked for preventing people from learning the facts of life, abridgment, condensation, abstracts, and anthologies are praised as the necessary tools by which a democratic people can learn the facts of life. More careful study of the rise of these practices and of their effects might make us more aware of and more wary of what we have been doing. An old joke is the report that a successful New York publisher is preparing an anthology of "The World's Three Best Commandments."

The history of techniques of art reproduction, in which André Malraux, in his *Voices of Silence: Man and His Art*

(1953) discovers far-reaching significance, must, for the most part, be dug out of the histories of particular techniques, like Gabor Peterdi, *Printmaking, Methods Old and New* (1959). Some writer with a knowledge both of the techniques of reproduction and of the history of art could give us an important book on modern technological transformations of our artistic experience. Enticing suggestions are found in Ernest Gombrich, *Art and Illusion* (1960).

On the interrelations of visual and literary art forms, the importance of new media and of widening audiences, Gilbert Seldes has some interesting general comments and critical insights offered with a professional's inside knowledge. See his *The Seven Lively Arts* (1924), *The Great Audience* (1950), and *The Public Arts* (1956).

The literature on the movies is enormous. But the subject has by no means attracted as much writing talent, energy, or industry as it merits from historians. A useful introduction is Richard Griffith and Arthur Mayer, *The Movies* (1957), a pictorial history written out of broad experience and long intimacy with the subject. Leo Rosten, *Hollywood* (1941) is an admirable sociological study of the movie capital still in its heyday. The atmosphere and preoccupations of Hollywood in the '40's and '50's are skillfully communicated in Ezra Goodman's richly anecdotal *Fifty-Year Decline and Fall of Hollywood* (1961). More specialized studies, especially related to the problems I discuss in this chapter are Margaret Farrand Thorp, *America at the Movies* (1939), a perceptive study of movie audiences, full of facts on box-office successes, on who was going to what movies, and on the effects of movie-going on cosmetics, costume, and morality; Hortense Powdermaker, *Hollywood, the Dream Factory* (1950), a self-consciously anthropological study, with interesting, but sometimes devious interpretations; Dore Schary (as told to Charles Palmer), *Case History of a Movie* (1950), a detailed account of the making of a single movie; Frank Getlein and Harold C. Gardiner, S.J., *Movies, Morals, and Art* (1961), a sensible critique from the Catholic point of view. On the star system, see Edgar Morin's bizarre *The Stars: An Account of the Star System in Motion Pictures* (translated from the French; Evergreen Profile Book #7, 1960), which collects much valuable detail and many insights around some contrived and occasionally precious concepts of liturgy, dream, etc. The relations between novels and movies are explored in Lester E. Asheim, "From Book to Film: A Comparative Analysis of the Content of Selected Novels and the Motion Pictures Based upon Them,"

(1949), an unpublished doctoral dissertation in the Graduate Library School of the University of Chicago, which comes to some surprising conclusions, carefully documented; George Bluestone, *Novels into Films* (1957), which traces the mutations in six specimen adaptations; and Erwin Panofsky's brilliant brief article, "Style and Medium in the Motion Pictures," *Transition*, XXVI (1937), 121–133.

On the significance of the technological changes of the last century for musical experience, we still need much research and writing. Paul S. Carpenter, *Music, An Art and a Business* (1950) looks primarily at the effects on the professions of musician and of musical composer. On Muzak, see Stanley Green's excellent article, "Music to Hear but Not to Listen To," *Saturday Review*, XL (Sept. 28, 1957), 55–56, 118; and the brief item "Omnipresent Music," *Musical America*, LXXVI (Jan. 15, 1956), 13. Katherine Hamill, "The Record Business—'It's Murder,'" *Fortune*, LXIII (May, 1961), pp. 148–151, 178–187, discusses the special problems of making a profit out of mass-circulation records. For the story on the broadcasts of music in Grand Central Terminal, see *Time*, LV (Jan. 2, 1950), p. 15, and (Jan. 9, 1950), p. 14.

The cataclysmic consequences of the increasing rate of progress of scientific knowledge and the increasing rate of production of printed matter for our very concept of knowledge are only beginning to be studied. Some stimulating suggestions are found in Jacques Barzun's sprightly and penetrating *House of Intellect* (1959). See Derek J. de Sola Price, *Science Since Babylon* (1961), a readable, incisive, and strikingly original book by a distinguished historian of science. This book points to some of the most exciting uncharted territories for students of twentieth-century intellectual history. It raises a number of profoundly disturbing questions about education and research in all areas bordering on the sciences. Francis Bello, "How to Cope with Information," *Fortune*, LXII (Sept. 1, 1960), 162–167, 180–92 deals briefly and graphically with some of these questions. A special supplement to *The New York Times* (April 30, 1961), "The Information Explosion," by International Business Machines Corporation, gives some intriguing hints of these problems and of how one adventurous company is facing them. See also, International Business Machines, "Language 'Translator' Publicly Demonstrated for First Time," Press Release dated for May 27, 1960, available from IBM in New York City. A full history of IBM would be an important contribution to an understanding of American civilization in the twentieth (and perhaps the twenty-first!) century.

Chapter 5. *From Ideal to Image:*
The Search for Self-Fulfilling Prophecies

AND

Chapter 6. *From the American Dream to American Illusions?*
The Self-Deceiving Magic of Prestige

The great changes in modes of thought are always more easily observed by later ages than by those undergoing them. To describe one's own way of thinking in one's own vocabulary is often as difficult as to see the color red through red-colored glasses. We are tempted to speak today, not of our thinking, but of our "image" of our thinking and of ourselves. The usual response of people to a critic who discovers some novelty in current ways of thinking is to say that he does not know his history, because people (at least sane or wise people) *always* thought just like us. Such acolytes of the familiar avoid recognizing the consequences of their own blindness by saying it is quite normal to be blind. Nowadays nearly everybody talks about images, but very few have yet admitted that this expresses an important change in our way of thinking: Wasn't Caesar also concerned about his public image? As a result, there is a meager literature about the epistemological and philosophic implications of the Graphic Revolution.

Almost everybody, strangely enough, likes to believe he is engaged in one of the world's oldest professions. Hence most histories of advertising begin with a cluster of plausible absurdities about the antiquity of advertising: Jesus, we are told, was the first advertising man; we are told of ancient advertisements for runaway slaves, etc., etc. Similarly, the most common attacks on new institutions, occupations, and techniques take the form of showing how these express the old vices. "Advertising," we are often told, violates all traditional criteria of honesty, of art, of productivity. In this way popular writers easily enlist the public-spirited interest and excite the tsk-tsk's of all respectable citizens. They attack Madison Avenue for dealing in untruths (of which it is seldom really guilty), and so distract attention from the deeper, more pervasive (and more disorienting) fact that the rise of advertising has brought a social redefinition of the very notion of truth.

Much of the material for all the earlier chapters is relevant also to Chapters 5 and 6 and to the general history of the rise of images. Advertising, despite its importance in the American economy and in our daily life, has attracted surprisingly few historians.

A useful introductory handbook is James Playsted Wood, *The Story of Advertising* (1958). Some notion of how much the profession and its problems have changed can be seen by comparing a recent textbook like Wood's with one like Frank Leroy Blanchard, *The Essentials of Advertising* (1921), which now looks as obsolete as a sixteenth-century introduction to physics. The advertising news in the business section of *The New York Times* is one of the handiest sources of news of the profession for the general reader. A remarkable piece of objective reporting is Martin Mayer, *Madison Avenue, U.S.A.* (1958; Cardinal paperback, 1960) which should be read by anyone with a more than casual interest in the subject. Mayer gives more information and in a fuller context than does Vance Packard's sensational and debunking *Hidden Persuaders* (1957). The popularity of Packard's book (and its numerous imitators) has evidenced the naiveté of the American consuming public and its desperation to find someone to blame.

An important reflective book, which explores the wider implications of advertising is Otis Pease, *The Responsibilities of American Advertising* (1958). An unromantic account of the tasks of the advertising agency is Rosser Reeves, *Reality in Advertising* (1961). On the testimonial endorsement I have made much use of William M. Freeman, *The Big Name* (1957).

Trademarks—with a long history in law and commercial practice—can still best be studied through practical handbooks like Clowry Chapman, *Trade-Marks* (1930); I. E. Lambert, *The Public Accepts: Stories behind Famous Trade-Marks, Names and Slogans* (1941), which collects facts not easily available elsewhere about the origins of American trademarks and trade slogans; Jessie V. Coles, *Standards and Labels for Consumers' Goods* (1949). *Trademark Management: A Guide for Businessmen* (published by the United States Trademark Association, 1955) is a circumstantial description of the problems of protecting trademarks, and of how "unpoliced" words escape into the language.

Some clues to the shift in popular attitudes to advertising are found in the contrast between the humor in *Ballyhoo,* a vulgar magazine of the '30's which spoofed advertising by travestying its extravagant claims, and *Mad,* an advertising-oriented magazine of the '50's and '60's aimed at a comparable audience, which reaches out to spoof reality itself. *Mad's* post-election issue in November, 1961, printed a congratulatory cover (identical except for the picture) at both ends of the magazine: one saying "We were with you all the way, Dick!" the other substituting "Jack" for "Dick."

Perhaps the best serious approach to the development of modern advertising is through one or another of the excellent company histories. Especially rich and readable is Boris Emmet and John E. Jeuck, *Catalogues and Counters: A History of Sears, Roebuck and Company* (1950). Works like this, done with depth and objectivity, admirably free of moralizing, tell us precisely which techniques succeeded or failed in selling particular products. A readable peripheral source on the place of advertising in American social history is Mark Sullivan, *Our Times: the United States, 1900–1925* (6 vols., 1926–1936), delightful for its witty and discriminating choice of detail. We have a few histories of advertising agencies, like Ralph M. Hower, *The History of an Advertising Agency* (Rev. ed., 1949). An indispensable aid for anyone seriously interested in these subjects is Henrietta M. Larson, *Guide to Business History* (1948).

Information on the rise of radio and television and their relation to advertising and other topics can be found in Leo Bogart, *The Age of Television: A study of viewing habits and the impact of television on American life* (2d ed., 1958) and in Sydney W. Head, *Broadcasting in America* (1956), which in a valuable and astonishing Appendix prints in parallel columns an item-by-item comparison of the three trade association codes of ethics for radio, television, and films. See also Joseph T. Klapper, *The Effects of Mass Communication: An Analysis of Research* . . . (1960), a guide to the literature. For a specialized study see Everett C. Parker and others, *The Television-Radio Audience and Religion* (1955), a study supervised by Yale University Divinity School. Stimson Bullitt gives some brilliant suggestions on the significance of the new media for American political life in *To Be a Politician* (1959), especially Chapter 5.

Biographies remain among the most authentic and entertaining sources of information on all these topics. One of the best is P. T. Barnum's autobiography, *Struggles and Triumphs* (1854) republished in numerous editions, for example under the title *Barnum's Own Story: The Autobiography of P. T. Barnum, Combined & Condensed from the various Editions published during his lifetime* (ed. Waldo R. Browne, 1927). Almost all the other major figures in the history of American advertising lack adequate biographies. John Gunther's *Taken at the Flood: The Story of Albert D. Lasker* (1960) is a disappointing, thin, and pious account of one of the most interesting figures in modern American social history. For the major figures we must still look to the magnificent *Dictionary of American Biography* (edited by Allen Johnson and Dumas Malone, 20 vols. and 2 supplements; 1928–1958) which, with its second supplement, includes prominent persons who died before Jan. 1, 1941; and the later and current volumes of *Who's Who in America*.

The history of public relations and the profession of the public relations counsel is especially elusive because many assignments remain confidential. Some individuals and companies have been as reluctant to confess their techniques of public relations as movie stars are to reveal their cosmetic and plastic surgery secrets. But for reasons I have suggested in this book, we are becoming sophisticated—or at least increasingly curious—about all these matters. For reading on this topic see the suggestions above, under Chapter 1.

On the history of public opinion polling, much of the knowledgeable writing has been defensive. See, for example, George Gallup and Saul Forbes Rae, *The Pulse of Democracy: The Public-Opinion Poll and How It Works* (1940). On the other side see Lindsay Rogers, *The Pollsters* (1949). The roots of interest in opinion polling, and the implications of polling were prophetically suggested in some of the writings of John Dewey, especially *The Public and its Problems* (1927), and in the early works of Walter Lippmann, *Public Opinion* (1922), *The Phantom Public* (1925), later explored in his *The Good Society* (1937). Mildred Parten, *Surveys, Polls, and Samples* (1950), though out of date, still introduces the layman to many practical and technical problems of polling. Later developments are described by Leopold J. Shapiro, "The Opinion Poll" (1956), an unpublished doctoral dissertation in the Department of Sociology of the University of Chicago, which treats the poll as a sociological phenomenon, and explores (with examples) the way people actually initiate, plan, and conduct opinion polls. It suggests some of the consequences, for example, of the intelligence, naiveté, or personal concerns of interviewers. On some of the reflexive problems of the polls, see Eric F. Goldman, "Poll on the Polls," *Public Opinion Quarterly*, VIII (Winter, 1944–1945), 461–467, and numerous other valuable articles in that professional journal of opinion polling.

Much of the well-earned appeal of Samuel Lubell's perceptive election reporting and predicting (*The Future of American Politics* (1952; Anchor paperback 1956); *The Revolt of the Moderates* (1956)) comes from the fact that in an era of statistical polling he deals not with images and norms of opinion, but with the motives, worries, and concerns (and in the very words) of actual individual voters.

One intriguing subject which I have been unable to pursue is the recent history of psychology, and especially the shifting focus of psychologists who are concerned with testing "intelligence" and "personality." I suspect that a study of this shift might reveal still wider implications of the preoccupation with images which I describe in this volume. "What the first war did for the development of techniques for assessing intellectual functioning," Dr. Gardner Lindzey remarks, "was almost exactly duplicated by World War II in the area of motivation." (Ed. Gardner Lindzey, *Assessment of Human Motives* (1958;1960), p. 5) The elaboration of "projective techniques" and similar testing devices expresses less interest in the person's capacity to handle the brute facts of life than in how he fits himself into an image. "The shift in focus for psychologists from the cognitive to the conative or motivational," Dr. Lindzey goes on, "is nicely reflected in the fact that during the past decade and a half the Rorschach Test [using the interpretation of ink blots] and unconscious motivation have become as widely known and discussed by the general public as were the intelligence test and IQ some twenty-five years earlier." What is often thus simply described as an increasing interest in "human motivation" may, from another point of view, also reveal an increasing interest in images, with some consequences suggested in my Chapters 5 and 6. Hints of these changing interests among psychologists, political scientists, and public administrators can be found in the massive *Studies in Social Psychology in World War II:* Vol. I, Samuel A. Stouffer and others, *The American Soldier: Adjustment During Army Life* (1949); Vol. II, Samuel A. Stouffer and others, *The American Soldier: Combat and its Aftermath* (1949); and Carl I. Hovland and others, *Experiments in Mass Communication* (1949). Special topics of interest in this connection can be followed in Hermann Rorschach, *Psychodiagnostics* (Berne, 1942); Silvan Tomkins, *The Thematic Apperception Test* (1947); Claire H. Schiller (ed.), *Instinctive Behavior: The Development of a Modern Concept* (1957). The historical development of some of these notions can be followed in Jay Wharton Fay, *American Psychology Before William James* (1939); J. C. Flugel, *A Hundred Years of Psychology* (2d ed., 1951); and A. A. Roback, *History of American Psychology* (1952). The subject of language is also obviously related to these developments; a history of logical positivism might offer helpful hints. Some of the subtlest way-opening questions were asked by Benjamin Lee Whorf, whose works can be conveniently approached through his *Language, Thought, and Reality* (ed. John B. Carol, 1956).

Some original suggestions on the place of crime in American life (and American news) are found in Daniel Bell, *The End of Ideology* (1960), especially Chapter 7, "Crime as an American Way of Life," and Chapter 8, "The Myth of Crime Waves." We still need more histories of American attitudes to sports and sports news.

A detailed history of American image-making efforts abroad would be of great value to the future historian of American life and morals. So far, some of the most perceptive studies have been by foreigners—for example, by the Italian journalist Luigi Barzini, *Americans Are Alone in the World* (1953). William J. Lederer and Eugene Burdick, *The Ugly American* (1958), seems to me more significant as an illustration than as a critique of what is the matter with our relations to other peoples. The authors criticize us for not doing better what we are already (but in my opinion should not be) trying to do, instead of asking whether we might not better be trying to do something else.

Acknowledgments

In the research for this book I have had the valuable aid of Harold D. Woodman, who superlatively combines the historian's respect for fact with an eye for the large significance of detail. Without his selfless assistance this book could hardly have been written. I am also indebted to numerous friends, colleagues, and students at the University of Chicago; especially to Albert U. Romasco, who encouraged me to undertake this volume and who read and criticized the entire manuscript, and to Roger Shugg, who gave freely of his superb editorial judgment. One of the pleasures of writing this book was the opportunity to renew an old friendship with Simon Michael Bessie of Atheneum Publishers, who has patiently and ruthlessly reviewed the manuscript in all its stages. I also want to thank my other friends at Atheneum, especially Hiram Haydn and Marc Friedlaender, who have found time to read and criticize the book in detail. The manuscript has been prepared, copied, and recopied by Mrs. Ed Stack of Homewood, Illinois, to whose intelligence, efficiency, concern for detail, and devotion to the enterprise I owe more than I can say. Much of this book grows out of my research in various areas of American history over the past several years. Some of the ideas were first presented in "Democracy and Culture in America," a paper at the conference on "Popular / Mass Culture: American Perspectives," at the Ohio State University, October 28, 1960; "The American Image," a talk to the Citizens' Board of the University of Chicago, November 30, 1960; and "Varieties of Historical Experience," a paper delivered at the annual meeting of the American Historical Association in New York City, December 29, 1960. A number of the notions and examples in this book were developed at the family dinner table and in discussions with my sons, Paul, Jonathan, and David. My principal editor, for this as for all my earlier books, has been my wife, Ruth F. Boorstin, who remains for me both final court of appeal and chief counsel.

Index

Afterword

George F. Will

THERE ARE BOOKS, and this is one, that change the way we think because they change the way we see and listen. Today we see that we are living in a society that increasingly resembles an echo chamber lined with mirrors. Amid the sensory blitzkrieg contemporary life, much that is spoken is merely audio wallpaper. It is there but not noticed. We do not even listen, really listen, to what we ourselves are saying. If we did we would find that our intelligence is being bewitched by alarming clues to what we are, willy-nilly, becoming.

Consider a phrase dearly beloved of all people in and around politics. The phrase is "photo opportunity." We know what we mean by it. A photo opportunity is an obviously staged and even clearly labeled ("photo op") event in which a public official or candidate for public office does something photogenic. He does it for the purpose of striking a pose useful in symbolizing an attitude or intimating a promise. You know the stuff. Candidate dons hard hat to show that he is jus' folks and is in harmony with the toiling classes. Candidate scowls at developers' bulldozers, or at toxic waste dumps, to show concern for all creatures great and small.

But wait. What in the world is *not* a "photo opportunity"— a thing suitable for a photograph? The Grand Canyon is a photo opportunity. Aunt Min standing at the rim of the Grand Canyon is a photo opportunity. For that matter, Aunt Min home from vacation and dozing in the porch swing is a photo opportunity. But neither Min nor the Canyon count as an "opportunity." A photo opportunity, properly understood, is someone important doing something solely for the purpose of

being seen to do it. The hope is that those who see the resulting pictures will not see the elements of calculation (not to say
cunning) that are behind the artifice.

Boorstin's book has changed the way we listen by making
us conscious of the jargon in the air. And the air has never
been thicker, and can hardly get thicker, with jargon. One effect of Boorstin's book has been to induce in readers a healthy
skepticism. It shows readers how to stand back and squint at
the world. Or to put the same point another way, the book
shows readers how to infer the behind-the-scenes apparatus—
the ropes and pulleys that move the curtains and scenery—of
our social life.

At first blush it might seem that Boorstin is like the boy
who blurted out the news that the emperor wore no clothes.
But the boy was being artless, saying something that others
could say if they would just shake off the blinders of convention. Boorstin is a sophisticate who patiently explains that
there is, all around us, both more and less than meets our eyes
and ears. There is less in the sense that there is a false-front,
papier-maché quality to much of the "news" and many of the
events that are brought to our attention. There is more in
the sense that behind the "news" and events there are real,
important intentions and calculations.

Boorstin's book has, I will wager, shaped the climate that
has, in turn, shaped the practice of political journalism. Nowadays campaigns are conducted on television. What candidates do outside of television studios they do for the feeding
of television cameras. (It has been well said that today a campaign rally is three people clustered around a television set.)
Fortunately—and our good fortune owes something to Boorstin—journalism has become dutiful and skillful at dissecting
the politicians' uses of the medium, explaining the intentions
behind the events. Journalism calls attention to the ropes and
pulleys of the theater (it is always that) of politics.

This edition of Boorstin's book comes at a propitious moment. How-to books are all the rage with the reading public,
and this is such a book. I know, I know: In his foreword twenty-

five years ago Boorstin called this a "how-not-to-do-it" book. But Homer nods and Boorstin, for once, erred.

Nowadays most how-to books tell us how to achieve thin thighs quickly or sexual ecstasy slowly. Boorstin's book tells us how to see and listen, and how to think about what we see and hear.

It used to be said that what Americans most avidly read were books on the Civil War or on animals, so the ideal title would be *I Was Lincoln's Vet*. For a large, discerning, and still-growing audience, a valued title is *The Image: A Guide to Pseudo-Events in America*.

DANIEL J. BOORSTIN

Daniel J. Boorstin was the Librarian of Congress Emeritus, one of our nation's most eminent and widely read historians, and author of the best-selling *The Discoverers,* translated into over twenty languages, and *The Creators,* among other books. His celebrated earlier trilogy *The Americans* was awarded the Pulitzer, Bancroft, and Parkman prizes. He won the Dexter Prize of the Society for the History of Technology and the Watson Davis Prize of the History of Science Society.

He directed the Library of Congress for twelve years. Before that he was Director of the National Museum of American History of the Smithsonian Institution, and earlier had been the Morton Distinguished Service Professor at the University of Chicago, where he taught for twenty-five years.

Born in Georgia and raised in Oklahoma, he received his B.A. *summa cum laude* from Harvard and his doctor's degree from Yale. He has spent a good deal of his life viewing America from the outside, first in England where he won a coveted "double first" while a Rhodes Scholar at Balliol College, Oxford, and was admitted as a barrister-at-law of the Inner Temple, London, and also as a professor in Rome, Paris, Cambridge, Kyoto, and Geneva. He lectured all over the world, and was decorated by the governments of France, Belgium, Portugal, and Japan. He died in 2004.

THE AMERICANS

THE COLONIAL EXPERIENCE
VOLUME I
Winner of the Bancroft Prize

Boorstin presents "a superb panorama of life in America from the first settlements on through the white-hot days of the Revolution" (*Saturday Review*).

"This is an ambitious book, well-documented throughout, with many stimulating ideas."

—Herbert Mitgang, *The New York Times*

History/0-394-70513-0/$12.00

THE NATIONAL EXPERIENCE
VOLUME II
Winner of the Francis Parkman Prize

The second volume of Boorstin's study of Americans explores problems of community and the search for a national identity.

"This exceptionally good book...abounds in concrete, entertaining details, and in bright, original ideas about those fascinating people, us."

—*The New Yorker*

History/0-394-70358-8/$13.00

THE DEMOCRATIC EXPERIENCE
VOLUME III
Winner of the Pulitzer Prize

The story of the last 100 years of American history is told "through countless little revolutions in economy, technology, and social rearrangements...illuminated by reflections that are original, judicious and sagacious" (Henry Steele Commager).

"An exhilarating adventure that carries us along the highways and byways of a national history like no other."

—John K. Hutchens, *Book-of-the-Month-Club News*

History/0-394-71011-8/$14.00

THE DISCOVERERS

This vivid, sweeping history of man's search to know his world and himself is written with "a verve, an audacity and a grasp of every sort of knowledge that is outrageous and wonderful" (Alistair Cooke).

History/0-394-72625-1/$14.00

HIDDEN HISTORY
Exploring Our Secret Past

A collection of 24 incisive essays which examine rhythms, patterns, and institutions of everyday American life: from intimate portraits of legendary figures to expansive discussions of historical phenomena.

"Highly representative of his awesome scope...eminently readable and provocative."

—*Washington Post Book World*

History/0-679-72223-8/$12.00